For the longest time, missional endeavors [*based approaches. These have often been co is significant to have this monograph, Arts A solution for the 21st century - with local creative arts engagement ... efforts. A "must read" for all who are willing to set free their missional paradigm.*

Lim Swee Hong (林瑞峰), Deer Park Associate Professor for Sacred Music and Director for the Master of Sacred Music program at Emmanuel College of Victoria University in the University of Toronto, Canada

This edited volume provides a comprehensive understanding on the issue of arts in mission taking balance between a global overview and a local perspective, between historical and cultural perspectives, between traditional and contemporary media, between past and future orientations, and between ethnomusical and ethnodoxological perspectives. There is an additional sense of balance between further reading and questions for reflection/discussion as well. There is a gorgeous integration of theological, historical, cultural, and missiological perspectives in this volume.

Steve Sang-Cheol Moon, PhD (President and CEO, Charis Institute for Intercultural Studies, Professor and Director of PhD Program in Intercultural Studies, Grace Mission University)

Arts Across Cultures, treads carefully along three lines of missions: the theoretical, practical and cultural. Adding a strong voice to the creative and effective use of all art forms, this book does not shy away from discussion on redeeming art, reimagining the Christian faith, the power of aesthetics for Gospel storytelling, or the expression of Christo-centric theology through local or global flavours.

For missions to truly begin a new phase of evolving transformation, this book does not only invite the artist in missions, or the arts practitioner. Integral to this dialogue, this book stirs up church leaders who are hungry for creativity in Gospel proclamation. It dares all Creative Arts heads to be courageous in the power of the Good News, propelled by brave artistic expressions. Mission agencies are invited to strengthen their strategies to embrace new and effective methods of communication with the ever-evolving new tribes and new generations among the nations of the world.

Dr Joseph S.G. Lee, Associate Professor, School of Church Music, Singapore Bible College (until Nov 2022) Executive Board Member, Global Consultation on Arts and Music in Missions (GCAMM) Senior Pastor, Bartley Christian Church, Singapore (from February 2023)

Christian artists can and must join God's mission to draw Asia and the world to himself! This vision is clearly presented in this book. Theological foundations of the arts in mission come to life through Asian case studies and insights, providing many resources and ideas. An invaluable resource for those who seek to join and support God's work in Asia and beyond through the arts.

Myrleene Grace Yap,
former Dean of the School of Church Music, Singapore Bible College

Combined with missiological reflections, rich experiences from the fields, and practical tools for contextualizing local arts and facilitating co-creating spaces, this is a valuable resource for kingdom leaders and the arts specialists serving in Asia and Asian diaspora contexts around the world.

Jaewoo Kim, Proskuneo Ministries

This edited volume provides valuable resources that investigate the intersection between missiology and the arts, which is currently underexplored. The diverse range of authors allows the volume to deepen yet widen the conversation in grounded theological and missiological principles. A must-read for Christian artists and practitioners who are passionate in engaging arts in their culture.

Dr Calida Chu FRSA FRAS, University of Edinburgh

Arts Across Cultures is a remarkable and wide ranging book. Contributors to the volume explore their specialist areas with breadth and depth, demonstrating how "the yeast of kingdom presence [is] at work in the world through the arts." With footnotes and references to a range of languages, plus case-studies and a rich variety of in-text book ideas and further reading – Arts Across Cultures is geared for a global readership. Whether or not your interest is Asia this is an indispensable book for understanding how the arts intersect with Christian theology, discipleship, worship and mission.

Peter Rowan, PhD, Co-National Director, OMF (UK)

This important book, in both thoughtful and practical ways, promotes the role of arts in Christian mission. But it also shows the centrality of peoples' art--their dances, songs and stories--to their identity and their worship practices, even to any theological deliberation. Reflection comes later, first come the visions and dreams of young and old, which Acts tells us always accompanies the wind of the Spirit.

William A Dyrness, Senior Professor of Theology and Culture,
Fuller Theological Seminary, Pasadena, California

Arts Across Cultures

Reimagining the Christian Faith in Asia

To Naomi,

wishing you God's blessing

in this season of Advent
& Christmas,

Wawe

Series Preface

Regnum Studies in Mission are born from the lived experience of Christians and Christian communities in mission, especially but not solely in the fast-growing churches among the people of the developing world. These churches have more to tell than stories of growth. They are making significant impacts on their cultures in the cause of Christ. They are producing 'cultural products' which express the reality of Christian faith, hope and love in their societies.

Regnum Studies in Mission are the fruit often of rigorous research to the highest international standards and always of authentic Christian engagement in the transformation of people and societies. These are for the world. The formation of Christian theology, missiology and practice in the twenty-first century will depend to a great extent on the active participation of growing churches contributing biblical and culturally appropriate expressions of Christian practice to inform World Christianity.

Regnum is supported by the generosity of EMW

Arts Across Cultures
Reimagining the Christian Faith in Asia

Edited by

Warren R. Beattie and Anne M. Y. Soh

First published 2022 by Regnum Books International

Regnum is an imprint of the Oxford Centre for Mission Studies
St. Philip and St. James Church
Woodstock Road
Oxford OX2 6HR, UK
www.regnumbooks.net

09 08 07 06 05 04 03 7 6 5 4 3 2 1

British Library Cataloguing in Publication Data
A catalogue record for this book is available from the British Library

ISBN: 978-1-914454-43-1

Typeset by Words by Design
Printed and bound in Great Britain
for Regnum Books International

Cover images: Job Tan (musician with angklung),
Ling Zi (embroidery and acrylic artwork), and Shrimathi Susanna
(Bharatanatyam dancer with her senior student Dhanya Mahadevan)

Dedication

The Prinsep Players

Contents

Preface

This volume, *Arts Across Cultures: Reimagining the Christian Faith in Asia*, considers the issues that arise in the artistic engagement with the Christian faith in different cultural settings across Asia. It forms part of a continuing discussion about the impact of context on different aspects of Christian faith in Asian cultural settings. What is distinctive about this book and its companion volume, *Ministry Across Cultures*, is a concern to focus on the practical elements of this discussion whilst connecting them to theory in a way that will stimulate practitioners to think further about the implications of culture on their ministry, in this case, in the area of the arts. At the heart of the book is the assumption that those engaged in the arts in mission and "reimagining the Christian faith in Asia" represent both local Christians and those who come from wider contexts as part of the process of transmission of Christian faith. Historically, these relationships have been complex and multilateral, varying from place to place and across time. This book recognises that artistic and theological sensitivity are required on both sides – whether international or local – but that the body of Christ is enriched by the fellowship of those who strive "to keep the unity of the Spirit through the bond of peace" (Ephesians 4:3) whatever their origin.

The idea for writing this book emerged from the development of a master's degree in Arts with Mission that was created at All Nations Christian College, Easneye, UK, in 2013.[1] A number of the postgraduate students and lecturers (including Associates) had interests in aspects of Asian culture. For this project, we selected several topics on the arts that were connected to specific cultural settings by Asian authors, and these form the heart of the book along with a chapter on cosmopolitan cities. These scenarios were supplemented with introductory reflections on issues such as the relationship between the arts and mission and what it means to be an artist facing missional, cross-cultural and artistic challenges, as well as opportunities, in local cultural contexts – themes that permeated the master's degree in Arts with Mission. The book concludes

---

[1] Warren was the MA Programme Leader and initiator of the new award along with Jill, the Arts tutor, who had long taught arts in relation to mission at BA level - Anne (and her husband Job) were members of the first cohort.

with a consideration of approaches to the nurture and training of practitioners as they seek to engage artistically and missionally across cultures in Asian contexts.

Throughout the book connections are made between theory and practice:[2] in the Introduction, and Chapters 1 & 2, "arts cameos", show how artists and groups from within Asia and from other cultures have contributed to arts in the life of the Asian church and its mission; Chapters 3 & 4 integrate extended case studies – the use of Chinese calligraphy in a creative arts workshop and a visual arts project for spiritual formation amongst the Wa people; in Chapter 5 there are three short case studies followed by further advice for practitioners; and in Chapter 6 each of the six models of intercultural worship includes an example of how these function in specific cosmopolitan church settings; in Chapter 7, as the focus shifts to Central Asia, local narratives illustrate how the church, in relative isolation, is incorporating arts within self-determined missional pathways; finally, in Chapter 8 the impact of the "Arts for a Better Future" (ABF) training course is illustrated through a range of arts activities showing how artists seek to make an impact for the kingdom of God in local contexts, supplemented with personal reflections from artists who have been nurtured through ABF.

Bibliography and Readings

As noted in the preface to the companion volume, there is a constant tension in writing about Asian contexts and connected themes, whether theological, missional or artistic, using English rather than local Asian languages. In both volumes we have strived to represent a spectrum of writers and thinkers – some from Asia and some from elsewhere. We hope that the kind of materials and authors that we point to will lead readers to materials connected more specifically to their cultures of interest, including those in local languages.

Throughout the chapters, we have devised a number of categories to highlight books of interest: "Book Idea" (a recent book which connects to the core theme of the chapter); "Suggested Reading" (which indicates introductory treatments of a subject) and "Further Reading" (which offers a wider range[3] of materials); those interested in greater detail can also pursue the materials in the footnotes and in the Select Bibliography at the end of the book. Although there are references in the text and footnotes to a range of languages, including Mandarin

---

[2] Compare Sara Schumacher's comments about "engaging theologically with the 'voice' of practice" in her book review of Michael J. Bauer, *Arts Ministry: Nurturing the Creative Life of God's People*, Calvin Institute of Christian Worship Liturgical Studies (Grand Rapids, MI: Eerdmans, 2013): Sara Schumacher, "Review: Arts Ministry: Nurturing the Creative Life of God's People," *Transpositions* (Nov 7, 2014), accessed Nov 7, 2021, http://www.transpositions.co.uk/review-arts-ministry-nurturing-the-creative-life-of-gods-people/.

[3] The recommendations in "Further Reading" occasionally point to important historical works where connections are made with mission and the arts or to Christian art in Asian settings – these can be found in academic or depository libraries.

and Korean, for the benefit of a global readership, these "Book Idea/Reading" materials are generally recent, accessible, and in English but they do include international and Asian publications.[4]

Further Reading on Theology and the Arts
Begbie, J. S., ed. *Beholding the Glory: Incarnation through the Arts*. Grand Rapids, MI: Baker Academic, 2001.[5] Bergmann, S. *In the Beginning is the Icon: A Liberative Theology of Images, Visual Arts and Culture*. London and New York: Routledge, 2014. García-Rivera, A. R. *A Wounded Innocence: Sketches for a Theology of Art*. Collegeville, MN: The Liturgical Press, 2003.

The theme of "the arts" crosses many of the boundaries of theological and missional disciplines and some of the best introductions and syntheses concerning "arts across cultures" or "arts in mission" are found in reference works that have an Asian or missional focus. Several missional and theological dictionaries contain reflections on the interplay between mission and Christian faith and the arts, aesthetics, liturgy and music which would be of interest to readers of this book. These include the *Dictionary of Mission Theology*,[6] the *Global Dictionary of Theology*[7] and the *Dictionary of Mission: Theology, History, Perspectives*.[8] In addition, *A Dictionary of Asian Christianity*[9] has

---

[4] The international character of the book means that readers need to be aware of the varieties of standard English that occur in the quotations, especially for recurring words like contextualisation and globalisation, and be understanding of the complexities of rendering three (or two) character Asian names like "Loh I-To" or "He Qi" – given the common Asian usage that puts family names first and differs from the inversion of names assumed by western systems of references and bibliography. Transliteration of Korean words and names follows usage at relevant moments in time (systems and conventions have shifted in recent decades).

[5] The first set of "Further Reading" introduces some key materials on the wider discussion between theology and the arts in the 21st century, with pointers towards global aspects of the debate. Begbie's edited book makes it clear that a wide range of "arts" can be included in discussions of Christian art. This volume, with its focus on mission (broadly understood), draws freely on a number of artistic forms.

[6] John Corrie, ed., *Dictionary of Mission Theology: Evangelical Foundations* (Downers Grove, IL: IVP, 2007).

[7] William A. Dyrness and Veli-Matti Kärkkäinen, eds., *Global Dictionary of Theology: A Resource for the Worldwide Church* (Downers Grove, IL; Nottingham: IVP Academic; IVP, 2008).

[8] Karl Müller, Theo Sundermeier, Stephen B. Bevans and Richard H. Bliese, eds., *Dictionary of Mission: Theology, History, Perspectives* (Maryknoll, NY: Orbis Books, 1997).

[9] Scott W. Sunquist, ed., and David Chu Sing Wu and John Hiang Chea Chew, associate eds., *A Dictionary of Asian Christianity* (Grand Rapids, MI: Eerdmans, 2001).

articles on "Art and Architecture" and "Music, Asian Christian"; its broad understanding of what is meant by "Asia" reflects the focus of this book.[10]

The Oxford Handbook of Christianity in Asia[11] and *The Oxford Handbook of Music and World Christianities*[12] both contain materials on the arts and music relating to Asia as well as wider themes. The article on "The Arts" in *The Oxford Handbook of Systematic Theology*[13] is an excellent critical introduction to theological discussions of the relationship between theology and the arts. Finally, although the focus is more centred on the arts and worship (and its primary audience is located in the global north), the recent bibliographical overview by David Taylor at the end of his book *Glimpses of the New Creation*[14] gives an excellent contemporary review of a range of topics connected to the arts and Christianity which would be of interest to artists who work across cultures.

Contextual Theology and the Arts

The relationship between the study of contextualisation theory and the arts is still very much at a formative stage. This book adopts an eclectic approach with individual authors drawing on materials that illustrate or inform their own discussions and contexts, so that many of the books and articles cited connect with the *practice* of contextualisation as it relates to the arts in Asia. In what follows, materials that engage with contextual *theory* in relation to the arts and mission are highlighted – they include both those that reflect particularly on Asia and some more general works.

Küster's recent article[15] on contextualisation and the arts offers a concise summary of issues from an ecumenical perspective which makes connections to

---

[10] With the addition of Central Asia in this volume – for a discussion of how "Asia" can be described in terms of Christianity see Sunquist *et al.*, *Dictionary of Asian Christianity*, xxiii.
[11] Felix Wilfred, ed., *The Oxford Handbook of Christianity in Asia*, Oxford Handbooks (Oxford: Oxford University Press, 2014).
[12] Suzel Ana Reily and Jonathan M. Dueck, eds., *The Oxford Handbook of Music and World Christianities*, Oxford Handbooks (Oxford: Oxford University Press, 2016); this volume also has relevant material on themes such as liturgy, world Christianity and globalisation.
[13] John Webster, Kathryn Tanner and Iain Torrance, eds., *The Oxford Handbook of Systematic Theology*, Oxford Handbooks (Oxford: Oxford University Press, 2009); for the article mentioned see: William A. Dyrness, "The Arts," 561-79.
[14] W. David O. Taylor, *Glimpses of the New Creation: Worship and the Formative Power of the Arts* (Grand Rapids, MI: Eerdmans, 2019). See the section "For Further Reading," 279-89.
[15] Volker Küster, "Contextualisation through the Arts," in *Contextual Theology: Skills and Practices of Liberating Faith*, eds. Sigurd Bergmann and Mika Vähäkangas (London and New York: Routledge, 2021), 205-20. See further on the editor Bergmann's contribution to the arts (including global dimensions) and to contextualisation: Sigurd Bergmann, *In the Beginning Is the Icon: A Liberative*

Christian art in Asia with a focus on visual arts. He traces the origin of the term "contextualisation", approving of its embrace of the dimensions of both inculturation and liberation.[16] In summarising key historical phases of missionary art, he suggests four categories of artists who engage with Christian themes – his third and fourth categories overlap with the discussion of "missional artists"[17] in this volume. He is insightful on how the debate on contextualisation and art may well edge more towards the discourse of glocalisation[18] into the future. Küster's reflections set out the contours of the discussion and offer useful analyses of certain categories of Christian art in terms of biblical and theological themes (including art in Asia). He takes a positive view of the potential of the arts and *local* artists to be innovative and creative in the way in which they communicate Christianity to cultures in Asia and the global south.

In the musical sphere, Loh I-To's writings[19] show the need to contextualise music in Asia, especially in the face of globalisation and homogenising pressures, and he looks at how Asian hymnody can reflect more closely Asian musical styles, instruments and the local context when it comes to setting words to music – in short, he proposes a more Asian synthesis of music, lyrics and worship. Ethnomusicologists such as Roberta King[20] and Robin Harris[21] offer practical advice for musicians who work across cultures applying contextual theory to music with implications for the arts more generally.

Theology of Images, Visual Arts and Culture (London and New York: Routledge, 2014) and Sigurd Bergmann, *God in Context: A Survey of Contextual Theology* (London: Routledge, 2017), Kindle.

[16] For Küster, both Protestant and Catholic approaches to inculturation around the arts have tended towards models of translation or accommodation rather than to more adventurous approaches.

[17] See Chapter 2.

[18] This term emphasises the way in which the local needs to be taken into account by the global and yet also reshapes the global towards the local in a new distinctive synthesis.

[19] I-To Loh, "Contextualization versus Globalization: A Glimpse of Sounds and Symbols in Asian Worship," *Colloquium: Music, Worship, Arts* 2 (2005): 125-39. See also I-To Loh, "Music, Asian Christian," in *A Dictionary of Asian Christianity*, eds. Scott W. Sunquist *et al.* (Grand Rapids, MI: Eerdmans, 2001), 569-74; for more on Loh see Chapters 2 and 6 of this book.

[20] Roberta R. King, "Singing the Lord's Song in a Global World: The Dynamics of Doing Critical Contextualization through Music," *Evangelical Missions Quarterly* 42, no. 1 (2006): 68-74.

[21] Robin P. Harris, "Contextualization: Exploring the Intersections of Form and Meaning," *Connections: The Journal of the WEA Mission Commission* 9, no. 2-3 (2010): 22-23.

Melba Maggay's Perspectives on Contextualisation in Asia

A distinctively Asian perspective on contextual theology comes from the Filipina theologian Melba P. Maggay.[22] Although her writings are not primarily about the arts,[23] Maggay connects her thinking on contextualisation to liturgy – with implications for the arts – and she has an interest in aesthetics.[24] For Maggay, expressions of theology are always connected to local cultures so there needs to be an engagement with the vernacular culture by local people which she describes as "a theological re-rooting and re-routing," drawing approvingly on words of José de Mesa,[25] a Catholic theologian in the Philippines.[26] An important idea for Maggay is that of contextualisation in relation to "deep structures": "underlying worldviews, a people's way of looking at the world, deep-seated beliefs and value systems that are largely unconscious."[27]

Maggay's concern is to move "towards contextualization from within" looking at "a culture's system of meaning" expressed in its own terms and through its own language:[28]

> ... people in a largely oral society such as the Philippines experience life as primary reality – passing events restored in memory and reinterpreted over time; thus the

---

[22] Melba P. Maggay was one of a group of "selected writers" on mission that the editor researched for his PhD. In what follows, as Maggay may be less familiar to some readers, this section highlights her distinctive way of expressing insights on Christianity and liturgy in her own cultural context.

[23] For a wider analysis of Maggay's contribution to mission, see Warren R. Beattie, "Transformational Missiology – An Emerging Trend in Evangelical Missiology in Asia: An Analysis with Reference to Selected Asian Writers" (PhD thesis, University of Edinburgh, 2006).

[24] See further Melba P. Maggay and William A. Dyrness, "Art and Aesthetics," in *Global Dictionary of Theology: A Resource for the Worldwide Church*, eds. William A. Dyrness and Veli-Matti Kärkkäinen (Downers Grove, IL; Nottingham: IVP Academic; IVP, 2008), 64-70. Reflecting on Asian aesthetics, Maggay critiques a range of topics from an Asian slant: humanity's relationship to nature, topics such as impermanence and melancholy, "perspective" (in the visual arts), as well as the impact of religious traditions and how "allusiveness" relates to the arts in Asia.

[25] For an accessible discussion on contextual theology that compares and contrasts the approaches of Maggay and de Mesa, see Andrea Roldan, "The Gospel in the Filipino Context: José M. de Mesa and Melba P. Maggay," *Mission Round Table: The OMF Journal for Reflective Practitioners* 13, no.1 (Jan-Apr 2018): 24-30.

[26] Melba Padilla Maggay, "Introduction – The Task of Contextualization: Issues in Reading, Appropriating, and Transmitting the Faith," in *The Gospel in Culture: Contextualization Issues through Asian Eyes*, ed. Melba Padilla Maggay (Manila: ISACC and OMF Literature, 2013), 7.

[27] Melba Padilla Maggay, *Global Kingdom, Global People: Living Faithfully in a Multicultural World* (Carlisle: Langham Global Library, 2017), 116.

[28] Melba P. Maggay, "Towards Contextualization from Within: Some Tools and Culture Themes," in *Doing Theology in the Philippines*, compiled by ATS Forum on Theology (Manila: OMF Literature and Asian Theological Seminary, 2005), 37-50.

sense that the world is unfixed, a dynamic, interpersonal system of encounters with people and other beings. ... Thought and expression are often highly organized, but in ways that are imaginative and intuitive rather than analytical and abstract. Concrete human experiences are distilled in proverbs, riddles, myths and parables, thus the cognitive preference for stories rather than abstract words.

Implications for Liturgy and Ritual

In the context of how the "deep structures" of a culture are worked out, in a section entitled "Redeeming the Image," she considers the idea of communication in ways that are in line with Filipino culture – a matter that is significant when it comes to liturgy and ritual:[29]

> ... communication must be highly symbolic, continuous, personal and engaged; paying attention to process rather than mere product which is concentrated on fixing a content believed to be finished once organized. Messages must be right-brain dominant, and the cultic forms centred on dance, drama, ritual and song, instead of the usual accent on linear preaching and the poverty of symbol that dominates Protestant worship.

She affirms Dyrness' insight that whilst, in the west, the "visual and symbolic" elements are reduced to a supporting role, in the "Filipino imagination" it is the opposite.[30] As to how Christianity connects with this kind of process of imagination, in terms of the liturgy, she suggests that "the stress on *proclamation* of the Word needs to be balanced by *presence*, or visible non-verbal signs that would serve as a persuasive context for the Word." Against the backdrop of her perception of the contrasts of western and Filipino cultural worlds, she makes the following observation, referring to the western church after the Reformation:[31]

> The liturgical centre of the west shifted from *altar* to *pulpit*, from *image* to the *Word*
> ... the West evolved a religious culture heavily on the side of abstract

---

[29] Image – this refers not just to arts and liturgy but also to theological categories – see the comment: "there is a need to strengthen the indigenous image of God as all-powerful and de-emphasize Christ as forever suffering." Melba Padilla Maggay, "A Religion of Guilt Encounters a Religion of Power: Missiological Implications and Consequences," in *The Gospel in Culture: Contextualization Issues through Asian Eyes*, ed. Melba Padilla Maggay (Manila: ISACC and OMF Literature, 2013), 44; longer quote, 50-51.

[30] Maggay, "Introduction – The Task of Contextualization," 12. She notes approvingly Dyrness' point that western culture moves from "abstract to concrete" whereas in the Philippines the reverse is felt to be true – "dramatic and visual are of the essence; abstract and dogmatic concerns would seem to be peripheral." See William A. Dyrness, *Invitation to Cross-Cultural Theology: Case Studies in Vernacular Theologies* (Grand Rapids, MI: Zondervan, 1992), 105.

[31] Maggay, "A Religion of Guilt Encounters a Religion of Power," 42 – emphasis from Maggay; longer quote, 51.

intellectualism, assuming that whatever it is that God is doing, He must be doing it in the head.

Maggay concludes by observing that for people in the Philippines "the strong cognitive ethos of Protestantism needs to be softened by a feeling for the romance of ritual and intuitive ways of expressing faith."[32] Maggay is aware of the implications of these matters for the liturgy in Protestant churches in the Philippines. She reckons that: "what we call 'folk religion' is really this ongoing dialectical interaction between the people's reading of their formal texts and traditions and their culture and historical situation as controlling contexts." Pursuing this contrast between Filipino and Protestant traditions (from the west) she observes:[33]

> Our liturgical use of the body and performative sense of ritual is evident, for instance, in the centrality of processions, festivals and images in our worship. This is in patent contrast to the emphasis in the West, on credal statements and abstract propositions where the Protestant religious imagination seems to be located, especially since the massive shift from image to the word, from the altar to the pulpit, in the wake of the Reformation.

For Maggay, the work of contextualisation draws on theological insights to make sense of this process of cultural change using theoretical categories but has application to many aspects of everyday life and practice in Christianity and church life. The examples above show ways in which this discussion on contextual theology and "deep structures" can inform approaches to the liturgy in the Philippines given its aesthetic and artistic character. The work of Miranda-Feliciano and others take this forward in relation to a range of art and expressive forms.[34] There are clear implications for artists working in other Asian contexts both in terms of an approach to contextual theology that takes account of local Asian perspectives and the relevance of such insights for the arts and artists in relation to local expressions of Christian liturgy and the life of the church and its mission.

Contextualisation – Arts in Mission (General)

At a general level of thinking about contextualisation, in addition to the widely acknowledged and important monographs such as Bevans' *Models of Contextual*

---

[32] Maggay, "A Religion of Guilt Encounters a Religion of Power," 56

[33] Maggay, "Introduction – The Task of Contextualization," 13; longer quote, 11.

[34] See chapter 1 for "arts cameos" about a liturgical procession led by Melba Maggay and the contribution to contextual liturgy in the Philippines by Evelyn Miranda-Feliciano (the latter refers to other artistic forms such as hymnody in her book).

Theology[35] and Schreiter's *Local Theologies*,[36] readers could note Flemming's work on *Contextualisation in the New Testament*[37] that assesses the way in which the Bible itself constantly responds to the context of its readers. Finally, the *one* volume from the global north on contextual theology that is both theologically grounded and highly inspirational for artists would be Clemens Sedmak's book, *Doing Local Theology*.[38] In the context of Thesis 6: "There are many ways of doing theology … ," Sedmak continues, "Theology is taught and written, danced and sung, sculpted and painted, even dreamed and cried." By way of explanation he adds, "Movies, novels, buildings, paintings, show implicit theologies." He goes on to share Henri Nouwen's comments on one of Rembrandt's paintings.[39] Not only does this book point to the arts in various ways in the text, but its interest in local cultures and local theology leans towards a wholehearted engagement and embrace. This is evidenced by one of its metaphors of the local theologian being like a cook who creates cuisine with local ingredients.[40] Eating is very much a communal activity in Asia; in some contexts, sharing communal meals can even be viewed as an act of identification, so Sedmak's stance reflects well the mindset and heart of those who want to identify with a local culture and connect with local people and local arts, as a missional artist should seek to do.

Contributors to This Research Project

We would like to express our thanks to the following people for their help at various stages with this project.

To the team at Regnum – especially Paul Bendor-Samuel, Elizabete Santos and Tony Gray in the long process of taking a book from conception to completion and for their support in the production of a companion volume to *Ministry Across Cultures* around the theme of "Missional Church in Asian Contexts."

---

[35] Stephen B. Bevans, *Models of Contextual Theology*, Faith and Cultures, Rev. and expanded ed. (Maryknoll, NY: Orbis Books, 2002).

[36] Robert J. Schreiter, *Constructing Local Theologies*, 30th anniv. ed. (Maryknoll, NY: Orbis Books, 2015).

[37] Dean E. Flemming, *Contextualization in the New Testament: Patterns for Theology and Mission* (Downers Grove, IL: IVP Academic, 2005).

[38] Clemens Sedmak, *Doing Local Theology: A Guide for Artisans of a New Humanity* (Maryknoll, NY: Orbis Books, 2002). The book is based around "50 Theses for Doing Local Theology," 162-68.

[39] Sedmak, *Doing Local Theology*, 11-12; the picture in question is Rembrandt's "The Pilgrims at Emmaus." See Chapter 4 for further connections between Sedmak's thinking and the visual arts.

[40] Sedmak, *Doing Local Theology*, 17-20. Thesis 9: "Many different images capture the work of a theologian. The idea of local theologies can be expressed through the image of the theologian as a village cook. Doing local theology is like cooking with local ingredients."

To all the writers – Hennie Chiu, Vivian Chiu, Ian Collinge, Jill Ford, Robin Harris, Brian Schrag and Julie Taylor – for being ready and willing to work together remotely over a period of years to bring this volume to publication and for their enthusiasm and energy in making connections between the arts and Christianity in many different cultural settings.

To Dr William D. Taylor for taking time in the midst of a particularly busy publishing schedule to write the Foreword, drawing on his own passion for the arts in and for mission and setting a book with an Asian focus in a global context – artistically and missionally – as well as sketching out contours for future reflections.

To all the students, visiting lecturers and participants on the BA and MA programmes at All Nations Christian College (UK) and the "Arts for a Better Future" training events: their contributions have helped us reflect more deeply on the role of the arts in mission. Warren has also appreciated the opportunity to interact with students around the arts on the MTh/MSc programmes at the Centre for the Study of World Christianity, New College, University of Edinburgh and the BA programme at the Highland Theological College, University of the Highlands and Islands.

To various colleagues who have been involved in the process from project to published book – and a special thanks to Julie for reviewing two of the editor's sections, to Anne for all her editorial work on texts and bibliography, and to Anna Watkins and Victoria Townsend who helped with ideas, bibliography and information around the chapter on creative arts workshops. Also to Derek Beattie for help with proof-reading in the final stages.

We are grateful to Job Tan (musician with angklung), Ling Zi (embroidery and acrylic artwork), and Shrimathi Susanna (Bharatanatyam dancer with her senior student Dhanya Mahadevan) for permission to use the respective photos in the book cover.

Warren would like to say a special thank you to Stroma for all her help during this project, for all the extra responsibilities that she took on to make it possible, and her constant encouragement and support.

The book is dedicated to "The Prinsep Players" – an instrumental ensemble who have played for the third Sunday morning service once a month at Prinsep Street Presbyterian Church in Singapore from December 2006 onwards – in gratitude to the friendship and collaboration of Ten Yeen, August, Yang'en, Kirk, Diana and Philip and the other church members and friends who joined on an occasional basis over the years, especially Ping and Mae. Making music in church, regularly, with the Prinsep Players who come from several nations was a genuinely creative experience in a congregation that continues to "embrace" the arts and artists, and welcome people from around the world.

Missional Church in Asian Contexts Series

When the first book *Ministry Across Cultures* was being developed around 2012, we realised that there was the possibility of sharing further reflections on themes that connect mission and the church in Asia. Although "the arts" was not a topic on the original list, it has emerged as an area of increasing importance and one that is challenging and fascinating at both an intellectual and an applied level. This companion volume represents the next step in that process of a series of books envisaged as *Missional Church in Asian Contexts*.[41]

Warren R. Beattie (Associate),
The Centre for the Study of World Christianity,
New College, University of Edinburgh.

Anne M. Y. Soh,
Arts Release, WEC International (Singapore).

---

[41] See the comments about this series at the end of the book – these include a brief discussion of the understanding of missional church which underpins these volumes.

Foreword

William D. Taylor

I will never forget the stunning autochthonous music, dance and song in Pattaya Thailand that inaugurated the global consultation convened by Mission Commission of World Evangelical Alliance MC 2008 consultation. It was like nothing I had seen before. The instruments, the music genre and style, the Thai vocalization, the stylized traditional dance forms—all contextualized by and into the Christian world view. I still see and hear them in my mind. While I did not understand a word of the lyrics, and the art form was new to me, I had this profound sense that I was witnessing a new creation that God was releasing worldwide. And he is doing just that. We concluded that consultation with a rousing Sakha, the Siberian round dance, led by Robin Harris, one of the authors of this book.

Before my three decades of global service with the Mission Commission, my family and I invested seventeen years in Latin America. Sadly, I suffered from a strange blindness during those years of cross-cultural mission. That is, I had no theology, neither theoretical nor practical, for the arts beyond the pre-evangelistic or purely evangelistic. That is strange, because I had married a classical pianist, Yvonne, whose gifts came from calling, training, skill and commitment to the Gospel proclamation. She regularly played in pre-evangelistic events, and God had surprised us with the gift of a grand piano during our second year in Latin America.

I had seen some "evangelistic street dramas" in Guatemala City, but they served only to introduce the Gospel. My crisis came in two moments. The first came with the question, "What do we do with Mildred and Manolo?" This musically gifted couple had been one of Guatemala's most popular singers in night clubs and other music festivals. When they came to faith and our relationship began, the question arose, "But what will *they* do now?" Well, that was relatively easy (to me): they should sing Christian songs. But should they totally leave their former world and friends? Thankfully they kept doors open to both.

A tougher nut to crack was what to do with Elias and Ana Elsy, professional ballet dancers and stars in Guatemala's National Ballet Company. Yvonne had led Ana Elsy to Christ, and Elías committed his life a few months later. There was no market nor money in sacred dance in Guatemala. Little did I know! Ana

Elsy transformed my mind and heart. Her stellar career concluded with the lead role in the ballet, Coppélia. It was magnificent, and that night in Guatemala's national theatre, something stirred deeply in me. After the finale, we met her in her dressing room where with radiant face she exclaimed, "Yvonne and Guillermo, as I listened to the orchestra's overture, waiting for the curtain to open, I dedicated Coppélia to Jesus Christ!" They became our Stephanie's ballet instructors. They also became lifelong friends. During a recent visit to Guatemala, they joyfully told us of the Bible studies and conversions of fellow ballet dancers in the succeeding years. They still teach classical ballet.

Those personal narratives lead me to express deep gratitude to the long-term project that produces this series of volumes, and specifically to Warren R. Beattie and Anne M. Y. Soh as editors of this multi-cultural companion to *Ministry Across Cultures: Sharing the Christian Faith in Asia, 2016*. It is encouraging to note how this book emerged in part from Lecturer Dr. Jill Ford's work at All Nations Christian College, UK, and its vision to equip cross cultural servants in art and mission.

And this book not only affirms these items, but it also lays out the path before us, a journey less travelled, urging us to explore and inhabit with God-given creativity. Thank God for this resource and its nine writers. Collectively they have opened many doors into the magnificent role that the creative arts play in God's kingdom. I was both stretched and encouraged as I worked through the book, and felt that this book could easily become a template for resources in other continents and regions of our world.

I encourage the authors to keep exploring critical topics. For example, we need a robust articulation of a theology of the *vocation* of the artist. This is deeper than just "doing art for evangelism's sake," or the exercise of a practical outworking of the missional dimensions of the artist and arts. We must validate a high calling upon those intuitive, Spirit-guided creatives who are called to be artists. Yes, they may see their art as skill and exhibit to be used for evangelism and mission, but their core vocation is deeper.[1] As reflectors of a creative God, many times their art product may not "look Christian," but by virtue of who they are and their vocation, it is very much Christian.

During a trip some years ago to India, I was honoured to meet and visit with Christian artist, Stephan Eicher, in his New Delhi studio. An artist-teacher, his vision crosses religions, it challenges the caste systems. His community studio is a classroom, and his exhibit area a prophetic visual feast. During our time together he explained his latest exhibit, the powerful way that prophetic art sends disturbing and subtle attacks against gendercide (i.e., sonograms used to abort baby girls), against systemic and personal injustice, in favour of the poor, the vulnerable, those desperately ill. Hindus, Christians, and those of other faith systems are invited into community to learn art, to listen to each other, to produce

---

[1] Editors' note: As suggested by the observations and caveats on p.34 & 47 and, more generally, in the works cited by Bauer and Seerveld.

excellent art that speaks to Indian cultures. And in that grace-filled context, issues of spiritual nature emerge, and the character of our personal, Triune, unique, God of justice and mercy are revealed.

I write this foreword as a witness to the arts *in* and *for* mission. I write as an elder servant who loves to bless, as one called to liberate these singular gifts. May this volume release artists around Asia, around the world, who share their passion, who are gifted in the arts, who desire all children, youth and adults to know of the gracious and radical love of the True God through his Son, the Christ, in the power of the Spirit.

William D. Taylor, PhD, President of TaylorGlobalConsult,
Former Executive Director of the Mission Commission of the
World Evangelical Alliance with 55 years in cross-cultural service

Introduction

The biblical studies theologian N. T. Wright has issued a challenge to Christians to think more deeply about the role and the importance of the arts in terms of Christianity:[1]

> The arts are not the pretty but irrelevant bits around the border of reality. They are highways into the centre of a reality which cannot be glimpsed, let alone grasped, any other way. The present world is good, but broken and in any case incomplete; art of all kinds enables us to understand that paradox and its many dimensions. … Perhaps art can help us to look beyond the immediate beauty with all its puzzles, and to glimpse that new creation which makes sense not only of beauty but of the world as a whole, and ourselves within it.

Writing recently, as both a theologian with an interest in the arts and as a musician, Jeremy Begbie has noted some encouraging developments:[2]

> The ferment of "theology and the arts" shows no sign of waning. It burgeons in colleges, universities and churches. Theological internet watchers observe its fast-expanding presence and publishers are beginning to see it as a serious niche market.

Arts in Mission

At a time when there is a renaissance of interest in the relation of the arts to Christianity, this book offers an informed and practical guide for one particular group of people: it seeks to explain the relevance and potential of the arts for Christians who work across cultures and who have artistic skills and gifts. By drawing on examples and studies from the field of Mission Studies as well as the Arts, this book aims to offer fresh perspectives and encourage those who want to share their faith through the arts as they serve across cultures.[3] Whether their identity is that of an artist now involved in missional projects or those in

---

[1] N. T. Wright, *Simply Christian: Why Christianity Makes Sense* (New York: HarperOne, 2010), 235-36.

[2] Jeremy S. Begbie, *A Peculiar Orthodoxy: Reflections on Theology and the Arts* (Grand Rapids, MI: Baker Academic, 2018), 182.

[3] In the case of local artists, "within" a culture. See further Chapters 1 and 2 which introduce a range of documents from Mission Studies in relation to the arts and artists.

Christian ministry who have artistic backgrounds and interests, they will find foundations, insights, ideas and resources and an introduction to a range of artists and artistic activities in Asian settings.

The book seeks to deepen an understanding and appreciation of arts and mission, both in theory and in practice, help readers in very practical ways to develop their artistic and cultural understanding, and enable them to engage more deeply with the arts in mission so that the arts do not remain "an untapped resource"[4] for mission.

Book Idea

Shreeves, K. *Art for Mission's Sake: Announcing the Gospel through the Creative Arts.* Grove Mission and Evangelism 119. Cambridge, UK: Grove Books, 2017.

With its focus on the missional dimensions of the arts, this booklet gives an informed but practical introduction to the topic. It takes a constructive approach to the arts in mission, builds a theological rationale, and then looks at how the arts can form part of a missional engagement in both the church and the world – recognising that there are sometimes barriers and misconceptions that need to be addressed.

Arts across Cultures

The phrase "arts across cultures" reminds us that as one journeys between cultures there will be a change of artistic experience. At the heart of this book is a stress on the importance of exploring the different expressions of the arts that artists who cross cultures will find in new cultural settings. Cultural learning and engaging with local culture and local arts are vital. However, there are some situations in our ever more connected global world where artistic forms "travel" – particularly into and away from cosmopolitan settings. The relationship of the global north and global south, the connection of the history of mission to European centres and to some extent European arts, all play their part in the complex issues that need to be negotiated.

There is a striking series of questions from John Mbiti[5] – directed at theologians in the global north who are aware mainly of global trends – which challenges them about how they engage with the local and, by implication, the "other" in terms of theology: "We know you theologically. The question is do you know us theologically?" If we were to replace the word artistically for theologically in Mbiti's

---

[4] See the opening of Chapter 1 for further discussion of this idea.
[5] John Mbiti as quoted in Kwame Bediako, *Christianity in Africa: The Renewal of a Non-western Religion*, Studies in World Christianity (Edinburgh; Maryknoll, NY: Edinburgh University Press; Orbis Books, 1995), 155.

sequence, it would prompt some searching questions for those who are missional artists[6] and who would like to engage in arts across cultures.

> We know you artistically. The question is do you know us artistically? Would you like to know us artistically? Can you know us artistically? And how can there be true artistic reciprocity and mutuality, if only one side knows the other fairly well, whilst the other side does not know or does not want to know the first side?

This stance of being open to other cultures is critical at many levels but it is especially important if missional artists are to have the capacity to identify with the choices that local Christians want to make in terms of local arts as opposed to global arts. Such identification demands that missional artists are open to the local so that they can appreciate, engage with and ultimately embrace local arts in a specific culture.[7]

Reimagining the Christian Faith

There is a critical connection between imagination and the arts that is seen in the reflections of artists, writers and, indeed, some institutions.[8] The title of this book is *Arts Across Cultures: Reimagining the Christian Faith in Asia*. The phrase "Reimagining the Christian faith in Asia" reminds us of the crucial role that the arts can play in helping to translate the Christian faith into other cultures. The question might be asked: why "reimagining" – why not just "imagining"? Reimagining is used in two senses. For missional artists who cross cultures there is a need to recognise that the cultural transition necessitates a reimagining of Christian faith from their own context to another context. Secondly, it is used to mean that in the engagement between missional artists, local artists and local Christians there is a *joint* labour of reimagining the faith as insiders and outsiders strive together to look at the gospel and the Christian faith with new eyes – an artistic outworking of Walls' envisaged global hermeneutical community.[9]

Implicit in this term is the idea that the life of the church is a constant reimagining of faith as the church interacts globally through time and as it encounters the kind of global–local interplays and pressures that are discussed in this book. For example, Ed Lapiz, who is engaged in projects adopting traditional and indigenous dances in the Philippines in relation to the Christian church, reimagines the role of local dance in Christian settings through a process of

---

[6] "Missional artist" is used to describe an artist who crosses cultures in mission – the term is introduced more fully in Chapter 2.

[7] See further in Chapter 1 and especially Chapter 2.

[8] For example, the University of St. Andrew's centre for theology and the arts is named – Institute for Theology, Imagination and the Arts.

[9] Andrew F. Walls, *The Missionary Movement in Christian History: Studies in the Transmission of Faith* (Maryknoll, NY: Orbis Books, 1996), 15.

"redefining" and "redeeming" indigenous dance.[10] Given the existing spread of Christianity in Asia, the role of "reimagining" is clearly not done by missional artists alone – but a sensitive appreciation of local arts can help missional artists to be catalysts and to offer perspectives on global arts, glocal expressions of the arts and the use of local arts in Asian settings. In many situations, missional artists will do this alongside local artists.

In some instances, local artists who are beyond the church may also be interested in the way the Christian faith can be interpreted through local artistic categories and may be willing to share their skills and resources.[11] Artists such as Roberta King have been interested in the relevance of inter-faith dialogue; there are situations in which shared artistic identity allows "space" for shared endeavour that can bring about fresh understandings and renewed perspectives.[12] Certainly, there needs to be empathy, openness and a sense of expectation in the process of engaging with arts across cultures and in the imagining and reimagining of Christian faith. This kind of interaction can be a rich and rewarding learning experience and offers the potential for engaging meaningfully with local people as well as local arts across cultures. It has a particular significance in the fact that an attitude of local identification, following the pattern of Jesus' incarnation, lies at the heart of what it means to be Christian and missional.

Further Reading on Imagination, Theology and the Arts
Dyrness, W. A. *Reformed Theology and Visual Culture: The Protestant Imagination from Calvin to Edwards*. Cambridge: CUP, 2004.
Hart, T., G. Hopps and J. S. Begbie. *Art, Imagination and Christian Hope: Patterns of Promise*. Ashgate Studies in Theology, Imagination and the Arts. London and New York: Routledge, 2016.
Kilby, C. S. [W. A. Dyrness and K. Call, eds.] *The Arts and the Christian Imagination: Essays on Art, Literature, and Aesthetics*. Brewster, MA and Barga: Paraclete Press, 2016.
Watkins, J. M. *Creativity as Sacrifice: Toward a Theological Model for Creativity in the Arts*. Minneapolis, MN: Fortress Press, 2015.

---

[10] Ed Lapiz, "The Christian and Dance: The Redemption of Dance for Use in Christian Worship," *Inspire* 2 (Jul 2001): 22-31, accessed Jul 26, 2021, https://icdf.com/sites/default/files/documents/redemption-of-dance-jan08.pdf.

[11] For reflections on Asian artists learning about Asian cultures and Asian art – even for Asians who are missional artists in their own culture – and for discussion about interacting with artists in multi-religious contexts see Masao Takenaka and Ron O'Grady, *The Bible through Asian Eyes* (Auckland: Pace Publishing, 1991), 10. See also Bauer's comments about "attempts to fence the table" referring to artists beyond the Christian community engaging in art around biblical and Christian themes; he suggests it is the *art works* that matter: Bauer, *Arts Ministry*, 21-22.

[12] See Roberta R. King and William A. Dyrness, eds., *The Arts as Witness in Multifaith Contexts*, Missiological Engagements (Downers Grove, IL: IVP Academic, 2019).

Insights from World Christianity

Those who work in the discipline of World Christianity[13] are well aware of the challenges of sharing faith and reimagining faith across cultures "to make the church 'A Place to Feel at Home.'"[14] Reflections and insights from World Christianity can usefully be applied to the arts and adopted with profit by missional artists. Concepts such as "translatability"[15] and the "promotion of the vernacular"[16] are relevant not just in general but also in relation to the arts in mission. These concepts all reflect the Christian interest in the theology of incarnation and its implications for identification with culture. The work of Lamin Sanneh has shown that where local languages are used in Bible translation, there is a real impact on identity and the sense of worth of local peoples. The act of Bible translation is not just an affirmation of the local character of Christian faith, but it is also an act of identification with the local culture which allows Christian ideas and concepts to be shaped by a local culture in its own terms. The idea of starting from a local language (and the Bible) and working out from that to promote local vernacular culture is both a profound insight and a powerful lever in strengthening identity and nurturing local cultures.[17]

At a deeper level, the promotion of vernacular cultures through acts of translation and of identification sends out an important message. It affirms that all cultures, though distinct and different, are valuable in God's sight and that each local culture can contribute through its artistic expressions to the global church. Melba Maggay has suggested that the reversal of the Babel event at Pentecost[18] is part of a process that continues towards the vision of the church at worship before the throne of God in the book of Revelation[19] – where representatives from every culture, language and tribe are present. Missional artists need to engage with local arts so they can share in that process of the

---

[13] For an informed and contemporary general assessment of World Christianity see Joel Cabrita, David Maxwell and Emma Wild-Wood, eds., *Relocating World Christianity: Interdisciplinary Studies in Universal and Local Expressions of the Christian Faith*, Theology and Mission in World Christianity 7 (Leiden: Brill, 2017).

[14] Walls, *The Missionary Movement in Christian History*, 7. The book title is by F. B. Welbourn and B. A. Ogot.

[15] See Walls, *The Missionary Movement in Christian History*, 26-42 on the "translation principle" and the need to address the "overwhelming foreign aspect of Christianity," 175 – where "aspect" embraces "image."

[16] See Lamin Sanneh, *Translating the Message: The Missionary Impact on Culture*, American Society of Missiology 42, Rev. and expanded ed. (Maryknoll, NY: Orbis Books, 2009), 213. Sanneh shows that translation of the scriptures into vernacular languages results in a wider "promotion of the vernacular" in terms of local cultures.

[17] See also Bill Harris, "The Church Planter and Artist: Becoming Partners in Ministry," *Connections: The Journal of the WEA Mission Commission* 9, no. 2-3 (2010): 34-35. Harris shows the power of identifying with local people using the Sakha language and local instruments in establishing a local church and in showing forth this local identity to those beyond the church.

[18] Maggay, *Global Kingdom, Global People*, 120-26.

[19] See, for example, Rev. 7:9-10.

promotion and appropriation of the local in their artistic work.[20] Such an endeavour begins with an engagement and embrace of local arts.[21]

De-westernising the Image of Asian Christianity

Asian voices within world Christianity offer a critique on the impact of global and, particularly, western influences on the transmission of the faith. Moonjang Lee suggests that the affirmation of local cultures often needs to include a turning away from the global, as typified by the western influences of Christianity. Lee talks about the need to deconstruct and reconstruct (and, we could add, reimagine) the *image* of Christianity in Asia so that it is perceived as a non-western religion or Asian religion. Indeed, Lee uses the phrase "the de-westernisation of the image of Christianity" to show that such a process needs to address the unnecessary elements by which Christianity is perceived to be western, especially in Asian contexts.[22]

> Sawai Chinnawook's images are striking, colourful and vibrant but they also evoke a strong sense of place in terms of South-East Asia.[23] The farmer in the picture "The Plentiful Harvest" has a bamboo hat in a tropical agricultural setting; the cattle in the "Thai Nativity" are local water buffalo that evoke Thailand (it feels as if the context of Koyama's *Water Buffalo Theology* is coming alive in front of the viewer's eyes)[24] and the whole scene appears to be shaped by Thai graphic forms offering a strong vernacular reimagining of the event.

---

[20] Maggay draws on Chomsky's idea of "deep structures" in linguistics as a conceptual springboard for contextualisation. See Maggay, *Global Kingdom, Global People*, 114-17. She attributes the lack of "Christianizing the native consciousness … as a failure to connect and engage the 'deep structures' of the indigenous imagination," 114.

[21] Ruth Wall's research on transformational learning in mission uses the sequence – encounter, engage, embrace – to show the intensification of contact that needs to happen when people function across cultures. With those concepts in mind, Chapter 1 on "Arts in Mission" considers encounter and intellectual engagement with local cultures against the global backdrop. Chapter 2 on "Artists in Mission" delves deeper into this journey of practical engagement with local cultures and the embrace of local arts. See Ruth Wall, "Preparing Adults for Crossing Cultures: A Study of a Transformative Approach to Christian Mission Training" (PhD thesis, Institute of Education, University College London, London, 2015), 188.

[22] Moonjang Lee, "Asianization of Theology and Theological Education," Unpublished paper, "Mission as Transformation in Twenty-First Century Asia" Conference, Trinity Theological College, Singapore, Dec 2003.

[23] An introduction to Chinnawong's work is found at "2003-2004 Artist: Sawai Chinnawong," Overseas Ministries Study Center, accessed Jul 19, 2021, https://www.omsc.org/sawai-chinnawong.

[24] Kosuke Koyama, *Water Buffalo Theology*, 25th anniv. ed., rev. and expanded (Maryknoll, NY: Orbis Books, 1999).

In a discussion of arts across cultures, the term "image"[25] is quite striking – although its primary focus is not just to the arts but to the wider ethos of Christianity.[26] It serves as a reminder of the way in which the living out of Christian faith in worship, witness and the transformation of the wider world, needs to be shaped by local cultural forms so that the perception of Christian faith is not seen falsely or unnecessarily as simply a "western religion."[27]

An Overview of the Book

Before exploring particular artistic journeys across cultures, the book starts by considering the theme of the arts and mission in relation to two key perspectives. The opening section of the book looks separately at the topics of arts and then artists in relation to mission. The chapter on the arts draws on selected late 20th and early 21st century mission documents, looks at the contemporary pressures on arts around global–local tensions and offers a simple three-fold framework of "worship, witness and transformation of the wider world" to suggest contours for the arts in mission. The chapter on artists introduces the term "missional artist," reflects on the development of artistic skills, the nature of missional vocation and the need for cultural learning and identification in relation to local cultures and arts.

The middle section of the book, Arts and Mission in Practice, looks at four themes and case studies, each in a particular cultural setting. Chapter 3 looks at how to use creative arts workshops to explore different art forms for transformational impact, drawing on a case study based around calligraphy in the Hong Kong Chinese context. Chapter 4 introduces a project that visualised and reimagined the accounts of the life, death, and resurrection of Jesus Christ in John's gospel by creating paintings as creative resources for Christian spiritual formation to stimulate further projects amongst the Wa people of China. Chapter 5 looks at two forms of digital media: Japanese anime and Korean drama. It explores how Christians can engage with these forms of storytelling in a range of ways, from interacting with other viewers to becoming producers of their own Christian stories, as part of the process of engaging with Asian societies around matters of faith. Chapter 6 describes an approach to worship in cosmopolitan cities by considering the relationship between intercultural churches and worship, around the key areas of culture and cultural diversity. It offers a careful

---

[25] Maggay talks about "redeeming the image" to complement "the Word" (in Protestant forms of Christianity in Asia) and to relate to Asian cultural processes – see Maggay, "A Religion of Guilt Encounters a Religion of Power," 24-56. See also the Preface.

[26] See further Maggay and Dyrness, "Art and Aesthetics", 64-70; 64-66 have a focus on Asian perspectives.

[27] African writers such as Kwame Bediako and Lamin Sanneh talk of Christianity as an African religion to underline that statistical shifts in the centre of gravity of Christianity make this a historical and contemporary reality. See, for example, Bediako, *Christianity in Africa.*

definition of intercultural worship and critiques several concrete approaches before concluding with new insights for practitioners.

The final section of the book looks at two examples of how the arts and artists can and need to be nurtured for Asian contexts. The penultimate chapter explores local Christian narratives that illustrate how expressive and communicative arts are contributing to the reimagining and growth of the church in Central Asia. The final chapter shows how skills for "arts across cultures" can be consciously developed. Using the "Arts for a Better Future" course as a case study, it suggests approaches to develop artistic projects with local communities that help missional artists to share effectively the good news of the kingdom of God with artistic and cultural sensitivity.

Part I

Setting the Scene –
Arts and Artists in Mission

1. Arts in Mission: Enhancing Worship, Witness and Transformation of the Wider World
Warren R. Beattie

The opening chapter explores the theme of arts in mission drawing on writings from mission studies that highlight the arts with a special interest in the relevance to contexts in Asia. There is a focus on the interplay in the contemporary world between the arts in local contexts and the impact of global influences. It concludes with a framework that looks at the implications of the arts in mission moving outwards from the church's worship on to witness and the transformation of the wider world.

Although many studies now exist on the arts and Christianity, informed yet practical discussion of the relationship between the arts and mission is harder to find. Embedded in the missional documents of the late 20th and early 21st century,[1] however, are thoughtful reflections on the role of the arts in mission that offer insights about both the challenges and opportunities facing artists who cross cultures in Asian contexts. *Arts Across Cultures* has a particular interest in how such ideas affect missional artists,[2] those with artistic gifts and interests who intentionally move into other cultures as Christians, and who seek to share the gospel of the kingdom of God made known through Jesus Christ. Testimony to this "good news" does not need to have a narrow, introverted focus. Christian faith begins in worship – whether personal or communal – but when expressed in human lives, it pushes Christians out to witness to God's purposes of redemption and transform the communities and societies around them by demonstrating the reality of the kingdom community and its kingdom lifestyle. Christians are to go into the wider world as disciples, followers of Christ Jesus, to share the good news with others so that lives and communities can be transformed.

This chapter aims to stimulate those with an interest in both the arts and mission to think about their interaction more creatively. It will show how

---

[1] Missional documents are drawn from the Lausanne Movement, the WEA Mission Commission and other selected groups with a focus on recent decades.

[2] "Missional artist" refers to both Christians with developed artistic skills who cross cultures (with missional intent) and local Christian artists who are involved in missional projects – see Chapter 2 for a fuller discussion.

missional documents *have* engaged with the arts in the late 20th and early 21st century and it will also suggest how to understand the global–local pressures that face Christianity in our era and negotiate these with integrity, giving particular attention to the importance of "the local." As people who cross cultures, missional artists need to interact deeply with local Christians and local arts – notwithstanding the complicated multi-faceted character of today's global world. The concluding sections will offer a simple but robust framework for what is understood by "mission" around which the arts can engage fruitfully in a range of ways. Taken together, these diverse elements can all contribute to the process of reimagining the Christian faith in Asia – a process that can involve missional artists who cross cultures working alongside those from within Asia.

Arts in Mission

In recent years, there has been a renewed interest within Mission Studies, as in Christianity more generally, about the importance of the arts:[3]

> We possess the gift of creativity because we bear the image of God. Art in its many forms is an integral part of what we do as humans and can reflect something of the beauty and truth of God. … the arts constitute one important way in which we can speak the truth of the gospel. Drama, dance, story, music and visual image can be expressions both of the reality of our brokenness, and of the hope that is centred in the gospel that all things will be made new. In the world of mission, the arts are an untapped resource. We actively encourage greater Christian involvement in the arts.

This comment comes from "The Cape Town Commitment (2010)" in a section entitled "Truth and the Arts in Mission." It shows real appreciation of the role of the arts and their relevance for worship, outreach and mission. It is evidence of how an informed interest in the arts, in relation to mission, is now being made explicit in contemporary missional statements. Viewed historically, the above comments have a context. Against the backdrop of the 1970s and a fresh critique of the global character of the church in the post-World War II era, there was a realisation that the church was in "a new missionary era" leading to a "re-evaluation of our missionary responsibility and role" which would lead to situations where "the universal character of Christ's Church will be more clearly exhibited."[4] From the late 20th century onwards, this meant that assessments[5] of

---

[3] Lausanne Movement, "The Cape Town Commitment (2010)," accessed Sep 6, 2021, https://lausanne.org/content/ctcommitment, Section IIA – 5 – Truth and the Arts in Mission.

[4] Lausanne Movement, "The Lausanne Covenant (1974)," accessed Sep 6, 2021, https://lausanne.org/content/covenant/lausanne-covenant, Section 8.

[5] Such reassessments occur periodically in history as with Constantini in the mid-1950s – see Andrew F. Walls, "The Western Discovery of Non-western Christian Art," in *The*

the worship and evangelism of the church would include a reappraisal of how vernacular cultures appropriated scripture, liturgical resources, music, arts and wider media, and show a deeper appreciation of the importance of local contexts and cultures.[6]

Mission Studies and the Arts in Mission

The readiness to engage with more creative and imaginative approaches to mission reflected in the Lausanne documents has been taken seriously by those involved in global mission. Deeper reflection and more nuanced critiques of the role of the arts have encouraged mission agencies and church leaders to embrace the arts in mission more fully and this has also been true in Asia. In an important observation, "The Lausanne Covenant (1974)" notes:[7]

> Missions have, all too frequently, exported with the gospel an alien culture, and churches have sometimes been in bondage to culture rather than to Scripture. Christ's evangelists must humbly seek to empty themselves of all but their personal authenticity in order to become the servants of others, and churches must seek to transform and enrich culture, all for the glory of God.

Such comments reflect a desire to develop resources for worship and mission which are local, and inspire missional artists to produce artistic outputs that will make an impact on local people in their own cultural settings. At the heart of Christian mission is the desire to share the good news of the kingdom of God and live lives that reflect its dynamic reality. There are times when this message is shared in a direct manner, but the arts can offer alternatives in which the gospel is communicated more indirectly. Part of the power of the arts is that they lend themselves to more symbolic and allusive modes of communication that can be made relevant in any cultural setting.[8]

A recent edition of the journal *Connections* dedicated to the "Arts in Mission"[9] highlights how the arts can be a point of invitation to others in mission, allowing them to consider Christian faith from fresh points of view. The capacity for the arts to facilitate this is described by concepts such as the "hospitable"

Missionary Movement in Christian History: Studies in the Transmission of Faith (Maryknoll, NY: Orbis Books, 1996), 173-86. Note Walls' comments about the "Tambaram International Missionary Conference" (1938) – in the 20th century – being the first Protestant missionary conference to discuss seriously "Christian Art," 180.

[6] Lausanne Covenant, Section 10.

[7] Lausanne Covenant, Section 10.

[8] Seerveld is a key exponent of the relevance of this concept – see Calvin Seerveld, *Bearing Fresh Olive Leaves: Alternative Steps in Understanding Art* (Carlisle: Piquant, 2000).

[9] "Arts in Mission," *Connections: The Journal of the WEA Mission Commission* 9, no. 2-3 (2010), available online: https://weamc.global/archive/Vol09No2-3_Arts.pdf.

character of the arts[10] – where they permit entry to a shared space, offering access to a range of people with different outlooks. The arts make it possible for people in diverse local cultures to express their identity as human beings, and for those who work across cultures there is space to explore a common shared humanity through artistic projects. The arts further encourage the use of "imagination" to engage with aspects of human life, especially the life-cycle from birth to death (or key moments in life), in specific cultures and even in particular places.[11] They are also able to "communicate" emotions and feelings, the complexity of the human condition, as well as the ideas and concepts that underpin the cultures people inhabit, and shape our shared experiences as human beings within culture and history.

Hospitality as both concept and practice has deep roots within the Christian faith.[12] The idea that the arts in mission can be a form of hospitality offers an insight that missional artists would do well to consider, exploring how the arts could be a point of invitation to "the other" in mission – enabling them to look at the world through different lenses. Franklin looks at how the arts might foster stances to mission that are contrasted with more head-on approaches: "... mission that is invitational, not coercive; vulnerable, not imperialistic; culturally sensitive not insensitive; and fully respectful of others."[13] Intellectually, there are two frames to Franklin's thinking. One is the manner in which the allusive character of the arts can help deliver a missional message that is less aggressive and assertive – less "top-down" or "from above" in its character. This may have relevance for a range of settings:[14]

> Could the arts soften the hard edge of our sometimes preachy style? Could the arts provide openings for exploring the big questions of human existence – which are essentially theological questions, questions with spiritual import? Art is certainly capable of bridging our differences and helping us to see what we as human beings hold in common.

He further notes that since cultures generally have a range of artistic traditions, local arts can be a source of cultural learning, affording opportunities

---

[10] See Cape Town Commitment, Section IIA – 5. Truth and the Arts in Mission. "Letting the arts serve as an hospitable environment in which we can acknowledge and come to know the neighbour and the stranger ..."

[11] Feature films often tend to exploit this specificity of locality – from art films dealing with travelling artists in South Korea, such as *Seopyeonje*, Taehung Pictures, directed by Im Kwon-Taek (1993), to socially provocative comedies set amongst Singapore's teenagers, in *I Not Stupid Too*, MediaCorp Raintree Pictures, directed by Jack Neo (2006).

[12] See, for example, Cathy Ross, "Creating Space: Hospitality as a Metaphor for Mission," *Anvil* 25, no. 3 (2008): 167-76.

[13] John Franklin, "Practising Hospitality: Arts and the Missional Task," *Connections: The Journal of the WEA Mission Commission* 9, no. 2-3 (2010): 6.

[14] Franklin, "Practising Hospitality," 6.

for identification that show respect for local cultures, and that they can make points of contact with the Christian faith that are of interest to local people. Such engagement is also intrinsically stimulating for artists and takes them to the heart of cultures and their arts. The interface between the arts and religious concepts has a capacity to create "intellectual space" and allow the re-evaluation of contrasting perspectives. As noted, the concept of imagination is used by both individuals and institutions in relation to the arts and Christian faith. Roberta King, one of a number of writers who have adopted this word in relation to the arts, offers another missional dimension – that of Christian dialogue with other religions[15] – when she notes that "scholars are realizing that arts can access the imagination in ways that inter-faith dialogue perhaps does not."[16]

Artistic forms can also be important in understanding how identity is shaped in local cultures. Local arts often reflect how ideas, concepts and emotions are shared and communicated in local cultures. Missional artists can understand more about a local culture, seeing how local arts reflect and express cultural identity. This local identity can be encouraged in worship, in the sharing of the story of the gospel, in evangelism, through music and song, through drama and other media. It can also help with transformation as the arts are invoked to address pressures and opportunities that local communities face. Missional artists can work with local arts to "help communities respond to the spiritual, social and physical challenges they face"[17] so that they bring out the identity and character of those communities and show how the message of the kingdom of God can bring about deep-seated and lasting transformation.

Further Reading on the Arts in Asia
Eubank, L. A. *Dance-Drama before the Throne: A Thai Experience.* Chiang Mai: TCF Press, 2004.
Lim, S. H. *Giving Voice to Asian Christians: An Appraisal of the Pioneering Work of I-To Loh in the Area of Congregational Song.* Saarbrücken: Verlag Dr Müller, 2008.
Takenaka, M. *The Place Where God Dwells: An Introduction to Church Architecture in Asia.* Hong Kong: Christian Conference of Asia, 1995.

---

[15] This also indicates the power of the arts to cross into different religious and cultural spheres – see Roberta R. King and William A. Dyrness, eds., *The Arts as Witness in Multifaith Contexts*, Missiological Engagements (Downers Grove, IL: IVP Academic, 2019).

[16] See Roberta R. King, "Christ Plays in Ten Thousand Places: Challenges and Possibilities for Music and the Arts in Mission," *Connections: The Journal of the WEA Mission Commission* 9, no. 2-3 (2010): 13.

[17] Brian Schrag, "Why Local Arts Are Central to Mission," *Connections: The Journal of the WEA Mission Commission* 9, no. 2-3 (2010): 15.

Global–Local Pressures

Any reflection on the arts in mission needs to take account of the interplay between the global and the local in today's world. For missional artists, global–local interactions can also be illumined by insights from world Christianity as that discipline highlights the importance of local players and local realities in any form of missional activity.[18] Missional artists must also learn from reflections by artists, generally, on how the arts could be developed in local contexts in our contemporary global world.[19] Our generation lives in a global, multicultural world where fusions of cultural elements can occur in surprising and unexpected ways. These currents reflect the complexity of the modern context and its interrelated character.[20] There are special challenges for missional artists going to other cultures. These include the negotiation of issues linked to the history of Christianity, including power and identity, especially where these relate to European arts from the global north which have enjoyed a privileged place in the global church. However, the history of art is full of examples of cultural interchange where the movements of people and ideas have created important artistic exchanges. Art from one culture penetrates the art of another and creates new syntheses.[21] In the visual arts, Western painters such as Van Gogh (and others) had a desire to explore Japanese art;[22] by contrast, modern day Chinese painters such as He Qi are aware of trends in western art[23] as they seek new pathways for their own distinctively Asian style.

Global Christianity faces a particular challenge. The global expansion and global presence of the church is an integral consequence of the church's mission

---

[18] World Christianity recognises that the transmission of the Christian faith is a polycentric activity – see Allan Yeh, *Polycentric Missiology: 21st-Century Mission from Everyone to Everywhere* (Downers Grove, IL: IVP Academic, 2016).

[19] Borrowing and reshaping artistic ideas across cultural (and even religious) boundaries has been a part of the artistic process over centuries – see introduction in Michael Church, ed., *The Other Classical Musics: Fifteen Great Traditions* (Woodbridge: Boydell Press, 2015), 1-23.

[20] See for example – Jehu J. Hanciles, *Beyond Christendom: Globalization, African Migration, and the Transformation of the West* (Maryknoll, NY: Orbis Books, 2008), and Suzel Ana Reily and Jonathan M. Dueck, eds., *The Oxford Handbook of Music and World Christianities*, Oxford Handbooks (Oxford: Oxford University Press, 2016).

[21] Michael Church makes the point that historically, music traditions have been part of global flows; for example, music traditions moved from the Mediterranean into north Africa and beyond into Asia – see Church, *The Other Classical Musics*, 10-13; 250-56. A reverse process takes place today as Silkroad Ensemble's music fuses western and eastern traditions in a new synthesis – see Yo-Yo Ma's Silkroad Ensemble. "Silkroad Ensemble," Silkroad, accessed Dec 22, 2020, https://www.silkroad.org/silkroad-ensemble.

[22] The Van Gogh museum in Amsterdam has a whole section devoted to the influence of Japanese arts. See for example, Vincent van Gogh, "Almond Blossom," Van Gogh Museum, accessed Dec 22, 2020, https://www.vangoghmuseum.nl/en/collection/s0176V1962.

[23] Qi He, *Look toward the Heavens: The Art of He Qi* (New Haven, CT: OMSC, 2006).

and God's concern for the nations. However, the transmission of the Christian faith[24] in the second millennium has *often,* though by no means always, been accomplished through Christians from the global north.[25]A combination of the flourishing of arts in the global north in this period and the contemporary power of the global north in terms of cultural institutions has meant that historically, and in the present, there is a disproportionate influence from the arts of the global north in the global church.[26] There are many situations where local people feel that such pressures have failed to affirm local cultures and local cultural expressions – this has led to a neglect or pushing aside of local cultural traditions and local arts. The negative impact on local cultures and particularly indigenous cultures and the unhelpful associations between Christianity and western culture has been clearly described by Ed Lapiz using the example of the Philippines.[27]

Negotiating Global–Local Tensions

Missional artists need to wrestle with the task of taking the arts across cultures in the midst of the complexities of the modern world with the simultaneous impact of the local and the global. They must negotiate global pressures so that they affirm local cultures and local arts, whilst allowing local people the scope to make their own artistic choices. Missional artists can function as catalysts to facilitate the local and give space to the local church and artists to affirm the place of their *own* culture. Missional documents from the Lausanne movement are helpful in showing the contours of this discussion. Local churches need to be able to celebrate their own culture: "We have emphasized that the church must be allowed to indigenize itself, and to 'celebrate, sing and dance' the gospel in its own cultural medium." But churches still have the liberty to draw on the global and elements beyond their own culture: "A church must be free to reject alien cultural forms and develop its own; it should also feel free to borrow from others."[28]

---

[24] On the serial expansion of Christianity see Andrew F. Walls, "Christianity in the Non-western World: A Study in the Serial Nature of Christian Expansion," in *The Cross-Cultural Process in Christian History: Studies in the Transmission and Appropriation of Faith* (Maryknoll, NY: Orbis Books, 2002), 27-48.

[25] Walls notes that, "By 1500, European Christianity possessed a coherent, largely homogenous artistic tradition. Art was generally speaking 'Christian art.' The Christianity which entered into engagement with the faiths of Asia … was in confident possession of an artistic tradition which had absorbed several vernacular artistic traditions." Walls, *The Missionary Movement in Christian History*, 174.

[26] See comments on "elitist" attitudes in Mark R. Francis, "Liturgy," in *Dictionary of Mission: Theology, History, Perspectives*, eds. Karl Müller, Theo Sundermeier, Stephen B. Bevans and Richard H. Bliese (Maryknoll, NY: Orbis Books, 1997), 284-87.

[27] See below for concerns about indigenous peoples; see also Ed Lapiz, "Where Every Nation Has a Contribution," *Connections: The Journal of the WEA Mission Commission* 9, no. 2-3 (2010): 7.

[28] Lausanne Movement, "The Willowbank Report: Consultation on Gospel and Culture," Lausanne Occasional Paper, no. 2 (1978), accessed Sep 6, 2021,

Some Christian communities have opted decisively towards the global and choose to give priority to global forms of Christian music. A Korean Christian leader was once asked after a typical Sunday Service: "Where is yours?" The questioner was wondering whether Korean music was being adequately included in worship. The Korean replied, "This *is* ours! We are a globalised society and this is the music we have chosen to adopt."[29] The choice towards global music by most of the churches in Korea is mirrored by an interest in the wider society of that same global music. In common with other north Asian and many elements of Chinese diaspora societies (in places such as Singapore, Malaysia, Indonesia and Thailand), global music derived from Europe and North America is common in both society and church.[30] On one side of the debate, an outstanding conductor such as Masako Suzuki (a Japanese Christian) would see global but western-derived forms of Christian music as being part of the *Asian* Christian heritage.[31]

Loh I-To, by contrast, has been an advocate for local music traditions and local hymnody. His input to the debate is exemplified in the compilation of the hymnal *Sound the Bamboo*.[32] His work as a composer and editor of hymns has challenged local musicians to both deeper contextualisation of global music and innovation across Asia. He encourages local Christians to compose hymns that reflect local musical styles and aesthetics as well as writing words that reflect the distinctive emotions and character of Asian settings.[33]

Missional artists need to respect opinions that favour the global. On the other hand, it is perfectly reasonable to encourage Asian churches to include music by musicians who come from their own cultures as in the Korean Protestant hymnbook and the hymnbooks edited by Loh I-To and others. It is vital that those who cross cultures as missional artists facilitate such artistic endeavours and

---

https://lausanne.org/content/lop/lop-2, Section 8 – Church and Culture: E – The Danger of Provincialism.

[29] Personal conversation with a Korean Christian, Mar 2002. See comments below on *Neulsori* for an example of a group that promotes traditional Korean music.

[30] See Michael N. C. Poon, "Music among Christians in South-East Asia," in *Christian Music: A Global History*, ed. Tim Dowley (Oxford: Lion, 2011), 219-20.

[31] Suzuki proposes that Asian *Christian* musicians are better placed to interpret Bach's church cantatas than *secular* European musicians as the former are more sympathetic to the Christian aesthetic and ethos that informs them. Paul T. McCain, "News Flash: J.S. Bach Was a Christian – Why Suzuki Gets Bach," *First Things* (Aug 1, 2010), accessed Jul 26, 2021,
http://firstthings.com/blogs/evangel/2010/01/news-flash-j-s-bach-was-a-christian-why-suzuki-gets-j-s-bach/.

[32] Christian Conference of Asia, *Sound the Bamboo: CCA Hymnal 2000* (Tainan: Taiwan Presbyterian Church Press, 2000).

[33] I-To Loh, "Contextualization versus Globalization: A Glimpse of Sounds and Symbols in Asian Worship," *Colloquium: Music, Worship, Arts* 2 (2005): 125-39. See also Chapter 6 on Loh and hymnody.

support local exponents of the arts. There is also much that can be learned from the writings and artistic endeavours of such Asian artists.[34] At a theological level, "The Willowbank Report (1978)" uses the book of Ephesians to remind Christians that individual churches are part of the "universal church" which crosses cultural divides:[35]

> Therefore, while rejoicing in our cultural inheritance and developing our own indigenous forms, we must always remember that our primary identity as Christians is not in our particular culture but in the one Lord and his one body.

As with other aspects of church life in relation to local contexts, there is a need for discernment and a willingness to recognise, ultimately, the choices made by local Christians whilst constantly affirming that our identity in Christ can be shaped by both local and global cultural elements.

Maintaining Sensitivity towards "The Local"

To some readers, this may seem an excessive, perhaps even a misplaced apologetic for the global. However, a balance needs to be struck between the push and pull of global forces, often boosted by history and power (and the cultural worlds that they inevitably create) with the role of the local in shaping alternative realities and ways of being in contemporary society. In what follows, this balance is redressed in terms of the local and this is an equally vital dimension of the discussion. The determination to respond to the undermining and neglect of the local in a global world is at the heart of the "Arts in Mission" special edition.[36] The danger and consequences of such neglect is eloquently, if somewhat starkly, expressed by Ed Lapiz:[37]

> Christianity came to the Philippines together with colonization. … Successful evangelization was often measured by the destruction of indigenous culture. The God of the Bible was presented as a western deity who could only be pleased with Western cultural expressions – in architecture, language or music. Liturgy had to conform to Western aesthetics. Indigenous culture was judged as demonic in a way.

Without such local input there is also a potential problem for Christian liturgy:[38] "The indigenous people became victims of singing the music and

---

[34] See the many examples of Asian artists, artistic activities, and writings and reflections related to them that are mentioned throughout this book.

[35] Willowbank Report, Section 8 – Church and Culture: E – The Danger of Provincialism.

[36] "Arts in Mission," *Connections*.

[37] Lapiz, "Where Every Nation Has a Contribution," 7.

[38] Midian is quoted in Neil R. Coulter, "Book Review of Andrew Midian's The Value of Indigenous Music in the Life and Ministry of the Church," *Connections: The Journal of the WEA Mission Commission* 9, no. 2-3 (2010): 16.

experiences of other people; they sing of what doesn't really concern them." These comments help the wider church to understand the predicament of local people who are marginalised even in their own culture.[39] Such negative attitudes towards the local people and culture meant that artistic expression tended to lean towards the arts of the global church but crucially, and negatively, turn away from indigenous or local cultures. As a result, when local Christians sought a Christian identity they often ended up taking on elements of an adopted global identity which turned them aside from their own culture. There are further challenges from history in this regard as suggested by "Redeeming the Arts (2004)":[40]

> Though the approach is changing, there are still groups of missionaries insisting on western art forms for indigenous churches. Based on the teaching they have received, many non-western churches have adopted this practice. It is a challenging task for local leadership to reclaim their traditional cultural practices.

The rejection of local arts can lead to people in local cultures feeling slighted.[41] The missional artist needs to be willing and poised to embrace local arts. Once there is an attitude of openness, the next steps that need to be taken are the actual learning about the local arts, then learning how they might be developed in relation to Christianity and the church's mission.[42]

> The work of Ed Lapiz and "Kaloob" shows the importance of affirming local arts and artists to redress the impact of global forces. "The goal is to see the Church use and reinterpret for contemporary worship the rich musical, dance and costume heritage of our people. … This is mainly because the dance and music vocabulary of the Filipino Christian church today, at least those that use dance in worship, needs enriching and Filipinization. … We should evolve a Filipino Christian liturgy."[43] Lapiz shows the importance of local arts at the level of contextualisation

---

[39] Ed Lapiz' work offers a model of how to protect and reinvigorate artistic resources so that they can be reclaimed in the culture and in the church. "This isn't dance; this is breathtaking research," Kaloob Dance, accessed Jul 26, 2021, http://www.kaloobdance.com/Vision.html.

[40] Lausanne Movement, "Redeeming the Arts: The Restoration of the Arts to God's Creational Intention," Lausanne Occasional Paper, no. 46 (2004), accessed Sep 6, 2021, https://lausanne.org/content/lop/redeeming-arts-restoration-arts-gods-creational-intention-lop-46, Act III – Scene II.

[41] Krabill tells a powerful story about how people from a mono-cultural background can fail to grasp the value of local arts. James R. Krabill, "These People Aren't Really Christian, Are They? A Mission Administrator's Plea for Ministry Training in Ethno-Arts," *Connections: The Journal of the WEA Mission Commission* 9, no. 2-3 (2010): 50-51.

[42] Terms such as "appropriation" and even "redeeming" of the arts are used – but these need to be handled with care.

[43] Lapiz, "Where Every Nation Has a Contribution," 8; see also Ed Lapiz, *Pagpapahiyang: Redeeming Culture and Indigenizing Christianity* (The Philippines, 2010), 171.

but also seeks to encourage indigenous traditions and arts and to strengthen a sense of identity and self-worth. Lapiz divides his activities into two categories, "performance" and "prayformance": the former is used in exhibitions, the latter is designed to be incorporated into worship.

Affirming Local Cultures in a Global World

This alternative perspective is expressed by artists such as Schrag and Spradlin, who affirm the global tapestry of creativity found in God's world expressed through local cultures and art forms.[44] Ideas from Mission Studies and the arts coalesce in the following quote with their implications for self-worth and identity as the arts become a conduit through which cultural identity and local cultural meanings can be communicated:[45]

> Our goal is to spark the emergence of enduring traditions of Scripture-infused song composition, drama, dance, story-telling, chanting, visual and other locally thriving arts, traditions that help communities respond to the spiritual, social and physical challenges they face.

Local visual arts and concepts are used creatively in *The Hope* film set in Tibet. Within the film, a travelling Tibetan storyteller and his daughter use four paintings in the local *thangka* visual arts style to illustrate the story of Christianity. The paintings share the characteristics of *thangka* paintings where multiple scenes are portrayed together (here in the form of four contemporary posters) to create a textured and nuanced sense of movement and flow in the story. Two of the paintings draw from the Old and two from the New Testament: through the storyteller's tales they offer a synopsis of the Christian faith with a local flavour and creatively address some of the misconceptions about the "good news" in that setting.[46]

The concept of "living theology" (from García-Rivera) indicates how local experiences of Christianity in worship are profoundly influenced by liturgical forms and, inevitably, these are shaped both by local theological emphases and by local arts. His insights have a particular relevance for local cultures. They affirm that all cultural expressions of Christianity shape it in a local image around the resources of the local culture – even when they draw on global liturgical

---

[44] See also Miriam Adeney, "Songs like Tropical Fish: Splashes of God's Creativity," *Connections: The Journal of the WEA Mission Commission* 9, no. 2-3 (2010): 46-47.

[45] Schrag, "Why Local Arts Are Central to Mission," 15.

[46] John Oswald, "Film and Art Open Tibetan Hearts to the Gospel," in *Worship and Mission for the Global Church: An Ethnodoxology Handbook*, eds. James R. Krabill, Frank Fortunato, Robin P. Harris and Brian Schrag (Pasadena, CA: William Carey Library, 2013), 305-307; see also hmsarthistorian, "Tibetan Christian Thangka Ministry," *Indigenous Christian* (Nov 22, 2011), accessed Jul 19, 2021, https://indigenousjesus.blogspot.com/2011/11/tibetan-christian-thangka-ministry.html.

forms.[47] Similarly, Spradlin affirms that local nuances inform all aspects of arts in a culture when he uses the language of "indigenous metaphors" and "symbols." He recognises that there is a distinctive dynamic at play in local cultures in line with their own aesthetic and artistic traditions. As a result, he is sensitive to the need for contextual expressions of Christianity to draw on local artistic categories (as expressed above by Schrag) but extends the list to include "ceremonies, liturgy, pageants, visual or movement expression, architecture" and similar cultural forms. On that basis, Spradlin redefines "artistic expression" so that it has a local character and makes a break with the global (often western-derived) artistic traditions that have characterised Protestant mission movements since the time of the Reformation. Such a view of the worth and distinctiveness of a whole range of artistic forms within a local culture gives an impetus to local artists to view themselves as God's "creative image bearers and our artistry as an integral part of life."[48]

> An example of a contextual liturgical procession is found in the response led by Melba Padilla Maggay, on behalf of the Institute for Studies in Asian Church and Culture (ISACC), to the disaster in the Philippines in 2013 caused by typhoon Yolanda. The procession was organised by Protestant Christians on Easter Sunday morning. It was a simple yet meaningful event – a journey on foot which culminated in a service of worship on the beach. Drawing on themes from John 21, there was a strong Filipino ethos and though some key participants were marked out by their white Easter clothing, most people were in ordinary casual dress. In the face of the powerful emotions experienced in the disaster, the procession and service evoked hope, expressed through Filipino rituals, refashioned as a Christian response to the aftermath of the typhoon and as a prelude to community-building by drawing out the local community's resources with the help of outside intermediaries.[49]

Late 20th century missional documents and the insights of World Christianity affirm the place of local cultures in a global world. "The Nairobi Statement on Worship and Culture (1996)" reminds missional artists that human cultures are valued and that worship and church life reflect four aspects of culture: the transcultural (essential elements that transcend culture); the contextual (key elements that reflect local culture); the counter-cultural (concepts that bring challenges to local cultures as needed); and the cross-cultural (local elements

[47] An introduction to García-Rivera's thinking is found in Michael J. Bauer, *Arts Ministry: Nurturing the Creative Life of God's People*, Calvin Institute of Christian Worship Liturgical Studies (Grand Rapids, MI: Eerdmans, 2013), 21. See further Alejandro R. García-Rivera, *A Wounded Innocence: Sketches for a Theology of Art* (Collegeville, MN: The Liturgical Press, 2003).
[48] Byron Spradlin, "Worship and the Arts in Ministry and Missions," *Connections: The Journal of the WEA Mission Commission* 9, no. 2-3 (2010): 49-50, for both quotes.
[49] See Melba P. Maggay, "Rise Up and Walk: Tacloban AVs," DVD (Manila: ISACC, n.d.), Resurrecting – Section III.

that are shared across the global church). Local styles are affirmed through both contextualisation and creative assimilation.[50]

> Although most Korean church music follows global patterns, *Neulsori* (a Korean traditional music mission group) is one ensemble that shows how church music sounds using the idiom of *gugak*[51] (Korean traditional music).[52] In their liturgical music-making, the group uses a mixture of sources including those from the standard Protestant Korean hymnbook and others derived from *gugak* styles. The instrumental and vocal accompaniment reflects a highly competent artistic model of how *gugak* can fit with liturgical and missional settings. An application to wider cultural forms is seen in a celebratory Korean dance "Bless the Lord!" where youngsters in *hanbok* (Korean traditional dress) sing and dance to *gugak* music.[53]

Local arts can speak powerfully into their own culture when handled by those who have an appropriate understanding. They can be a powerful channel for missional artists. Franklin makes an important point about local arts (thinking primarily of global south cultures):[54]

> When we consider the way in which music, dance, visual art, story and craft are woven into the fabric of indigenous cultures in the majority world, it is evident that the arts are an untapped resource for missions.

As noted above, local arts help with cultural learning and offer opportunities to identify with local cultures. They also offer fresh opportunities to link culture to Christian faith.[55] The challenge for missional artists is to learn the new culture

---

[50] "… creative assimilation enriches the liturgical ordo – not by culturally re-expressing its elements, but by adding to it new elements from local culture." Lutheran World Federation, "The Nairobi Statement on Worship and Culture: Contemporary Challenges and Possibilities (1996)," Calvin Institute of Christian Worship (Jun 16, 2014), accessed Jul 27, 2021, https://worship.calvin.edu/resources/resource-library/nairobi-statement-on-worship-and-culture-full-text, Section 3 – Worship as Contextual. This site gives helpful contextual details.

[51] For an introduction to the modern world of *gugak* (Korean traditional music) see National Gugak Center, accessed Sep 20, 2021, https://www.gugak.go.kr/site/main/index001.

[52] See "늘소리 국악선교단 - 1집" [*Nul-Soree* (sic.) Korean traditional music mission group – Volume 1], CD (Pusan: 다솔 [DaSol] Studio, 2001).

[53] CGNTV KIDS, "[워십] 축복하세 - 늘소리국악선교단 @나는야 주의 어린이 143회" [Worship – Bless the Lord! – Neulsori Traditional Music Mission Group@Me? I'm a Child of the Lord! Ep. 143], YouTube, accessed Jul 26, 2021, https://youtu.be/Dk3RA4G9t-c.

[54] John Franklin, "Arts and Mission Taskforce," *Connections: The Journal of the WEA Mission Commission* 9, no. 2-3 (2010): 5. See also Cape Town Commitment, Section IIA – 5.

[55] Franklin, "Practising Hospitality," 6-7.

adequately in order to understand the character of local arts and to explore (with local artists) how new artistic forms might be developed with integrity in missional contexts. At our current moment in history the challenges of mission necessitate greater scrutiny and possibly, for some, greater openness to the use of the arts in mission.

Arts in Mission – A Practical Framework

In what follows, a practical framework for the arts in mission is sketched out.[56] It suggests some concrete directions as to how the arts can be incorporated into mission. It will serve as a frame against which historical, contemporary and practical understandings of the arts in mission can be made. The spheres of focus will be described as follows: worship, witness and the transformation of the wider world.[57]

Worship, Witness and Transformation of the Wider World

Worship is used to refer, primarily, to services in church contexts; witness points to the fact that the gospel can be shared both within churches and outside their doors in local communities; "transformation of the wider world" indicates how the good news needs to spread out beyond the church in mission and, in so doing, transform both the church and the world beyond the church.

Worship and the Arts – Reimagining Our Encounter with God

The initial focus on "worship" underlines that Christian faith is expressed primarily within churches in their services of worship. All major denominations in the 21st century acknowledge the importance of culture and its implications for worship and liturgy following two thousand years of mission and the rise of the global church.[58] Scholars of mission such as Andrew Walls have noted the various ways in which the arts have been embraced in worship, with differing emphases depending on church traditions. Protestant churches, for example, have drawn on the arts to reflect local cultures and creativity in relation to the scriptures and the language of worship and liturgy and for hymnody; other

---

[56] See also the framework in Bauer, *Arts Ministry*, 122-23, which speaks of evangelism, community, social justice and the cosmos.
[57] Such a framework is meant to be suggestive rather than definitive – indicating that the potential relevance of the arts in relation to mission is wide-ranging.
[58] The term "liturgy" has a range of meanings that include the shape of services of worship (especially Sunday services), and the ordering of worship over the period of a year, hence ideas of the "liturgical calendar." See, for example, The Nairobi Statement on Worship and Culture.

traditions, such as Catholicism,[59] have drawn more on the visual or the performing arts and often have a wider range of musical styles.[60]

The history of mission, and of the church, is full of examples of how the arts have enriched Christian worship down through the centuries and across the world.[61] The Willowbank Report recognises that mission has led through history to "a rich inheritance of Christian theology, liturgy and devotion" although this is not to "be imposed on any church, but rather be made available to those who can use it as a valuable resource material."[62] Liturgical resources need to be shaped or reimagined locally but the transmission of Christian faith through the global church has generated materials that can enrich local churches wherever they are. These are important insights for mission as they show that, despite the treasury of liturgical resources accumulated over the centuries, balancing the needs and demands of the local and global in our worship, at any moment in time, is a delicate juggling act.[63]

> Miranda-Feliciano believes that "liturgy must be seen … as composing the present and local image of the church." She offers a range of ideas to help create a local flavour for worship in the Philippines. Beginning with a stress on vernacular languages, "experience is embedded in language," she further notes the importance of local arts by offering the architectural illustration of a chapel in a *salakot* (the local native palm hat) style as a metaphor of God's sheltering and protection. More stretching examples show how indigenous forms of communication for teaching, response and reflection could be adapted and drawn into the liturgy: *barangay* is a forum for discussion that allows participation between the people and the elders; *balagtasan* is a poetical debate chaired by a moderator. She concludes with the importance of "a distinct kind of music that is Filipino in essence and character"

---

[59] See Walls, *The Missionary Movement in Christian History,* 174-76, for a discussion of Catholic perspectives on missionary art centring on Constantini but setting his work in historical context. See further "Sancrosanctum Concilium (1963)," Vatican, accessed Jul 27, 2021,
https://www.vatican.va/archive/hist_councils/ii_vatican_council/documents/vat-ii_const_19631204_sacrosanctum-concilium_en.html, Sections 21 and 37-40.

[60] See also Laurel Gasque, "Art," in *Dictionary of Mission Theology: Evangelical Foundations*, ed. John Corrie (Downers Grove, IL: IVP, 2007), 26-29. Within Protestant denominations, Anglicanism and Lutheranism, in general, have broader musical traditions.

[61] See, for example, Andrew Wilson-Dickson, *The Story of Christian Music: From Gregorian Chant to Black Gospel* (Oxford: Lion, 2003), and Rowena Loverance, *Christian Art* (London: British Museum Press, 2007).

[62] Willowbank Report, Section 4 – Understanding God's Word Today: C – The Learning Community.

[63] Reflections within the Lausanne Movement imply that traditions across the globe have faced challenges around the arts across cultures and in mission.

that draws on local musical forms and instruments to create a Filipino ethos in worship.[64]

The ideas here draw out how the arts can illumine and enhance the community's liturgy and worship and include the choice and use of language both in worship and for the translation of the Christian scriptures, as well as the adoption of music and other arts in liturgical settings.

Suggested Reading on Worship and the Arts
Brown, F. B. *Inclusive Yet Discerning: Navigating Worship Artfully*. Calvin Institute of Christian Worship Liturgical Studies. Grand Rapids, MI: Eerdmans, 2009. Kapikian, C. *Art in Service of the Sacred: Symbol and Design for Worship Spaces*. Nashville, TN: Abingdon Press, 2006. Miranda-Feliciano, E. *Of Songs, Words and Gestures*: *Rethinking Filipino Liturgy*. Manila: ISACC, 2000. Taylor, W. D. O. *Glimpses of the New Creation: Worship and the Formative Power of the Arts*. Grand Rapids, MI: Eerdmans, 2019.

Witness – Telling God's Story through the Arts

"Witness" points to how the gospel – the life-changing story given by God to the church (the good news of the kingdom) – is shared so that it can be heard, understood and embraced by the world beyond the church.[65] Evangelism does not just take place outside the church but it can be helpful to think of the scope and potential of the arts in helping to relate the Christian story to the world beyond the church, as well as within. The sharing of the gospel, God's story, has an important place in the witness of the church: "The first task of evangelism is to tell the dramatic story of salvation history, the narratives that are foundational to the life of faith."[66] As an artist, Bauer is convinced that the sharing of the Christian story – the good news of the kingdom – can be enhanced by the appropriate use of the arts. Such a view is supported by the biblical scholar Michael Green.[67] The gospel of the kingdom is a timeless message but needs to be given expression in local and contemporary terms. Green shows how the flexibility demonstrated by the early church can be mirrored in creative and artistic ways of sharing the good news in the modern world. He gives examples[68]

---

[64] Evelyn Miranda-Feliciano, *Of Songs, Words and Gestures: Rethinking Filipino Liturgy* (Manila: ISACC, 2000), 7, 16 and 30 – for the quotes.

[65] See the Cape Town Commitment, Preamble and onwards, for the centrality of "witness."

[66] Bauer, *Arts Ministry*, 128.

[67] See Michael Green, *Acts for Today: First Century Christianity for Twentieth Century Christians* (London: Hodder & Stoughton, 1993).

[68] Green's examples fit the cultural settings of global Anglican/Episcopal churches in the 1980s and 1990s.

of Christians who "proclaim the gospel in drama, dance and preaching," perform "sketches," engage in "circle dancing to … folk tunes," use a "sketch-board," and sing in choirs.[69]

> Prinsep Street Presbyterian Church in Singapore encourages the arts and music as part of the church's life and outreach: "Enjoy God's gifts of arts and music with our performing groups and fellowships, and serve the church with your talents!" Included in the various music groups and choirs are "The Believers" who perform music and drama in a contemporary style. The Believers[70] put on musical dramas that have a Christian message: "Wandering Heart" shows how they combine music, drama and dance to share the good news in the contemporary Singaporean context in ways that really connect with local people and their lives.[71]

To share the good news of the kingdom within and beyond the church, missional artists need a good understanding of the *kerygma* – the key elements of the Christian faith. They also need imagination to think how the arts can contribute to the church's witness by sharing the Christian faith creatively through the retelling of the story of the gospel across cultures in a manner that reflects the diversity of the church worldwide.

Suggested Reading on Witness and the Arts
Bauer, M. J. *Arts Ministry: Nurturing the Creative Life of God's People.* Calvin Institute of Christian Worship Liturgical Studies. Grand Rapids, MI: Eerdmans, 2013.
Campbell, C. R. *Outreach and the Artist: Sharing the Gospel with the Arts.* Grand Rapids, MI: Zondervan, 2013.
King, R. R. *Global Arts and Christian Witness: Exegeting Culture, Translating the Message, and Communicating Christ.* Mission in Global Community. Grand Rapids, MI: Baker Academic, 2019.

---

[69] Green anticipates the attitudes and ideas developed in J. Nathan Corbitt and Vivian Nix-Early, *Taking It to the Streets: Using the Arts to Transform Your Community* (Grand Rapids, MI: Baker Books, 2003).

[70] "The Believers," Prinsep Street Presbyterian Church, accessed Jul 26, 2021, http://www.pspc.org.sg/ministries/arts-and-music/the-believers; and Jaime Wong, "Wandering Heart Trailer," YouTube, accessed Sep 20, 2021, https://youtu.be/wV5n-Bz5iHA.

[71] The church is also committed to outreach by members who are artists to the arts schools situated near the church building and has a range of artistic groups that share in the life of the church. See The Arts Fellowship, accessed Sep 20, 2021, https://www.pspc.org.sg/ministries/arts-and-music/the-arts-fellowship.

Transformation of the Wider World –
the Power of the Arts to Bring Change

The language of "transformation" and the idea of "the wider world" underlines that mission is not simply about the gospel as a story to share.[72] Rather, it includes how communities and societies are transformed through the mission of the church which is expressed, not just in the message of the kingdom, but by the example and model of the kingdom community. Although theologians of "mission as transformation" have not, to date, dealt extensively with the arts, they do show how the presence and character of Christians in a society can make a difference to the wider community. By reflecting Christian values, the arts can foster and contribute to transformation, and missional artists can draw creatively on the imaginative power of the arts to help people envisage different possibilities for their lives. The church's mission in the wider world requires empathy and understanding in terms of the arts but when properly embraced they can help bring about transformation, acknowledging that there are limits to what can be accomplished through the arts alone:

> We must state here that art, in and of itself, cannot transform; only Christ can transform the human condition. With that clarification as context, we can show that the arts allow for diversity as they "witness" in verbal and nonverbal ways to the truth about the human condition and incarnationally "show" God's redemptive purposes. They can also draw people to Christ when linked to acts of compassion and service. The arts enable cross-cultural and cross-generational communication and contextualization. Social and economic barriers can be overcome through collaborative art making, and arts used in therapies can invigorate health and healing.[73]

The arts, however, can be helpful in reaching out to groups and communities beyond the church, as they point to the transformative power[74] and life-changing character of the gospel at work both in the church and in the community around it. Bringing about genuine transformation requires both missional understanding and thoughtful artistic practice that draw deeply on the power of the arts to challenge how people view their everyday lives in order to invoke the possibility of change and point them in the direction of the kingdom and the God who sustains it.

---

[72] The idea of "mission as transformation" has wider roots but the core intention of transforming communities is shared in several sources of the arts and mission literature. See also Vinay Samuel and Chris Sugden, eds., *Mission as Transformation: A Theology of the Whole Gospel* (Oxford: Regnum Books, 1999).

[73] Redeeming the Arts, Prologue.

[74] "Transformation" also describes how Christian communities bring about change through mission – see, for example, Al Tizon, *Transformation after Lausanne: Radical Evangelical Mission in Global–Local Perspective* (Oxford: Regnum Books, 2008).

Personally affected in his own cultural setting by the events of the 9/11 attacks, the Japanese-American artist Makoto Fujimura has shown by example, and also in his writings and presentations, the importance for Christian artists of contributing constructively to culture by using their artistic gifts and ways of seeing the world to show the love and transformative power of God. As an artist working in both Asia and the west, he stresses the need for Christian artists to use art as a means to be nurturing *in* culture – recognising the goodness and bounty of God in the created world – rather than be distracted with defending "entrenched cultural identities."[75]

Suggested Reading on Transformation of the Wider World and the Arts

Corbitt, J. N., and V. Nix-Early. *Taking It to the Streets: Using the Arts to Transform Your Community*. Grand Rapids, MI: Baker Books, 2003.

de Gruchy, J. W. *Christianity, Art and Transformation: Theological Aesthetics in the Struggle for Justice*. Cambridge: Cambridge University Press, 2001.

Fujimura, M. *Culture Care: Reconnecting with Beauty for Our Common Life*. Downers Grove, IL: IVP Books, 2017.

Mitchell, J., G. Vincett, T. Hawksley and H. Culbertson, eds. *Peacebuilding and the Arts*. Rethinking Peace and Conflict Studies. Cham, Switzerland: Palgrave Macmillan, 2020.

Conclusion

This chapter shows the relevance of the arts in mission and the potential for the arts to express Christian concepts in new cultural contexts. It indicates how the concept of arts across cultures can help with the reimagining of Christian faith as an integral part of the missional process. It points to how contemporary Christians can draw on the resources of the arts to respond more creatively to the missional challenges that confront them and to recognise the potential of fresh approaches that put greater emphasis on the arts:[76]

There is a need for a paradigm shift in how we view the arts – a fresh vision to help us understand how the recovery of the imagination and the affirmation of the gift of artistic creativity can be both celebrative and significant for the church.

The time is ripe for churches and mission agencies to find a fresh vision for the arts so that they can harness the potential of the arts to enhance the sharing and living out of the gospel and Christian faith, showing how "symbols, rituals, dances, and musical instruments can be renewed, restored, and refocused to the

---

[75] Makoto Fujimura, *Culture Care: Reconnecting with Beauty for Our Common Life* (Downers Grove, IL: IVP Books, 2017). See also Makoto Fujimura, "Make Good Lecture: Culture Care," Morphē, accessed Jul 22, 2021, https://www.morphearts.org/resources/make-good-lecture-culture-care.

[76] Redeeming the Arts, Prologue.

glory of God."[77] In the language of this book, these sentiments indicate how Christian faith can be *reimagined* through the arts. The western world in its post-Christendom phase has reached the point where the perspectives of many and their "imaginations" are untouched by Christianity. Asia is a continent where many have not yet encountered Christian ideas, but the arts can be used to reimagine and revitalise Christian faith. Takenaka and his colleagues encourage viewing *The Bible through Asian Eyes* and such a process draws on artistic "ways of seeing" to shape the continuing sharing and transmission of the Christian faith.[78] The role of the arts in renewing God's world and human communities is to offer the church a dynamic that helps it be creative in a rounded and holistic manner – to be missional so that the kingdom of God is not just communicated, but lived out and given vibrant expression in the Christian community and through the lives of its members in the society around them. Missional artists need to engage deeply with local cultures, to understand the potential of local arts, and to learn and embrace new artistic forms so that they can draw on them with integrity in conjunction with local artists. In so doing, they will make a creative impact in worship, witness and the transformation of the wider world, throughout the diverse cultures and societies of Asia, and will contribute to the ongoing task of reimagining the Christian faith in the 21st century.

Questions for Reflection/Discussion

1. How do the Lausanne documents from the Covenant to the Cape Town Commitment encourage us to look afresh at the arts in mission? How do categories such as "hospitality" and "imagination" broaden our understanding of what the arts can contribute?

2. The discussion of global "pressures" that can favour the global at the expense of the local is a reality in many regions. How do missional artists and local Christians "negotiate" these tensions in your context? There is also a section on how "the local" can be affirmed. How do the examples from the Philippines point to ways in which such "affirmation" can take place?

3. The "image of Christianity" and "the de-westernisation of the image" of Christianity:[79] how might these theological concepts inform artistic practice in Asia?

4. "Worship, witness and transformation of the wider world." How do these categories offer a range of possibilities for the arts in mission? Are all three categories reflected in your own context in relation to the arts in mission? If not, are there ideas that might inspire further engagement?

---

[77] Redeeming the Arts, Epilogue.

[78] Masao Takenaka and Ron O'Grady, *The Bible through Asian Eyes* (Auckland: Pace Publishing, 1991), 7-13.

[79] See also the ideas of Melba Maggay (in the Preface) and Moonjang Lee (in the Introduction).

2. Artists in Mission:
Becoming Missional Artists across Cultures
Warren R. Beattie

This chapter develops the idea of "missional artists" and analyses how they can interact with local cultures and develop the skills needed to enter the world of local arts. Learning to engage with local arts has parallels to learning local languages: the development of artistic skills is a process which involves ongoing cultural engagement and embrace in a deep and sustained manner. The closing sections reflect on the nurture of missional artists at both an individual and organisational level.

The opening chapter considers how the *arts* are connected to mission. In this chapter the focus will be on *artists*. The realisation that artists as well as arts are important in mission is made clear in the following quote from "The Cape Town Commitment (2010)":[1]

> Artists at their best are truth-tellers and so the arts constitute one important way in which we can speak the truth of the gospel. Drama, dance, story, music and visual image can be expressions both of the reality of our brokenness, and of the hope that is centred in the gospel that all things will be made new.

The Cape Town Commitment reminds us that such artists are not simply inventing ideas and art forms as they react to the world around them – rather, they are speaking *truth* to the world, in all its need and disarray, and are helping others to approach this truth from a variety of perspectives through their artistic creations. When Colin Harbinson looks at artists in terms of the concepts of authenticity and witness he makes similar points. Witnesses are people who encounter a significant moment in life and feel "compelled to make known to others what we know." For Harbinson, such witness viewed in artistic terms will have a "ring of truth."[2] By coming at issues from fresh perspectives, but moving from the "familiar to the unfamiliar," the artist opens up concepts and their artistic medium becomes a "window" on reality. He reminds us that good art does not take us away from reality. Rather, it functions as an authentic witness and in doing so helps others experience the world around us in a fresh manner:[3]

---

[1] Cape Town Commitment, Section 5.
[2] Colin Harbinson, "Art as Authentic Witness," *Connections: The Journal of the WEA Mission Commission* 9, no. 2-3 (2010): 10 – echoing T. S. Eliot.
[3] Harbinson, "Art as Authentic Witness," 11.

For a work of art to be a true witness it must be deeply authentic in its portrayal of life as we experience it, yet thoroughly biblical in the breadth of its vision and worldview. As artists we must embrace God's command and Christ's commission to be faithful witnesses of what we have seen and heard.

The idea of biblical truth is instructive here, as it acts as a lens on what the Cape Town Commitment calls "brokenness" and "hope"[4] – helping artists to think about the fallen nature of humanity but also the hope and possibility of redemption that is held out in the Christian scriptures and faith.

Missional Artists

The term chosen to best describe the kind of person for whom this book is intended – an artist who lives, works and creates art *across cultures* – is a "*missional artist.*" Both of these words, taken individually and together, are important: missional artists have a *missional* vocation but their identity as *artists* and the artistic dimensions of their vocation are indispensable facets of who they are. What it means to be a missional artist is clearly expressed in "Redeeming the Arts (2004)" through three lenses: missional artists have 1) a *perspective*, a way of seeing that allows ideas to be shaped and formed by the artist through 2) the medium of their *artistic discipline*, and this process of artistic endeavour and creation, in turn 3) facilitates *an interaction and response* back to the wider community through works of art.[5]

> Artists not only see the world in unique ways, they also use their design sense in any art form to interpret and arrange their responses to the world. Devices such as composition, story line, choreography, screenplay, and many subsets of those skills shape the finished product for the audience, so that our experience of it is largely controlled by the artist.

From the sphere of aesthetics, Calvin Seerveld writes that "artists provide binoculars for helping us look at the world and imaginatively to understand it more"[6] and he puts a similar premium on the act of "seeing" (or "envisioning") which lies behind such artistic activity. This does not take away from the process of developing skills and the elements of a craft, shaped by education and practice, and enhanced over time with commitment and engagement. Rather, all these elements melded together underpin the vocation of skilled artists and result in the emergence of works of art.[7]

The links between missional vocation, artistic identity and artistic skills are brought out in the following comment: "Artistic expression is meaningful work

---

[4] Cape Town Commitment, Section 5.
[5] Redeeming the Arts, Act II – Scene II: How Artists Design.
[6] Seerveld, *Bearing Fresh Olive Leaves*, 59.
[7] Seerveld, *Bearing Fresh Olive Leaves,* 49-51.

in the kingdom of God in any culture and is worthy of study, apprenticeship, and the cultivation of mastery. There are no short cuts to excellence."[8] By affirming the value and challenges of the artistic calling, this observation brings out two important points. Firstly, the missional artist is one who essentially contributes to the life of the kingdom of God through their *artistic* vocation, skills and outputs. As we have seen, missional activity can include worship, witness and transformation. Like others involved in mission who contribute through their vocational identity – as teachers and lecturers, in the health sector, in management and administration, or in church-related ministry roles – so missional artists contribute through their artistic vocation to the kingdom of God. Secondly, the missional artist is engaged in a *cultural* journey as well as an artistic one. Indeed, the engagement with a new culture as an artist involves general cultural learning as well as artistic explorations. Not only does the missional artist have to identify with their new culture at a personal, human level, they also need to adopt as their own the artistic traditions of the culture. Such an embrace takes the existing artistic experience and expertise gained in their own culture and allows it to be contextualised as they enter more fully into the artistic traditions of another culture.[9]

The Cape Town Commitment makes the point that the arts can be a dimension of Christian discipleship and speaks of: "Bringing the arts back into the life of the faith community as a valid and valuable component of our call to discipleship."[10] This suggests that the arts need to be part of the life of discipleship for all Christians, recognised as a medium through which disciples can gain more profound insight about their faith. However, implicit in such a description is the idea that for some their very calling as disciples,[11] as followers of Christ, is to be artists.[12] In its opening section, Redeeming the Arts also stresses the link for artists between discipleship and the biblical and theological foundations that are at the heart of Christian life:[13]

> … to understand discipleship for artists as participants in the church's mission in the world, we need to understand with more empathy and perspective some of the

---

[8] Redeeming the Arts, Act II – Scene II: Artistic Mastery.
[9] The title of Scott's book reflects this journey – see Joyce Scott, *Tuning in to a Different Song: Using a Music Bridge to Cross Cultural Differences* (Pretoria: University of Pretoria Institute for Missiological and Ecumenical Research, 2000).
[10] Cape Town Commitment, Section IIA – 5. Truth and the Arts in Mission.
[11] Precursors for these roles can be seen in the Old Testament people of God. Peterson uses the model of "Bezalel as an artist" (after Ex. 31). See Eugene Peterson, "The Pastor: How Artists Shape Pastoral Identity," in *For the Beauty of the Church: Casting a Vision for the Arts*, ed. W. David O. Taylor (Grand Rapids, MI: Baker Books, 2010), 89-96.
[12] For artists who are musicians, there are examples in the Old Testament (1 Chron. 6:31-47) – see Jeremy S. Begbie, *Resounding Truth: Christian Wisdom in the World of Music*, Engaging Culture (Grand Rapids, MI: Baker Academic, 2007), 60-67.
[13] Redeeming the Arts, Prologue. (See also Act II – Discipleship.)

key issues that affect their involvement … the discipleship of the artist shaped by a kingdom view … as uniquely gifted and vital parts of the Body of Christ – who like us all are called to work under the lordship of Christ, the creative Head of the Body which is the church.

The whole of "Act II" on Discipleship takes this theme further by encouraging Christian artists to see aspects of discipleship – in terms of character and relationships – as integral to Christian artistic formation.

Arts Ministry

The discourse of "arts ministry" offers a useful bridge between the vocational identity and training of missional artists and the application of artistic skills to various spheres of ministry. Arts ministry offers an approach that helps missional artists shift "attention from the inner life of the artist, from a focus on God and human formation to the outer life, where we examine the various ways in which artists and arts ministers are embedded in the world."[14] In their vocation, missional artists, like other artists, need to move from concepts and imaginings to create actual works of art that will connect with other people in worship, witness and the transformation of the wider world.

In his book on arts ministry, Bauer uses terms such as "intuition" to speak of the capacity of artists to look inwards spiritually and theologically; but he is aware that artists also need to have a "social imagination" that allows them to integrate their ideas about faith in a manner congruent with the kingdom of God, and the artistic and ministry vision to make their works of art relate to and engage with the wider world.[15] Redeeming the Arts makes similar comments in relation to what they term the "marketplace" – the everyday world.[16] It sees the missional artist on a journey that combines artistic and missional elements parallel to the journey of Christian discipleship.

Suggested Reading on Artists and Imagination
McElroy, J. S. *Finding Divine Inspiration: Working with the Holy Spirit in Your Creativity.* Shippensburg, PA: Destiny Image, 2008. Shaw, L. *Breath for the Bones: Art, Imagination and Spirit.* Nashville, TN: Thomas Nelson, 2007.

---

[14] Bauer, *Arts Ministry,* 122; Redeeming the Arts, Prologue: "Christian Art"? "Christian Artists"? – makes it clear that Christian artists are by no means "constrained" to the missional sphere; nor should the art created by Christians be evaluated in a limited or utilitarian manner. See further Su-Chi Lin, *Spaces of Mediation: Christian Art and Visual Culture in Taiwan*, Contact Zone Explorations in Intercultural Theology 24 (Leipzig: Evangelische Verlagsanstalt, 2019), 11-12 – footnote on Christian Art.
[15] Bauer, *Arts Ministry*, 29, 32 and 122.
[16] "Marketplace" has an equivalent sense to "the wider world." Redeeming the Arts, Act III Transformation – Arts, Mission and the Marketplace. See also Act II Discipleship.

Turner, S. *Imagine: A Vision for Christians in the Arts*. Rev. and expanded ed. Downers Grove, IL: IVP Books, 2016.

Missional Artists and Local Cultures

Entering any new Asian culture, the missional artist soon encounters not only the challenges of the unfamiliar languages and cultural forms but the many different artistic traditions and media that flourish. These are fashioned by different approaches to aesthetics and often have their own distinctive ethos.[17] The implications of this affect artists whether they enter a traditional oral culture, such as those of the indigenous groups of the Philippines or a modern urban society, such as South Korea with its combination of ancient cultural traditions, "hi-tech" devices and contemporary media showcasing *Hallyu* (the "Korean wave").

Engaging with a Local Culture

Identification with a new culture involves our whole being and our lifestyle, not just detached, intellectual reflection on ideas and concepts.[18] A missional artist who identifies with a local context must not only understand local arts but also the culture in its entirety. Such cultural learning is foundational for anyone working *across cultures* but for missional artists it forms an essential part of the process of learning about, engaging with and, ultimately, embracing a new culture. Jim Chew's framework for contextual mission uses terms such as message, lifestyle and ministry – where the concept of ministry underlines the shift that has to take place in a local culture, from theory to practice, and how ideas are embedded and reimagined in the ebb and flow of everyday activities.[19] The importance of lifestyle is echoed by Anthony Gittins: those who cross cultures, such as missional artists, need to move "from a monocultural to an intercultural lifestyle."[20] Such a transition is not always easy as it represents an experiential journey which involves social transitions as well as psychological and spiritual elements.

Gittins has a background as an anthropologist. He is by no means naïve about the challenges of cultural learning and gives informed advice to those who cross

---

[17] See, for example, Melba Padilla Maggay and William A. Dyrness, "Art and Aesthetics," in *Global Dictionary of Theology: A Resource for the Worldwide Church*, eds. William A. Dyrness and Veli-Matti Kärkkäinen (Downers Grove, IL; Nottingham: IVP Academic; IVP, 2008), 64-70.

[18] Jim Chew, *When You Cross Cultures: Vital Issues Facing Christian Missions*, New ed., rev. & updated (Singapore: Nav Media, 2009).

[19] This parallels Bauer's concept of arts ministry (above): the flow from the inward sphere, the artist's ideas, to the outward, the embodying of ideas in concrete works of art.

[20] Anthony J. Gittins, *Living Mission Interculturally: Faith, Culture, and the Renewal of Praxis* (Collegeville, MN: Liturgical Press, 2015), 15-28.

cultures. He reflects on the need to develop "ethno-cultural competence" and the ability to move from attitudes of "ethno-centrism" towards "ethno-relativism."[21] In short, how to transition from having intellectual and emotional links to just *one* culture to having the capacity to engage wholeheartedly with *another* culture. Gittins wonders whether someone who is unwilling to make this cultural journey, or worse, unaware of the need to do this, is like the person who goes to another culture and says, "Come join us, and we will teach you to do things our way – as we always have done."[22] His writings are as relevant to missional artists as to those who are on a journey of cultural learning and identification. It is clear that the opposite of cultural embrace is an alternative, to some degree, of cultural rejection. Such rejection can cause damage to local people, not just in the neglect of their local cultures and the loss of resources of local arts, but also in the corresponding impact on their identity and self-esteem. Missional artists, by contrast, need to engage with local arts and empathise with local artists if they are to facilitate the use of local artistic resources that can enhance the church's life and help it to flourish through local expressions of Christianity.

> Annie Baird was a missionary and music educator involved in the production of an important songbook in Korea, *Ch'angkajip* (*The Book of Songs)* in the 1910s. The motivation for this songbook reflected an increasing missional awareness and sensitivity to Korean culture in music education. The musicologist Kim shows how *The Book of Songs* took account of differences in musical styles found in indigenous Korean approaches to music – the adoption of certain rhythmic patterns, the favouring of pentatonic scales, and the avoidance of semitones – and so made a conscious effort to reflect local musical preferences. Baird also showed real proficiency in the Korean language and sensitivity in setting Korean words to music. Her collaboration with Choi Ja-Kyung, a highly skilled Korean colleague, further indicates that Baird had a genuine appreciation of the contribution local people can and should be encouraged to make to artistic endeavours in their own cultures.[23]

---

[21] Gittins, *Living Mission Interculturally*, 98-114.
[22] Gittins, *Living Mission Interculturally*, 24-30.
[23] S. Kim, "Korean Responses to Western Music Collaboration in the Early Twentieth Century" (Research Seminar, University of Edinburgh, Sep 2018). Kim has a PhD (2017), in historical musicology from Ehwa Womans University in Seoul, South Korea, where she researched the contribution of Baird and colleagues to Korean musical culture in relation to the *Ch'angkajip* and its era.

Book Idea

Loh, I. T. [M. N. C. Poon, ed.] *In Search for Asian Sounds and Symbols in Worship.* Singapore: Trinity Theological College, 2012.

The musician and hymnbook editor, Loh I-To, is a significant figure in Asian church music. This volume introduces his work in relation to hymnody and music for Asian contexts and helps foster an understanding of both theoretical and practical elements by drawing out the unique contributions made by Loh. The book also highlights the importance of contextualisation for church music in Asian settings.[24]

Becoming Bilingual and Bicultural – Implications for Missional Artists

When a person moves to a new culture there is a pressing need to become competent in a new language – a process described by the term bilingualism. Those who cross cultures use the term "becoming bicultural" as an extension of the idea of becoming bilingual. This can be seen in "The Willowbank Report (1978)": "Indeed, we believe it is enriching for Christians, if they have the opportunity, to develop a bi-cultural (sic) and even a multi-cultural existence."[25] Mastering a language involves learning, practice, effort and perseverance. This example of cultural learning points to the energy and time that are needed if missional artists are to develop a similar competence in the artistic traditions of a new culture. Redeeming the Arts is very conscious of both the idea that the arts are themselves a kind of language and the potential of local art forms to offer real possibilities for communicating aspects of the Christian faith in mission:[26]

> The arts provide a window to the language of the heart. Such a language is able to bypass obstacles that keep us from relating to one another. It takes time to do the research that will unravel the meanings of indigenous art, and weave well the threads and patterns of indigenous Christianity, so that the gospel can be poured into indigenous forms.

---

[24] The volume is edited by Michael Poon and includes concluding reflections from Lim Swee Hong – both of whom are important advocates of Asian hymnody and share an interest in Loh I-To's contribution to its development.

[25] Willowbank Report, Section 8. Church and Culture – G. The Church's Influence on Culture. This is an important insight: applied to local churches it stimulates them to have horizons beyond local worship rather than being constrained *only* by local cultural elements.

[26] Redeeming the Arts, Act III – Scene II: The Arts, Evangelism, and Contextualization in Mission.

Local arts and "languages of the heart" also offer a challenge to artists in that they need to learn these new media of communication.[27] The idea of mastering a new artistic tradition and its cultural forms, such as a music tradition, has been expressed in the term "bi-musical."[28] The ability to acquire such skills begins with the cultivation and development of a mindset that is open to "the other" (and their local culture) and to local forms of cultural and artistic expression. However, the learning journey does not stop there. It must go beyond openness and identification with a local culture and local arts by the missional artist to a deeper engagement with local artistic traditions, local aesthetics and local artistic know-how so that the missional artist embraces and makes these their own. Then, and only then, will they be able to draw on their newly acquired intercultural artistic knowledge as they apply their skills to the interface between the arts and mission.

Implicit in Gittin's conception of the shift to an intercultural lifestyle is the idea of "integration." By this he means that one is able to understand cultural experience in an integrated manner from a range of perspectives. Such integration is also necessary for the missional artist with their palette of artistic and aesthetic skills as they approach a range of projects as missional artists in a local culture. Applied to missional artists, these ideas push them to move beyond their own monocultural,[29] linguistic and artistic frameworks to become bicultural, bilingual, bi-musical and, ultimately, have a capacity for "multi-arts."

> Tibetan songs which help give local flavour to *The Hope* film project were developed by a bi-musical artist who had knowledge of local musical styles and instruments. "Five lyrical songs reinforce the film's storyline and provide time for reflection. Two use an indigenous question-and-answer format and, in keeping with Tibetans' love of music videos, four are choreographed with Tibetan regional dances. The third song is a poignant lament in soaring nomadic style. The final song is a call to the nations to dance the dance of faith in Christ illustrated … by diverse Tibetan styles. … In all five songs, videography features the striking lament of the high-altitude plateau." Extensive knowledge of a local music tradition – being bi-musical – allows an engagement with local ethos, emotions and aesthetics and can facilitate points of contact with other artistic genres.[30]

---

[27] For the benefits of indigenous arts see Lapiz, "Where Every Nation Has a Contribution," 7-9.

[28] Brain Schrag, "Becoming Bi-musical: The Importance and Possibility of Missionary Involvement in Music," *Missiology: An International Review* 17, no. 3 (Jul 1989): 311-19.

[29] Not all missional artists come from monocultural backgrounds but the term stresses the shift from predominantly one culture to two or many cultures.

[30] Oswald, "Film and Art Open Tibetan Hearts to the Gospel," 305-307. See also John Oswald, *A New Song Rising in Tibetan Hearts: Tibetan Christian Worship in the Early 21st Century* (Chang Mai: Central Asia Publishing, 2001).

A key challenge for Christian missional artists is that they would not be able to identify deeply with the choices that local Christians make either *towards* the local or *away* from the local if they themselves are unable to appreciate local arts. A missional artist who only knows their own language, their own style of worship and their own artistic tradition, will struggle to be a catalyst towards the local; one who is more bicultural and who can appreciate and develop "bi-artistic" (or "multi-arts") skills will be better able to empathise with both trajectories, even if local Christians ultimately decide to make artistic choices towards the global.[31]

Embracing Local Arts in a Local Culture

Over the centuries, theological ideas and frameworks that have drawn heavily on global or western patterns[32] have been transmitted without adequate reference to local issues: the same can be true for the arts in mission. There are reasons, derived from the history of Christianity and the flows of the transmission of faith, as to why European art forms have taken precedence in certain situations.[33] However, these realities have sometimes inhibited Christian groups who want to draw on their own local arts. There is a need for missional artists to be willing to become advocates of local art forms and to give special attention to those where necessary:[34]

> Missionaries need to champion the value of arts done by the local people in their own style, rhythm, and language, allowing them to express their praise to God. Art and music shaped by western society is present everywhere in the world. Instead of allowing this to erode interest and respect for the traditional indigenous culture, a strong church will accept the healthy challenge to worship freely with both western and indigenous music styles.

Missional artists need to engage intensely with the local community, the local cultures and local arts. They need to remember that, whilst learning local arts is an act of identification, care needs to be taken about the role of an artist coming into another's world and creating art works there. Missional artists need to be aware of the character of specific cultures and develop a thorough cultural grounding. Moving beyond the global to the local involves complex issues of identity and identification at a human level and these issues influence the arts and artists as they function at the local level as well. In addition to authentic

---

[31] See the Nairobi Statement on Worship and Culture, Section 5 – Worship as Cross-Cultural. It is, of course, possible to make some artistic choices that reflect global dimensions and other choices that lean to the local.

[32] See, for example, Melba Padilla Maggay, *Filipino Religious Consciousness: Some Implications to Missions* (Quezon City: ISACC, 1999).

[33] See Walls, *The Missionary Movement in Christian History*, 173-86.

[34] Redeeming the Arts, Act III – Scene II: Contextualization.

witness the idea of authentic *presence* in the local also becomes important. Missional artists who cross cultures need to give time and energy to the discovery of local artistic traditions. If they are in a culture where these artistic traditions are part of the church's world, they can engage with what already exists. If not, there needs to be a degree of humility and cooperation with local artists in order for missional artists to draw on local artistic traditions for a missional purpose. It is important to discuss with local people how this might best work out in practice. In some instances, these efforts of artistic learning can lead to more meaningful engagement with local people around the Christian message and how it is expressed in local arts.[35]

> Jim Chew shares about an artist whose appreciation of *gamelan* music and local dramatic arts led them to draw on traditional music and drama to express biblical themes through cultural art forms. The thematic focus included songs based on the Christmas story from texts in Isaiah and Luke using the *gendhing* art form which combines musical and instrumental elements. The story of Joseph was told using the *ketoprak* form, a kind of musical drama whose traditional links to historical stories fitted well. For the artist, this involved a process of cultural learning that involved a real engagement with the local culture and a deeper appreciation of some of the aesthetic and cultural dimensions of the art forms. It also led to better relationships with artists – musicians and actor-dancers – and fostered a growth in artistic imagination as the artist pondered how to express biblical themes in new cultural forms.[36]

Interacting with Local Artists

Missional artists not only have to learn *from* local artists, it is imperative that they learn to collaborate *with* local artists. Local artists have a much broader understanding of what local art forms mean to local people. They are better placed to contextualise skilfully the gospel, taking full advantage of the local art forms, especially those that could be invoked in the retelling of the gospel story. Bill Harris shares his confidence that local artists can be "trusted to depict the gospel in culturally familiar terms and nourish the hearts of growing believers with spiritual truth embedded in familiar forms."[37] He gives a concise sketch of how the discernment of local artists can contribute to the refinement of local arts in mission:[38]

---

[35] See the discussion in Takenaka and O'Grady, *The Bible through Asian Eyes*, 7-13.
[36] Jim Chew gives an example of engagement with local arts practitioners in a South Asian culture – Chew, "An Example of Contextualised Ministry among Javanese," in *When You Cross Cultures*, 45-50 – chap. 7.
[37] Bill Harris, "The Church Planter and Artist: Becoming Partners in Ministry," *Connections: The Journal of the WEA Mission Commission* 9, no. 2-3 (2010): 35.
[38] Harris, "The Church Planter and Artist," 34.

In a few fledgling church plants among the Sakha (Siberia), I have seen missionaries encourage local artists to examine their own culture and decide for themselves which elements of their indigenous arts might be appropriate to bring into worship services.

For local arts to prosper in relation to mission, there needs to be a genuine and ongoing commitment to developing and nurturing local artists. This means "identifying and mentoring" as well as inspiring artists who have gifts that can contribute to the arts in mission, helping to create contextual expressions of worship, witness and transformation of the wider world.[39]

> Alice Compain describes how playing the violin at night in her early days in mission brought her into contact with a younger person who taught her some national melodies in Laos which she transcribed, noting their rhythmic complexity. Later, she contributed some of those melodies as the basis for a local hymnal for young people. Interactions with Khmer people in the 1970s and '80s around the use of traditional melodies and the creation of new lyrics as well as, sadly, the death of many local Christians and musicians, led to Compain becoming a key coordinator for a Khmer hymnbook project. These projects reflected Compain's ability to combine specialist musical skills and develop close relationships with local people to work together to produce local hymnody.[40]

Suggested Reading on Local Artists in Asia
Bowden, S., J. Hesselink, M. Fujimura and J. A. Kohan. *Beauty Given by Grace: The Biblical Prints of Sadao Watanabe*. Baltimore, MD: Square Halo Books, 2012.

Bowden, S., J. Hesselink, M. Fujimura and J. A. Kohan. *Beauty Given by Grace: The Biblical Prints of Sadao Watanabe*. Baltimore, MD: Square Halo Books, 2012.
He, Q. *The Art of He Qi*. Roseville, MN: He Qi Arts, 2013.[41]
Lapiz, E. *Pagpapahiyang: Redeeming Culture and Indigenizing Christianity*. The Philippines, 2010.

Cultural Learning in Asia

Cultural learning needs to take account of a region's history.[42] For any artistic focus to have due regard for the depth and range of the local culture it must deal

---

[39] Redeeming the Arts, Act II – Scene II: Artistic Development of the Artist.
[40] OMF International, "A Musician on the Mission Field," Issuu, accessed Jul 21, 2021, https://issuu.com/omf_international/docs/alice_compain_booklet. See also Alice Compain, "Born across Borders, Raised in a Refugee Camp: The History of the Cambodian Hymnal," in *Worship and Mission for the Global Church: An Ethnodoxology Handbook*, eds. James R. Krabill, Frank Fortunato, Robin P. Harris and Brian Schrag (Pasadena, CA: William Carey Library, 2013), 313-15 – chap. 94.
[41] This is a second book of He Qi's art.
[42] Takenaka and O'Grady, *The Bible through Asian Eyes*, 8-10. This book reflects on Asian artists learning about Asian cultures and Asian art – including Asians who are missional artists in their own culture – and discusses interacting with artists in multi-religious contexts. See 7-13.

with the relevant cultural, historical and religious issues. Cultural learning also involves an awareness of the suffering and challenges that have come from the impact of global migrations and colonial powers from Europe and, sometimes, through the role of major powers such as China and Japan from within Asia. These historical forces have created economic and cultural pressures and prompted a quest for identity that has intensified in the late 20th and early 21st centuries. They have also created a desire for societies to be free from external pressures – though sometimes internal pressures are very real as well.[43] This rich history with its artistic and aesthetic traditions has been a source of inspiration for artists as they seek to mine the resources of the past:[44]

> ... there are several Asian artists searching their own nation's cultural history to find an authentic indigenous basis for their art. Ketut Lasia uses the disciplined Balinese style of art to paint biblical stories; ... Kim Hak Soo and Kim Ki Chang have found inspiration in Korean folk art; many Chinese artists are using brush paintings and promising young artists from Thailand and Burma, Sawai Chinnawong and Saw Edward, are exploring the traditional art styles of their countries.

There is also a need to be aware of the religious dimensions of the Asian cultures as "Asia remains the heart of the world's great religions."[45] This serves as a reminder that cultural learning has a broad agenda that has to include learning about the religious settings of a new culture. For those engaged in creating Christian art in Asia, there is a need to learn a new context and a new aesthetic – it is not simply a matter of taking ideas from the past or from outside. There needs to be a reworking as the local cultures and local (indigenous) arts are reimagined through the lens of Christianity. Local artists are conscious that local arts are a key resource that will help interactions about Christian faith: "Many Asian Christian artists believe that the use of indigenous art enables them to communicate biblical messages more directly with their own people."[46]

This reimagining has been expressed by Takenaka and O'Grady as an act of "seeing" in a very practical sense – using the language of "the Bible through Asian eyes" – by remaining sensitive to the distinctive nuances and shades of meaning that are perceived by these local artists. They make the point that Christian artists in Asia are exploring what constitutes local art when they respond as artists to the Bible. For many, this means a response as Christian artists; for others it means responding to the Christian scriptures from within

---

[43] For an informed, eirenic and yet provocative discussion around *Asian* views of Asia see Kishore Mahbubani, *20 Years of Can Asians Think?* Commemorative ed. (Singapore: Marshall Cavendish Editions, 2018).

[44] Takenaka and O'Grady, *The Bible through Asian Eyes*, 10. See also 36-39.

[45] Takenaka and O'Grady, *The Bible through Asian Eyes*, 8.

[46] Takenaka and O'Grady, *The Bible through Asian Eyes*, 10.

wider expressions and forms of Asian arts (hence the perception or reading of the Bible with *Asian* eyes and not simply *Christian* eyes).

> The artist He Qi has expressed a desire to create a contemporary kind of Chinese Christian art that is Chinese in character yet draws on elements and techniques of western art. "He Qi hopes to change the 'foreign' image of Christianity in China through art, and, at the same time, to supplement Chinese art as Buddhist art did in ancient times. In his works, He Qi offers a fresh blending of Chinese folk customs and traditional Chinese painting techniques with Western art of the Middle Ages and modern era." Motivated by a desire to create a genuinely Chinese art that reflects Chinese Christian identity viewing the Bible through "Chinese eyes," he has created a distinctive and dynamic body of work widely appreciated by the global Christian community.[47]

Nurturing Missional Artists

Missional artists need to have confidence that they have a role to play; the wider church also needs to recognise the potential of the arts. Redeeming the Arts notes the rewards possible where Christian artists are developed and nurtured and can contribute to the wider church:[48]

> Faith communities that affirm their artists and the arts may draw on their gifts to pass on the transforming story of the gospel through the arts, and address the whole person through the engagement of the imagination.

These words were written against the backdrop of a real concern about the marginalisation of artists in the church[49] and a perception that the lack of vision for the arts has limited the nurture and involvement of artists in the life of the church. Similar issues can be found in missional contexts, and there is a pressing need to address the nurture of missional artists not just in terms of their artistic skills but in terms of their readiness for cultural learning as well as in the areas of spirituality and discipleship.[50]

---

[47] He, *Look toward the Heavens*, 12-13 – for quotes.

[48] Redeeming the Arts, Act II – Discipleship: Character, Artistic and Relational Development of the Artist – Discipleship for Artists is Complicated by Their History.

[49] Redeeming the Arts was written at a time in the early 21st century to strengthen ties between churches and Christian organisations and to foster greater appreciation and nurture of artists in mission.

[50] The growth of specialist arts ministries may reflect the fact that such nurture and education need to take place outside of the church. For the implications towards mission and cross-cultural settings see Krabill *et al.*, eds., *Worship and Mission for the Global Church*, 358-419 (chaps. 117-29) and Schrag on the "Arts for a Better Future" training course in Chapter 8 of this book.

Creating a Climate of Nurture

In Redeeming the Arts, recommendations for the future tend to focus on the church but nonetheless certain core ideas transfer readily to the arts in mission: a) the need to develop a theology of the arts and creativity in mission;[51] b) the willingness to support and nurture artists in mission; c) the importance of nurturing creative-process skills that are relevant for mission including mission across cultures; and d) the development of an "articulate artistic 'voice' through critical insight"[52] where the latter is applied to historical and contemporary examples of creativity in missional contexts. Given the potential of the arts to speak into a range of cultural situations and to share the biblical story at different levels and using different media, Redeeming the Arts notes the surprising hesitancy of traditional mission agencies to be receptive to the arts:[53]

> The arts can be of immense value for cross-cultural communication. It is surprising just how reluctant most mission organizations have been to take up the arts and put them to work in the task of mission.

Sometimes churches and mission agencies are willing to rise to the challenge – at other times, they retreat into safety.[54] In many situations, where the story of the gospel cannot easily be heard due to the constraints of context, the arts and the work of artists may allow unexpected points of contact with local people.

The work of the film-maker Paul Nethercott in Japan shows the capacity of art to tell stories that create a space for Christian perspectives. Paul gave up his role as a traditional church-planter to focus on film-making: in *Finding Beauty in the Rubble* he looks at how one Japanese woman responds to the tsunami by using beach-combing as a method of finding hope and rebuilding her life after a traumatic natural disaster; in *Wadaiko & Black Gospel* he shows how ancient traditions of *taiko* drumming have combined with black gospel music, in a creative synthesis, to touch the lives of thousands of people. These films show how to connect Christian values to Japanese culture creatively and with imagination.[55]

Mission agencies and churches must ensure that artists are given the encouragement that they require to develop their vision and their vocation in

---

[51] See "Further Reading" in the Preface for resources on this topic.

[52] Redeeming the Arts, Act II – Scene II: Artistic Development of the Artist – Obstacles.

[53] Redeeming the Arts, Act II – Scene III: Relational Development of the Artist – Art that Serves.

[54] For changes in the general attitudes of Christian groups including mission agencies see comments by Franklin, "Arts and Mission Taskforce," 5.

[55] See Paul W. Nethercott, "Wadaiko & Black Gospel Music Video," Vimeo, accessed Jul 21, 2021, https://vimeo.com/12277828; Paul W. Nethercott, "Finding Beauty in the Rubble「がれきの中に見つけた美」," Vimeo, accessed Sep 20, 2021, https://vimeo.com/125076439.

training and in ministry. The Cape Town Commitment speaks of the need for "supporting those with artistic gifts, especially sisters and brothers in Christ, so that they may flourish in their work."[56] This reminds us that artists need space to develop and hone their artistic gifts and that such a process requires both nurture and encouragement. Positively, this process sets free new voices, develops and releases creative gifts that can create an impact, and produces new works for the body of Christ. Conversely, if artists are not nurtured there can be negative consequences: where they sense a lack of encouragement, or if they feel slighted, there is a risk they might lose their way and their gifts and talents will languish – this can further result in artists feeling marginalised or even rejected within the church and Christian organisations.

All Christians need to be encouraged in their faith at a personal level and in their vocations, recognising that there are different aspects of nurture. There is the encouragement that comes from relationships and community and the development of skills that emerges through learning and training from experienced teachers. This is relevant for artists as for other missional vocations, but given the complexity of relating the arts to worship, witness and transformation, there are special challenges for missional artists. There is a need for the kind of nurture that allows the space to think and reflect, to explore and experiment, so that artistic creation can take place and artists are helped to relate their art to the world around them. When Bauer states that even "creating a context in which artists can connect their faith and their craft is huge," he is making an important point.[57] Equipping artists to make a link between their arts and the Christian faith in concrete ways requires not just theological (or missional) awareness and developed artistic skills, but a commitment to take these artistic insights and capacities and draw on them to produce actual works of art that connect to an audience. The missional artist needs to have confidence not only in their missional vocation but also in themselves as artists including their experiences in the new cultural setting, with its related traditions of local arts, to be able to function effectively. Even then, there will be times when artistic projects may not work out: "In every community artists and craftspeople need support. They take risks in their work, and sometimes they fail."[58] The Christian community needs to be as ready to encourage missional artists in these situations as they are when the arts contribute with a greater degree of local acceptance.[59]

| **Suggested Reading on Artists and Their Vocation** |
| Anderson, C. J. *The Faithful Artist: A Vision for Evangelicalism and the* |

---

[56] Cape Town Commitment, Section IIA – 5. Truth and the Arts in Mission.

[57] Bauer, *Arts Ministry*, 28-29.

[58] Bauer, *Arts Ministry*, 184. Artists need community support even when they stretch boundaries.

[59] Bauer stresses that individuals should connect to a community for nurture and moral support in their vocation as missional artists – see Bauer, *Arts Ministry*, 182-85.

Arts. Studies in Theology and the Arts. Downers Grove, IL: IVP
      Academic, 2016.
Fujimura, M. *Art and Faith: A Theology of Making*. New Haven, CT: Yale
      University Press, 2020.
L'Engle, M. *Walking on Water: Reflections on Faith and Art*. New York:
      Convergent Books, 2016.
Noland, R. *The Heart of the Artist: A Character Building Guide for You and
      Your Ministry Team*. 2nd ed. Grand Rapids, MI: Zondervan Reflective, 2021.

Sustaining a Community of Nurture

An artistic community can play a critical role in the development of missional
artists. It provides support, a forum to nurture the role of the arts in worship,
witness and transformation in specific cultural settings; additionally, it can be a
forum for sharing artistic, cultural and missional ideas. This process allows for
the fashioning of creative ideas but against a measured backdrop of "aesthetic
criticism and accountability."[60] It also means that those with greater artistic and
missional experience can share what they have been learning over time.
Missional artists and agencies can learn from the framework proposed in
Redeeming the Arts which has various "levels" of nurture. It starts with
education and the *development of artistic skills*, goes on to the *opportunities* that
organisations[61] can create for artists and then finally shows how they can *sustain*
both artists and artistic opportunities.[62] The end-point of such a process would
be to usher in a culture of reflexivity and self-critical artistic vision that would
allow for thoughtful artistic creativity to continue in the long term within a
Christian community.[63]

> "Arts Release" is a ministry currently working in Singapore and Europe that has
> encouraged the nurture of local artists. The music group offers workshops that help
> develop skills in multicultural worship as they "teach a number of songs from
> around the world and help worship leaders, singers and musicians know how best

---

[60] Bauer, *Arts Ministry,* 183. Implicit in these sentiments is the idea of artists
ministering in relation to a nurturing community – see further below.
[61] See OM's Inspiro Arts Alliance, accessed Sep 20, 2021,
https://www.om.org/en/ministry-profile/inspiro-arts-alliance; SIL's EthnoArts, accessed
Nov13, 2021, http://ethnoarts.sil.org/ and WEC's Arts Release (see discussion above) –
these groups all show evidence of nurture and support within mission agencies.
[62] For a suggested framework see Redeeming the Arts, Act II – Scene III: Relational
Development of the Artist – Strategies. The above discussion adjusts the order and
simplifies the steps.
[63] Seerveld compares "arts advocates" in churches to farmers – taking a long view to
"plant" ideas and pathways for the future so that there is a fruitful influence and
ultimately "harvest" of the arts across the generations through to the grandchildren of
the current generation and beyond. Seerveld, *Bearing Fresh Olive Leaves*, 142.

to introduce them into their church life."[64] These include opportunities for playing music in worship and other settings. Short-term trips allow participants to experience the arts and music of other local traditions and to receive training which helps them to employ these in outreach efforts. Arts Release organises regular Creative Studio sessions where artists from multiple disciplines come together to study the Bible, intercede through art-making, and learn from experienced missional artists who share about their artistic endeavours. Such activities help artists and musicians to recognise the profound impact of culture as they relate their art to missional contexts.

Artistic Mastery

At a deeper level, missional artists need to be able to integrate the different dimensions of their vocation and this requires strong links and deep roots in a Christian community. The foundations of such a vocation will be formed in a church context, but longer strides in combining arts in mission will involve specialist training and nurture that will likely be best accomplished in colleges, mission agencies and specialist groups. Missional artists who are thoroughly grounded in their faith and their arts will be able to make a real contribution through their artistic skills. The missional artist needs to be able to respond to and shape culture not just echo or reflect it. They need to explore how to express Christian ideas in new forms and in fresh, creative ways. Some spheres such as music and the visual arts have a long history of involvement by Christian artists. Other areas, such as contemporary media, are still being explored. As noted earlier, the unique vision of artists must be treasured and developed: "How an artist sees the world can be a valuable asset for the church as it engages its mission."[65] This can be true not just for artists in their own context, but also for missional artists who cross cultures. Such artistry needs to be grounded in biblical, theological and cultural understanding and must strive to be genuinely creative.[66] Like all dedicated artists, missional artists need to maintain and develop their capacity as artists.[67] In this regard, Redeeming the Arts makes pertinent reflections on the ongoing need to strive for artistic mastery and what this represents: [68]

---

[64] "Arts Release," WEC International Singapore, accessed Jul 21, 2021, https://wec-sing.org/arts-release/.
[65] Redeeming the Arts, Epilogue: Developing an Artistic Voice.
[66] An inspiring example of this is found in Fujimura's artistic vision as expressed in his book about the relationship between the arts and faith, Makoto Fujimura, *Refractions: A Journey of Faith, Art, and Culture* (Colorado Springs, CO: NavPress, 2009).
[67] Missional artists need a theological and ethical foundation drawn from the Christian scriptures but developed in relation to other cultures to help foster artistic integrity. Missional training can help to develop greater insight around the cultural dimensions of integrity.
[68] Redeeming the Arts, Act II – Scene II: Artistic Development of the Artist – Artistic Mastery. The vocation of the missional artist can have a wide range of application and need not be restricted to any particular focus.

Artistic mastery, in any culture, is confirmed by that culture's artistic values and is always the result of extensive study and apprenticeship, often over many years. ... Mastery is more than skill, knowledge, and understanding. ... It involves the wisdom to apply those qualities in the creative process of what is being formed. In the hands of a master craftsman, artistic expression can be a powerful vehicle for the perception and reframing of 'truth telling.'

Such skills can be used to open up God's word to people, help Christians and others to reassess their spiritual lives and "provoke" change in individuals and communities.

Conclusion

For the arts in mission to thrive, churches and mission agencies need to recognise the importance of the arts and nurture, encourage and appreciate missional artists. As we have seen, the Cape Town Commitment makes points about both the arts and artists which are worth underlining. There is a need to develop a climate which sees "the Church in all cultures energetically engaging the arts as a context for mission."[69] There is real scope for the arts to make a much greater contribution to the task of mission and this includes a unique role for missional artists who are rooted as disciples in Christ Jesus and whose Christian life and artistry are at the service of the kingdom as "truth-tellers" opening up the rich global tapestry of the Christian faith. It is such a perspective – a vision for missional artists who take the arts across cultures into Asian contexts and share with local artists and Christians as they reimagine and retell the Christian faith – that lies at the heart of this volume.

Questions for Reflection/Discussion
1. How do the themes of artists as "truth-tellers" and "witnesses" help you understand the identity of missional artists? What could you do to cultivate arts which are grounded in a scriptural understanding of life and resonate with "a ring of truth"?
2. Missional artists have both a missional vocation and an artistic vocation. How do the ideas of "hospitality" and "seeing" further deepen your understanding of missional artists? Have you created solid foundations for your *missional* vocation?
3. How does the concept of bilingualism help as a metaphor for the kinds of cultural learning needed in terms of the development of artistic skills across cultures? How do categories such as "bi-artistic" or "bi-musical" offer insights into the process of engaging and identifying with a local culture and local arts?

---

[69] Cape Town Commitment, Section IIA – 5. Truth and the Arts in Mission.

4. Given the special challenges of being artists "across cultures," what lessons can be learned from the discussion of "nurture" for you and your organisation? How might such nurture encourage "artistic mastery"?

Part II

Arts and Mission in Practice

3. Creative Arts Workshops
for Change and Transformation
Jill Ford and Vivian Chiu

The arts constitute a particular way of explaining human experience and behaviour in the world in which we live. The arts, separately and collectively, enable us to ask the deeper questions of life. This chapter looks at the way creative arts workshops train and empower groups of people to develop their capacity to engage with the arts, recognising that involvement in and with the arts can have important and beneficial consequences for the quality of our lives, relationships, work and education. At the heart of the chapter is a case study of a creative arts workshop on Chinese calligraphy with a women's group.

Creative arts workshops (CAW) enable missional artists to connect with a spectrum of community groups to bring about insight, change and transformation through the arts. Missional artists can use CAW to explore how biblical values and Christian principles connect to social issues in a way that is open-ended and engaging. These workshops allow for creative and fresh approaches through the arts to address issues in local cultures and contexts that can lead to thought-provoking and beneficial outcomes. The participatory nature of CAW, is particularly important as it enables participants from a broad range of social and cultural groups to be educated, challenged and empowered as they interact with a variety of art forms. In what follows, the term "facilitator" refers to the role of the workshop leader, and "participant" will be used for those who share as workshop group members. This is a reminder that whilst the facilitator will have (developed) artistic skills, these are not the only skills needed to plan, deliver and bring to closure successful CAW. The word "participant" serves to underline that those who share in the workshop "participate" – in other words they are also key "agents" in the process whose engagement must be encouraged. The artistic activities need to be devised in such a way that they are accessible to participants, allowing that each participant will have a different level of artistic competency.

Before embarking on specific projects, it is helpful to understand and appreciate the educational and artistic benefits that come from CAW. The chapter will consider how such projects need to be conceived and developed, how they are refined and modified and also suggest how review and evaluation can help improve quality and effectiveness on subsequent occasions of delivery.

At the heart of the chapter is a case study that explores the theme of identity, and what it means to be a woman in contemporary Asia.[1] This offers an example of a CAW that draws on the use of Chinese calligraphy in relation to Proverbs 31, set in Hong Kong – a Chinese cultural context.

Creative Arts Workshops – The Concept

CAW encourage the exploration of social and moral issues through the arts. In CAW, artists (as facilitators) take elements and practices of creative arts and connect them to specific contemporary situations according to the needs, skills and expectations of the participants. A range of art forms can be drawn on to engage with the issues or problems that come from social contexts and to suggest possible ways of responding. In this way, creative arts are used to address the issues raised as well as simply offering insights by looking at them from different angles. CAW help with awareness and education, but the experience of artistic engagement and the workshop format can and should lead to action and even transformation. The use of creative arts that come from the local settings themselves can allow issues to be addressed in a contextual way and help explore and address issues that are locally rooted.[2]

Suggested Reading on Creativity
Bass, A. *The Creative Life: A Workbook for Unearthing the Christian Imagination.* Downers Grove, IL: IVP, 2001. Kindle.
Card, M. *Scribbling in the Sand: Christ and Creativity.* Downers Grove, IL: IVP, 2004.
Elsheimer, J. *The Creative Call.* Colorado Springs, CO: Waterbrook Press, 2001.
Fujimura, M. *Refractions: A Journey of Faith, Art, and Culture.* Colorado Springs, CO: NavPress, 2009.
Schrag, B., and J. Rowe. *Community Arts for God's Purposes: How to Create Local Artistry Together.* Pasadena, CA: William Carey Publishing, 2020.

Missional artists can use these CAW to devise culturally relevant ways of engaging with a local culture and foster the development of artistic abilities of the participants in a way that has potential in local cultural settings. This is because workshops allow the exploration of biblical, social and moral issues through local art forms. CAW have the potential to work with groups in both church settings (worship) and in community settings (witness and transformation

---

[1] Vivian Chiu, "'You Are Precious' – A Series of Art-Based Workshops on the Subject of the 'Noble Character of a Woman' in Proverbs 31" (BA research paper, All Nations Christian College, Easneye, UK, 2016).

[2] Brian Schrag, *Creating Local Arts Together: A Manual to Help Communities Reach Their Kingdom Goals* (Pasadena, CA: William Carey Library, 2013).

of the wider world).[3] Working across cultures, those leading the workshops need to have or develop the relevant artistic skills to create and deliver CAW in context. In many instances, the shift from a knowledge of one area of the arts – such as the visual arts or music – in their own context to a knowledge of the local arts of the new context is a significant part of the learning experience for leaders.[4] There will also be a shift in understanding of what "delivery" looks like in their own context to the implications of "delivery" in the new cultural context.

Suggested Reading on Workshops
Hamilton, P. *The Workshop Book: How to Design and Lead Successful Workshops*. Harlow: Pearson Education, 2016.[5] Chambers, R. *Participatory Workshops: A Sourcebook of 21 Sets of Ideas and Activities*. London and New York: Earthscan, 2002.[6]

Facilitators

For those leading such workshops there are several skills to develop. The development of CAW includes the stages of Discovery, Design, Delivery and Debriefing. These involve the preliminary creative processes which engage with local contexts and local people; planning and creating; facilitation of the workshops proper; and then the evaluation and review of the process as the CAW moves to closure. As facilitators, missional artists need to prepare, deliver and evaluate their own artistic material as well as gain understanding in creative arts skills, teaching and educating. Also, facilitators need to identify the progression of activities that are required in a workshop setting. The process of preparing for workshops includes the ability to evaluate how ideas will function in the workshop setting and assess their suitability for specific age groups, types of people and contexts. CAW are enhanced if the facilitators can devise and teach appropriate warm-up activities (including games and improvisations) and artistic activities using a range of creative stimuli.

Suggested Reading on Warm-Up, Improvisation and Games
Johnstone, K. *Impro: Improvisation and the Theatre*. Performance Books. London and New York: Methuen Drama, 2017. Johnston, C. *The Improvisation Game: Discovering the Secrets of Spontaneous Performance*. London: Nick Hern Books, 2006.

---

[3] Here the focus is more on the latter – in line with the case study.

[4] See the Creating Local Arts Together (CLAT) model for this idea. Missional artists need to learn to identify with their new contexts – thinking of the parallel with the word "incarnation" which points to the model of Jesus becoming flesh and entering a new human culture. See Schrag, *Creating Local Arts Together*, xv-xxxiv.

[5] An excellent general introduction to workshops.

[6] A text associated with "empowerment" through participatory learning.

Johnston, C. *Drama Games for Those Who Like to Say No*. London: Nick
    Hern Books, 2010.
Boal, A. *Games for Actors and Non-actors*. 2nd ed. London and New York:
    Routledge, 2002.

At the outset of a specific project, the CAW facilitator needs to gain a level
of awareness and assess the educational, artistic and cultural needs and
expectations of the participants – whether implicit or explicit, hidden or open.
Where possible, the facilitator's research can include space for local people in
the context to identify their own issues, needs, and expectations through
discussion or even focus groups or more elaborate projects.[7] Facilitators need to
tailor the workshop to specific contemporary issues that are relevant to their
audience and their context. For example, in the case study at the heart of this
chapter, the use of Chinese calligraphy, a highly valued Chinese art form, was
used to explore the particular issue of a woman's identity in relation to biblical
teaching.[8]

Suggested Reading on Arts Workshops (Drama/Theatre Focus)
Swale, J. *Drama Games for Classrooms and Workshops*. London: Nick Hern Books, 2010. Dixon, L. *Play-Acting: A Guide to Theatre Workshops*. London: Methuen Drama, 2003. Hahlo, R. and P. Reynolds. *Dramatic Events: How to Run a Successful Workshop*. New York: St. Martin's Griffin, 2000. Trefor-Jones, G. *Drama Menu: Theatre Games in Three Courses*. London: Nick Hern Books, 2015.

The creative and organisational skills required to run CAW varies with
different age groups and cultures and this needs to be kept in mind when
preparing for groups in church settings or in the wider community. Also,
facilitators need to remember that a workshop is different from a classroom or
lecture setting and different from environments in church (such as the sermon)
where the teaching is taking place in one direction. The ability to develop
creative ideas and adapt activities according to cultural contexts is a key
missional skill as is the ability to adapt to situations and contexts where the
unexpected happens.

---

[7] See the section of CLAT – Meet the Community (Steps 1-3) in Schrag, *Creating Local Arts Together*, 1-58.
[8] In Chinese contexts, such as Hong Kong, the general population uses the Chinese writing system or *hanzi* – adapted in Japan (*kanji*) and in Korea (*hanja*) – sometimes designated "pictographs" or "logographs" indicating the complexity of a system that represents words in a sophisticated symbolic form. In a workshop setting, with demonstrations, materials and support at hand, participants could engage in a simple calligraphy project.

Participants

In terms of those who participate, CAW can take different forms and provoke different kinds of reactions. Through the artistic activities, participants are encouraged to engage with the material and respond with their own questions and ideas throughout the workshops. CAW encourage experiential learning which means that in addition to the cognitive dimensions of learning, there are affective dimensions as participants are touched personally by what happens in the workshop through the activities and the human interactions.

As suggested in the section on facilitation, the greater the involvement of participants in the initial phases, the more the workshops will be tailored to their needs. Although there may be occasions when missional artists (as facilitators) have to identify issues on behalf of a group, it is much better to do that together with the local participants. This avoids top-down approaches to the design of the CAW and paves the way for context-driven input fashioning the processes of transformation which, in turn, will lead to greater engagement and self-reliance on the part of participants. The ability to shape the workshops with local insights and local input will help to encourage the personal dimensions of participation and this will make possible the sense of validation of each person who shares in the workshop. This is where transformation begins to happen. If facilitators can help foster an environment of empowerment and acceptance then the participants will be able to contribute at a deeper level and, ultimately, will gain greater benefit from what takes place.

Further Reading on Drama Training and Applied Theatre
Chadderton, D. *Practical Drama: The Secret of Theatre Arts Revealed.* Abergele: Studymates, 2013. Kindle.
James, S. *Drama for Real Life: 16 Scripts about the Choices That Shape Us.* Downers Grove, IL: IVP Books, 2006.
Johnston, C. *House of Games: Making Theatre from Everyday Life.* Rev. ed. London: Nick Hern Books, 2005.
Koppett, K. *Training Using Drama: Successful Development Techniques from Theatre and Improvisation.* London: Kogan Page, 2002.
Nicholson, H. *Applied Drama: The Gift of Theatre.* Theatre and Performance Practices. 2nd ed. New York: Red Globe Press, 2015.
Preston, S. *Applied Theatre: Facilitation: Pedagogies, Practices, Resilience.* Applied Theatre. London and New York: Methuen Drama, 2016.

Setting the Scene –
Understanding the Flow and Sequence of Creative Arts Workshops

Although the delivery and facilitation phase is at the heart of CAW, the four stages of Discovery, Design, Delivery and Debriefing need careful consideration.

Discovery – People, Issues and Art Forms in Context

- The facilitator and participants consider issues and problems in context
  The process draws on skills from both groups
- The insights of participants are brought into the melting pot
  Local knowledge is brought to bear on the local context
- The facilitator considers how the creative arts can be brought to bear
  The creative skills of facilitators are filtered through a local lens

The "Discovery" stage allows the facilitator to get to know the context, the issues and local people before the workshop which is helpful both for understanding the environment in which a workshop takes place and to allow some possible limitations – such as artistic ability or confidence and self-esteem – to be addressed ahead of time. If participants share in identifying the issues and problems that need to feature in the workshop then the whole process of teasing out responses through the artistic activities will be more fruitful and the whole experience will be more effective in terms of enabling change and transformation. These insights will feed into the facilitator's mind as they seek to ponder creatively the kind of artistic elements which will stimulate engagement with the issues and problems that need to be explored and addressed.

Design – Planning the Creative Arts Workshop

- Artistic focus for the workshop in relation to the facilitator
  Developing artistic skills and applications
- Group analysis
  Planning and creating workshops for different ages/contexts
- Synthesis – putting group, topic and arts together
  Analysing, organising and adapting creative materials in relation
  to the group, topic and specific artistic focus

At an early stage of the design process of the CAW there needs to be a consideration of the facilitator's artistic skills and capabilities. Depending on the kind of missional artist that they are, the CAW facilitator will have a palette of artistic skills from which to draw. Also, there needs to be reflection on the group of participants.

- What kind of interests do they have?
- What kind of artistic medium would work with the themes?
- What kind of level of artistic engagement is possible?
- What can be done in a way that is stimulating and engaging?
- How will the choice of artistic medium help get the point of the CAW across?

These two sets of constraints – the facilitator's artistic skills and the interests and abilities of participants – need to be teased out around the kind of topic and ethos that will be accomplished in the given setting within the timeframes that are available.

Delivery – Facilitation: Putting Ideas into Practice

- Delivering and facilitating creative arts workshops

Once the above issues of design have been worked through, the facilitator must think about the delivery of the workshop. The theme needs to be addressed systematically in stages as artistic activities are introduced with space for warm-up and winding-down at the beginning and the end (allowing time for the human interactions to be developed and for closure at the end of the process).

Debriefing – Evaluation and Review

- Debriefing

The final phase of the CAW is that of debriefing. Debriefing recognises that at the end of a workshop it is helpful for participants and facilitators to take time to consider what has been accomplished. For those participating, the focus is on what they personally have gained and what they have learned from the process. For facilitators, it embraces those dimensions but also allows an analysis of the workshop – both the process of delivery and the effectiveness of the content – for that specific occasion and for the future.

This phase gives space for feedback and review both at a personal level (for the participants) and in terms of evaluation (for the facilitator) of aspects of the workshop that worked well and other areas where development or enhancement could take place. It gives space to articulate the educational impact of the workshops – changes of perspective, things learned, what the next steps might be and so on. It allows for participants to try to take their insights and go further than simply having 'a nice experience' to really expressing what they have learned and what changes need to happen next in their own lives or in the lives of their community.

The Flow of Creative Arts Workshops – From Discovery to Design, Delivery and Debriefing

As suggested, CAW in this context are typically shaped around a Christian perspective on a particular issue (or issues), through the medium of a specific artistic approach. However, a wider variety of artistic forms may be used in the introduction, ice-breaker (warm-up) phases and the time of debriefing where response and review occur.

From Discovery to Design – Create, Present, and Respond

There are three main components that need consideration when designing a CAW that draws on art forms which connect to the learning experience and are at the core of the workshop experience.[9]

---

[9] See Andy Kempe, *The GCSE Drama Coursebook*, 2nd ed. (Cheltenham: Stanley Thornes, 1997), x-xiv. "Create, Present and Respond" is an adaptation of Andy

Create: What is the group going to create and which art form is appropriate?
- From discovery to design –
  Background issues that are worked through prior to delivery

The word *create* takes into account both the art form and what is to be created. It represents a core dimension of the design process. For example, if a story is going to be told, decisions need to be made about how the story is to be delivered. Will it be read? Or acted? Or presented in visual form? Or through a video clip? The word *create* is aimed at helping the missional artist as facilitator to make choices about artistic forms at the very outset and begin to connect them to the workshop proper.

Present: What are the stages that need to be completed that will lead to the presentation of the artistic product?
- From design to delivery –
  Presentation – stages that lead to how the group presents/performs

The word *present* takes into account *how* the group will prepare to present or perform the art work that has been created. As the preparation for the workshop makes connections between design and delivery, the idea of present comes to the fore. For example, if a visual art form such as calligraphy is going to be at the heart of the project, then *present* would embrace all the elements of the creative process from the initial introduction of the brush strokes on to the thematic focus of the project and through to the final production of the pages of calligraphy that are going to be produced.

Respond: What is being communicated through the art form? How could it be improved and what has been learned?
- From delivery to debriefing –
  Response phase – evaluation and review

The word *respond* takes into account the need to allow for response and review. This is the key activity in the debriefing phase. At the conclusion of the workshop, there needs to be space for discussion and reflection that allows feedback. This would likely include elements of analysis and evaluation, though other elements will bring affirmation and some may even bring a note of challenge. Where issues are explored for the purposes of education, change, advocacy, or empowerment, this stage should include opportunities to vocalise what is learned, and action points to take forward. In such instances, this phase of the CAW will bring more than just a challenge, it will provide space for changes of mindset to evolve that will lead inexorably to action. This is particularly important when working with vulnerable people. Allowing them to

---

Kempe's study of Drama and the activities required for creating performance. These can be aligned to other artistic forms.

articulate the changes they notice in themselves as a result of engaging in the workshop is crucial.

These three components – ***create***, ***present***, and ***respond*** – are intended to help frame the workshop and provide helpful headings when planning it. As well as creating a foundation on which the design of the project can be based, they help to create a dynamic that envisages the project as a whole and moves it forward step-by-step from the conception to the facilitation and on to the evaluation.

The Crux of Delivery – Putting the "Nuts and Bolts" Together

The process of delivery for the CAW needs to move from effective design to clear facilitation in a way that will help participants to understand the art form and the issues that are raised during the creative process. Hopefully, the response section will allow for a new understanding and perspective regarding the issues that have been explored and as a result of their own participation. To some extent, workshop designers and facilitators act as catalysts – at times, they need to be able to draw out individuals and groups in a way that will enhance their learning and their experiences.

The workshop facilitator should have the skills to draw participants into the activities so that issues can be explored safely. Envisaging a workshop environment is not just about enhancing learning and the related cognitive and affective experiences, it also involves creating a space of safety so that participants feel free and able to access a sense of empowerment, to challenge their thoughts, and find the capacity to change their circumstances. To do this effectively, the facilitator needs to give adequate thought to the design phase, as well as that of delivery.[10]

In terms of the flow of a CAW, there are a number of steps which need to be addressed and this section will consider these one-by-one:

* warm-up/thematic exploration/focus/body of work/reflection/ wind-down[11]

Through the various stages of the workshop, a degree of bonding occurs at a relational level and helps the participants to connect with the chosen topic and work towards an increasing level of engagement with the issues through the duration of the workshop. This is enhanced by their involvement in the artistic process. The following elements (outlined one-by-one) represent the flow of activity that brings the group together, allows them to think about themes and engage with them in an artistic way, takes ideas further at the level of personal

---

[10] For successful workshop training techniques see Kat Koppett, *Training Using Drama: Successful Development Techniques from Theatre and Improvisation* (London: Kogan Page, 2002).

[11] Adapted from the "Crash Course in Drama Workshop Leading" course, Bigfoot Arts Education, accessed Jun 15, 2021,
http://bigfootartseducation.co.uk/app/uploads/2015/08/ACTOR-AS-EDUCATOR.pdf.
See also http://bigfootartseducation.co.uk/.

reflection and impact, and then brings the proceedings to an appropriate closure.[12] Using a "Workshop Circle" helps to emphasise the sequence of the phases and gives a clear sense of the whole flow of the workshop at a glance.[13]

Workshop Circle

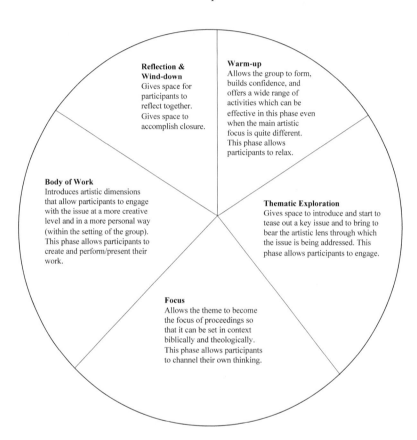

Reflection & Wind-down
Gives space for participants to reflect together. Gives space to accomplish closure.

Warm-up
Allows the group to form, builds confidence, and offers a wide range of activities which can be effective in this phase even when the main artistic focus is quite different. This phase allows participants to relax.

Body of Work
Introduces artistic dimensions that allow participants to engage with the issue at a more creative level and in a more personal way (within the setting of the group). This phase allows participants to create and perform/present their work.

Thematic Exploration
Gives space to introduce and start to tease out a key issue and to bring to bear the artistic lens through which the issue is being addressed. This phase allows participants to engage.

Focus
Allows the theme to become the focus of proceedings so that it can be set in context biblically and theologically. This phase allows participants to channel their own thinking.

---

[12] See the case study below – "A Chinese Calligraphy Creative Arts Workshop" – for an example of what this might look like in practice.

[13] Notes can be added to emphasise key points and ideas in each phase. The illustration has five sections: "Wind-down" is more applicable to performing arts (drama-based) workshops where people have taken on roles but could be added if required.

- Warm-up

Allows the group to form and build confidence (the world of drama education[14] offers a wide range of activities which can be effective in this phase even when the main artistic focus is quite different). This phase allows participants to relax.

- Thematic exploration

Gives space to introduce and start to tease out a key issue and bring to bear the artistic lens[15] through which the issue is being addressed. This phase allows participants to engage.

- Focus

Allows the theme to become the focus of proceedings so that it can be set in context biblically and theologically. This phase allows participants to channel their own thinking.

- Body of work

Introduces artistic dimensions that allow participants to engage with the issue at a more creative level and in a more personal way (within the setting of the group).

This phase allows participants to create and perform/present their work.

- Reflection

Gives space for individuals to take things further and work out what has been significant for them, showing how the artistic engagement has brought new learning and insight (it also includes space for challenge, empowerment and the resolve to move in new directions after the workshop). This phase allows participants to reflect.

- Wind-down

Time to bring proceedings to a halt gently and give space for the group to accomplish closure. This phase allows participants to resume daily life.

---

[14] See the suggested/further reading.
[15] This stage needs to introduce and explore the artistic skills required to achieve the body of work; it allows time to master skills to the point where deeper engagement is possible later. See the example of Chinese calligraphy in the case study.

Debriefing as Transition –
From Assessment to Closure and Back to Everyday Life

The final phase of the workshop (and to some extent a process that continues after delivery into everyday life for the participants and into the next workshop for the facilitator) is that of debriefing. This allows for both the facilitator and the participants to engage in the important task of responding to what has gone on in the CAW. This can include personal, artistic and theological reflections. For the participants it is one way of showing how the CAW made an impact on them and also ways in which these could have been heightened. For the facilitator it is an opportunity to take stock of the various elements of design and delivery, thinking partly about what has happened in this particular workshop but also how elements could be enhanced and refashioned on other occasions for maximum impact in participants' lives when they leave the workshop.

At the level of the facilitator, there may be deeper issues relating to the discovery and design phases, or of the process of delivery (as well as the conception) which need reflection and review. At the convergence of the interests of the participants and the facilitator are the ways in which the process has brought about transformation, change and insight in the lives and hearts of those who shared. It may also be an opportunity to think about further learning and practice in the artistic sphere or at the level of Christian faith, belief and understanding.

- How has this workshop contributed to the life of discipleship for those who are believers?
- How has it helped to make sense of the Christian faith for those, as yet, beyond the Christian community?

These are the kinds of questions which can be addressed in the debriefing phase.

Case Study: A Chinese Calligraphy Creative Arts Workshop: "The Noble Character of a Wife"

This case study will outline a specific creative arts workshop which was based on Chapter 31 in the book of Proverbs, on the theme of "The Noble Character of a Wife" in order to engage with women in Chinese culture in a way that allowed them to discuss and explore their character as women positively in their culture. The case study shows in a practical way how to connect a theme (identity in Proverbs 31) and the group (Chinese women) with the art form (Chinese calligraphy). It also illustrates the creative journey from Discovery to Design on to Delivery and Debriefing.

A Woman's Identity in Chinese Society – Discovery

The workshop was set up to focus on women and arts for women around the theme of Proverbs 31, with the intention of highlighting feminine characteristics relevant to Asian societies. The aim was to bring out characteristics such as wisdom, nobility and blessing, and underline that women are "precious" and to be valued. The focus of this particular workshop, set in Hong Kong, was that of Chinese calligraphy. Drawing on the book of Proverbs enabled women in an Asian culture to explore shared common values of what it means to be a good wife and have a noble character as a woman. The perspectives of Proverbs 31 were used both as a source of wisdom and a repository of ideas. Interacting with these ideas stimulated fresh perceptions about being a woman in contemporary Asia. It encouraged the participants to rethink their identity as women in their own culture, and empowered them to engage with and develop the concept of "a woman of noble character" from a biblical perspective.

The initial inspiration for the theme of this workshop came from interacting with the topic of child marriage around Asia[16] and reflections from the CAW facilitator's own Chinese cultural background. A woman's identity in traditional Asian cultures and in China is shaped by a number of influences. There is a complex interplay between the family's esteem and love of their daughters and a range of social and familial pressures which can push daughters into marriage, even at a relatively young age. In very conservative contexts, especially where societies are unsettled and there are threats of violence, many girls need to stop their education, marry and have children very early on in their marriage. In such environments, this sequence of life events actually reflects the desire of their families to protect women. Reflecting on these issues in contemporary Asia caused the facilitator of the case study to think about the history of bygone times in China, where child marriages often happened because of similar considerations such as war and economic factors. On the other hand, the old Chinese idiom also expresses parental love towards the daughter: "掌上明珠" (*zhǎng shàng míng zhū*), which means "you are a bright pearl in my palm"[17] – a meaning similar to "you are the apple of my eye." The status of women in such societies needs to be viewed through a complex of perspectives that draw on local cultural insights.

There are good reasons why the book of Proverbs could be used as a springboard for a workshop that wants to encourage contemporary women to explore afresh the nature of a woman's identity. From a cultural point of view, proverbial wisdom is generally open-ended and when it borrows concepts or ideas from other cultures, it tends to reshape them with its own understanding of their usefulness in its own context.[18] In the ancient Near Eastern culture of the

---

[16] See "Child Marriage," United Nations Population Fund, accessed Jun 15, 2021, https://www.unfpa.org/child-marriage.

[17] "掌上明珠" [a bright pearl in the palm], 沪江小学资源网 [Hujiang Resources for Primary School], accessed Jun 5, 2016, http://xiaoxue.hujiang.com/cyu/zhangshangmingzhu/ (in Chinese).

[18] Riad Aziz Kassis, *The Book of Proverbs and Arabic Proverbial Works* (Leiden: Brill, 1999), 115.

Bible, the book of Proverbs has a focus on younger people, what we would probably now term teenagers or young adults, and tries to instil both cultural and spiritual values about the nature of wisdom and its value for living.

Given the way in which the book of Proverbs is both culturally determined but deals also with universal themes and proverbial wisdom, which has a spiritual focus yet is culturally open, it can be a good book for approaching different cultures as an introduction to both wisdom and to spirituality. Writing for culturally traditional contexts, Bert de Ruiter suggests that Proverbs has several features that can make it an effective biblical book to use in situations of witness and transformation. For example, its content has a universal character that is widely applicable to people in many periods in history, and its inclusion of well-known concepts and expressions from the surrounding world of the Middle East lends it credibility to many Asian societies with more traditional values and family structures[19] even in the context of the contemporary urban world.[20] Proverbs 31:10-31 poetically presents the noble character of a wife. This is a fascinating passage with which to approach women in Asian cultures to discuss what it means to be a wife and offer space for reflection. This, in turn, can empower them to build their character and their identity as a woman.

Creative Responses to the Workshop Theme through Calligraphy – Design

The idea of designing a CAW for women to explore and to rethink their identity offered a space for empowerment where they could think about how to develop their character. The facilitator had experience of working in China, Japan and Nepal with women who had suffered from the trauma of earthquakes. From these experiences, the facilitator observed that when women were making something creative together in groups, they found it easier to share their stories and it helped to lift their mood, especially when they were experiencing times of suffering. The facilitator had the conviction that if people could engage in creative projects it would help to improve their sense of well-being and even bring them joy. At a theological level, Christians can see how the foundation for their creativity comes from the model of the creativity of God our Creator, whose character[21] we share, because we are made in the image of God.[22]

---

[19] Bert de Ruiter, *A Single Hand Cannot Applaud: The Value of Using the Book of Proverbs in Sharing the Gospel with Muslims* (Nürnberg: VTR Publications, 2011), 61. The references to wisdom are couched in a feminine form which has prompted the translation of passages about wisdom in a metaphorical way as "lady wisdom."
[20] Ruiter, *A Single Hand Cannot Applaud,* 79.
[21] For ways in which the creativity of God can inspire us in a range of vocational pursuits – some of which have a more artistic focus and some are more practical – see Robert Banks, *God the Worker: Journeys into the Mind, Heart, and Imagination of God*, Reprint ed. (Eugene, OR: Wipf and Stock, 2008).
[22] See Alice Bass, *The Creative Life: A Workbook for Unearthing the Christian Imagination* (Downers Grove, IL: IVP, 2001), 121, Kindle.

For CAW, specific art forms can be used to highlight a range of themes in slightly different ways. The use of Chinese calligraphy in relation to Proverbs 31 was designed to bring out ideas of beauty and uniqueness focused on the concept of names. For other CAW dealing with women in other cultural settings – such as refugees in the west, or women in the Middle East – the facilitator found ways to use different art forms, such as drama, handicrafts and body movement, but for women in a Chinese context, the idea of Chinese calligraphy as the chosen art form was considered more meaningful.[23]

In terms of the "Workshop Circle" – the case study had the following format in line with the aims and intentions outlined above:

Workshop Circle – Case Study

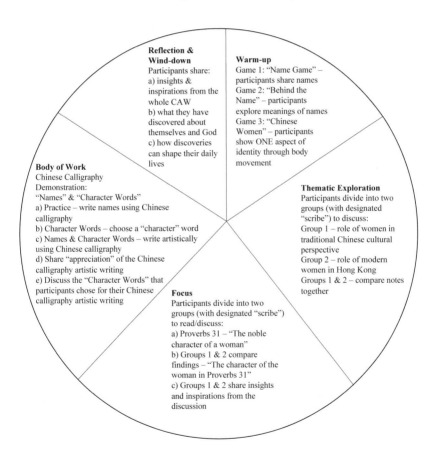

Reflection & Wind-down
Participants share:
a) insights & inspirations from the whole CAW
b) what they have discovered about themselves and God
c) how discoveries can shape their daily lives

Warm-up
Game 1: "Name Game" – participants share names
Game 2: "Behind the Name" – participants explore meanings of names
Game 3: "Chinese Women" – participants show ONE aspect of identity through body movement

Body of Work
Chinese Calligraphy Demonstration:
"Names" & "Character Words"
a) Practice – write names using Chinese calligraphy
b) Character Words – choose a "character" word
c) Names & Character Words – write artistically using Chinese calligraphy
d) Share "appreciation" of the Chinese calligraphy artistic writing
e) Discuss the "Character Words" that participants chose for their Chinese calligraphy artistic writing

Thematic Exploration
Participants divide into two groups (with designated "scribe") to discuss:
Group 1 – role of women in traditional Chinese cultural perspective
Group 2 – role of modern women in Hong Kong
Groups 1 & 2 – compare notes together

Focus
Participants divide into two groups (with designated "scribe") to read/discuss:
a) Proverbs 31 – "The noble character of a woman"
b) Groups 1 & 2 compare findings – "The character of the woman in Proverbs 31"
c) Groups 1 & 2 share insights and inspirations from the discussion

---

[23] See Vivian Chiu, "You Are Precious," Appendix on Workshops – Chinese Calligraphy. This particular appendix on the Chinese calligraphy workshop gives details on the process and comments from the participants.

Overview of Elements and Flow of the Case Study – Delivery

For the specific setting of the CAW that used Chinese calligraphy to explore a woman's identity in relation to Proverbs 31, the following description outlines the elements that were used.

- Warm-up

Games and group discussion for the women. This enabled them to feel confident with one another and at ease with the workshop setting.

- Thematic exploration

The theme of a woman's identity was introduced including the following key elements: traditional roles, the struggles of modern women, and the most important issues for contemporary women (as expressed by the group members themselves); the idea of using Chinese calligraphy to express "names" and "character" was introduced here.

- Focus

The women explored Christian character in Proverbs 31, identifying key terms and reflecting back their understanding.

- Body of work

This section was given over to the creation of Chinese calligraphy based on names that drew on concepts from Proverbs 31.

- Reflection

The women were given time to reflect on what had been learned and how the creative process had offered new insights to them; they were given the chance to express what they had discovered about themselves and about God.

- Wind-down

Taking the themes and ideas of the workshop, the women were given space to reflect on the implications for their everyday lives and how they might take this forward; time was given to bring proceedings to a halt and give space for the group to accomplish closure

Chinese Calligraphy at the Heart of a Creative Arts Workshop

Reviewing the core elements of the workshop in the section above, the following points are worth highlighting. Calligraphy is one of the traditional arts popular with Chinese people. It links well with their cultural identity. Using their name, written out, as a starting point, the women were invited to share their family's expectations for them as encapsulated in their names.[24] In Chinese culture, names

---

[24] Chiu, "You Are Precious," Appendix on Workshops.

and the characters which describe them are rich with meaning and the elements of a given name reflect some of the ways in which Chinese people invest and imbue their hopes for a daughter at the time of their birth.

In the first phase of the workshop, the women were introduced to a new style of calligraphy, and a different way of writing. Using Proverbs 31 (in Chinese) as a source of inspiration, they were encouraged to integrate their names and some character words that they really admired. They were invited to put the ideas together to make a new design or painting. This moment of artistic activity and discovery gave them the opportunity to draw on existing descriptions of themselves (as expressed in their names), and the inspiration of the graphic nature of words related to character (from Chinese pictographs), which led to new creative reflections about themselves in the new design or painting. The whole process allowed a period of time for the women to reflect on their thoughts and feelings about their names and their identities and come up with new insights and new ideas as a result of the artistic process and the group experience.[25]

One participant put her name (meaning "elegance") in the middle of the calligraphy and put different qualities inspired by Proverbs 31 around it: love, faith, generous, magnify the Lord, perseverance, awe ("fear"), kindness, and gentle ("soft"). Her prayer was that these concepts would shape her life.

---

[25] Xiting Huang and Zhenyong Wang, "書法經驗對心理健康及注意能力的影響" [The Influence of Calligraphy Experience on Mental Health and Attention Span], in 書法心理治療 [*Chinese Calligraphic Therapy*], ed. Shangren Gao (Hong Kong: Hong Kong University Press, 2000), 194 (in Chinese).

Lessons Learned from a Creative Arts Workshop – Debriefing

The CAW revealed that the participants found it fascinating to have an opportunity to compare the traditional Chinese expectations of women with the biblical perspective in Proverbs 31, and indicated that this was a new experience for them. It was also the first time they had seen Chinese calligraphy which featured their own names connected to words that are related to the concept of noble character. Both of these experiences made an impact on the participants.

Feedback on the Identity of Women in Chinese Society

The feedback demonstrated that the participants appreciated reflecting on their identity as women and their cultural identity. The exploration into the identity of the woman in Proverbs 31 from a different cultural background enabled fresh thinking which led to positive and empowering outcomes. One participant said: "Through reading the Bible, the discussion, investigation and reflection, I found out more about my own character and which elements I admire." In addition, through the biblical text they had an opportunity to reflect on the social and cultural setting of the woman in Proverbs 31 and the picture of womanhood that it portrays: "The workshop helped me to understand and appreciate the differences concerning women and identity in the Bible, and in Chinese culture."[26] The CAW allowed participants to have a deeper understanding of the biblical passage and they were able to discover that it offered different, yet positive perspectives compared to the views they had encountered in the world around them.

The use of an art form such as Chinese calligraphy was of real benefit in helping the women to explore and engage with their cultural identity, as well as express themselves in relation to this. It also helped them experience the potential of creativity through the arts for its own sake which they really enjoyed, so much so that they requested more time to interact with the art pieces that they were creating. There was a deep sense that these art pieces reflected their own character and identity. To this extent the CAW did accomplish its objective: "We can be very creative. Chinese calligraphy helped me be more creative."[27]

Reflections

When it came to the creative elements, different participants needed varying amounts of time which meant that it was difficult to finish the workshop on time. Facilitators need to remember that time is always a constraint in workshops.[28] There is a need for differentiating tasks depending on skills and how the participants engage. A realistic idea of what you want them to produce and share

---

[26] Chiu, "You Are Precious," Appendix on Workshops.
[27] Chiu, "You Are Precious," Appendix on Workshops.
[28] The "Discovery" stage of getting to know the context, issues and people *before* the workshop is helpful for addressing some of these limitations.

is needed.[29] When using visual arts, the facilitator needs to emphasise that the process of engagement is as important as the quality of the finished product and that this allows the participants the freedom to engage without fear of failure, or getting frustrated if they feel that they cannot finish the task in the given time.

Some participants who had not learned the artistic skills needed for calligraphy found it harder to enjoy the creative process, but they still enjoyed the workshop as a whole. This suggests that facilitators need to differentiate the various tasks and expectations in a workshop clearly so that participants are able to engage with the material at their own level. Certain participants who had experienced negative situations in their lives asked for more time so that they could share more fully.[30] Such responses suggest that the experience of engaging with art forms in a group setting made them want to express their feelings more deeply. As a result, the facilitator was encouraged that the CAW produced such positive results and saw this as a mandate to try further workshops of a similar kind with women's groups.

In terms of future developments, a series of Bible studies focusing on different women in the Bible, together with the use of art forms such as calligraphy would seem to be a good way to build on this idea of "noble character." The art forms could be developed in groups and this would empower the women to support each other, work collaboratively and develop their understanding of "women of noble character" together.

The purpose of this creative arts workshop was to enable a group of Hong Kong Chinese women to explore and rethink their identities in light of the "noble woman" from Proverbs 31 through the artistic medium of Chinese calligraphy. To a large degree, it was deemed successful by the participants as most of them really enjoyed using calligraphy to express these themes. During training on leading creative arts workshops in local cultural settings, the facilitator encountered the idea: "Art provides meaningful ways to engage with other cultures and point them to God."[31] This particular workshop offered support and confirmation of such an idea. Through the different phases of the project, the facilitator learned how to design a CAW in an appropriate way for a specific group of people in their cultural context, drawing on a local and valued art form (in this instance, Chinese calligraphy). Such experiences led the facilitator to take an interest in learning more about group work and the potential of CAW for women, especially those who suffer from trauma or similar issues.

---

[29] For example, some groups are very skilled and so can get more done in the time given. Others may only manage limited responses; having different levels of expectation can be helpful in such situations.

[30] This feedback serves as a reminder of why it is important to *signpost* to other phases (and activities) during the workshop and suggest how ideas can be taken further at later stages.

[31] See "Course Notes for 'Art, Culture and Identity'" (BA module [3rd year] by Jill Ford, All Nations Christian College, Easneye, UK, Apr-Jun 2016).

Conclusion

The creative arts are a powerful means to develop the imagination and creative expression. Involvement in CAW can be empowering as participants can explore new ways of understanding and new paths of personal and social discovery. CAW can help foster communication skills which enable group cooperation and the means to reconcile personal and social circumstances. CAW are valuable for education, mission and ministry because they provide a vital space for exploration, change and transformation.

Questions for Reflection for Facilitators of Creative Arts Workshops
1. As you review the process, was the workshop structured, designed and delivered in a manner which best suited the subject matter and allowed for positive engagement with the participants?
2. Were you confident that all matters concerning the management of the creative environment were considered and addressed?
3. How aware were you of the needs of participants? Was the workshop designed in a way that gave adequate room for creative flexibility?
4. Did you communicate your ideas for the workshop in a manner that enabled participants to flourish? Were there areas to consider for the future in terms of the development of the workshop?

4. Contextual Art for Spiritual Formation amongst the Wa People

Hennie Chiu

Hennie Chiu considers the potential of the visual arts for spiritual formation. She considers aspects of Wa culture, arts and aesthetics and connects this to a wider discussion about aesthetics and theology as they relate to contextual art and its potential for spiritual formation. The chapter then considers the specific project "The Divine Journey" – its conception, the contours of the project around four works of visual art – and the contribution that it makes to spiritual formation for the Wa people.

"A Divine Journey" –
Contextual Visual Arts and Spiritual Formation for the Wa

The art forms at the heart of this chapter were developed as an exploratory project for the contextualisation of visual art amongst the Wa.[1] Entitled "A Divine Journey" the project was designed to take the Wa people on a journey of spiritual formation through creative visual arts as they reflected on the divine journey of Jesus. The project aimed to create four paintings – "In the Beginning," "Turning Water into Wine," "The Conversation by the Well," and "From Humiliation to Glory" to inspire the Wa people to reflect on their journey with God. The idea was that these paintings would be visual resources that would help Wa Christians to understand the Bible and connect with stories around the life, ministry, death and resurrection of Jesus through what could be termed visual conceptualisations of the biblical narrative in a way that was sympathetic to local arts in Wa culture and society. In short, it represents a reimagining of the Christian faith and "the Bible through Asian eyes"[2] – suitable for a minority group whose heritage, that of the Wa people, had been largely oral.

---

[1] Hennie Chiu, "A Visual Re-Conception Using the Stories and Accounts of the Life, Death and Resurrection of Jesus Christ in John's Gospel to Encourage Christian Spiritual Formation for the Wa People in Yunnan Province" (MA thesis, All Nations Christian College, Easneye, UK, 2016).

[2] The phrase comes from the title of Takenaka and O'Grady, *The Bible through Asian Eyes*.

The project was created to act as a stimulus to prompt the Wa themselves to consider creating contextual art that would encourage spiritual formation of a Christian kind in line with their local cultural ethos and drawing on local arts traditions. In terms of the categories of missional artist considered earlier in the book, it represents the work of an Asian visual artist from a neighbouring country who has had a long connection with the culture and the art forms of the Wa people.

The Wa People – Culture, Arts and Aesthetics

The Wa people are an ethnic minority people group in Yunnan province in China with an oral culture whose lives traditionally have been centred around agriculture. They have received the Christian faith relatively recently. The first exposure to the Christian faith for the majority Wa people was over a hundred years ago. William Marcus Young, an American missionary, devised the Latin-script transcription for the Wa.[3] The language used in the Wa Bible is a composite language based on several varieties and is called the "Standard Bible Wa."[4] Christian resources in their culture and language are scarce. Having the Bible in their own language is an important foundation for spiritual life and leads to questions of how the Wa can develop further contextual resources to help with spiritual growth in their Christian life. In the early 21st century, now that they have their own version of the Bible and churches, they are at the point where they need a wider range of contextual resources to aid them in their spiritual growth.[5]

The Wa people are located in the south-west of Yunnan province in China and the north-eastern Shan State in Myanmar. Despite encouragements to adopt more fruitful methods of agriculture, many Wa people maintain their traditional way of life[6] and agriculture in remote mountainous areas. The Wa used to be animists and are known for having deeply religious sentiments.[7] Traditionally,

---

[3] Wa Dictionary Project, "The Young Family's Work with the Wa People," Humanities Computing Laboratory, accessed Aug 2, 2021,
http://www.humancomp.org/wadict/young_family.html.
[4] "Wa – Parauk," in *Ethnologue: Languages of the World*, 24th ed., eds. David M. Eberhard, Gary F. Simons and Charles D. Fennig (Dallas, TX: SIL International, 2021), accessed Aug 2, 2021, http://www.ethnologue.com/language/prk.
[5] This illustrates Lamin Sanneh's point that a translation of the Bible into a local language has encouraged deeper promotion of vernacular culture – in this case in terms of the visual arts – in ways appropriate to the local culture. See Lamin Sanneh, *Translating the Message: The Missionary Impact on Culture*, American Society of Missiology 42, Rev. and expanded ed. (Maryknoll, NY: Orbis Books, 2009), 213.
[6] Lei Shi, 佤族审美文化 [*The Cultural Aesthetics of the Wa*] (Kunming: Yunnan University Press, 2008), 75 (in Chinese).
[7] "The Wa Nationality," Ethnic China, accessed Aug 2, 2021, http://www.ethnic-china.com/Wa/waindex.htm.

festivals and events such as weddings, births and funerals have been marked with animal sacrifices and chicken bone divination. They have a long history of involvement in the worship of nature, spirits and ancestors because of their fear of them. Decades ago, they still practised head-hunting for spirit-sacrifice until their interactions with a wider Chinese society and representatives of the government of the People's Republic of China encouraged alternative approaches.

Arts and Aesthetics

The Wa people are considered to be one of the most ancient ethnic people groups in China.[8] As a result, a study of the history and culture of the Wa has been of interest to many scholars and researchers.[9] The Wa have an oral culture with an abundant heritage of oral legends, myths, stories, poems, proverbs and riddles. A number of rock paintings[10] in caves in Cangyuan County were discovered in 1965 and the themes depicted in those are closely related to the history, customs and lives of the Wa people; some of these customs continue to this day.[11] These rock paintings reflect how visual and imaginative they were, using visual art and symbols as a means of recording their lives, showing, for example, villages, hunting, dancing, sacrifice and history, and reflecting their wisdom and imagination.

Aspects of Wa Arts and Aesthetics

According to anthropological studies, Wa have a rich and abundant cultural heritage of various art forms such as dance, wine-making and weaving. Their lifestyle influences their aesthetic criteria. For instance, a woman who is considered beautiful in Wa culture is typically a woman who has a dark complexion with long black hair and a fairly sturdy and robust body. A woman with a light, fair complexion might be deemed as lazy and not willing to work hard and is therefore considered not "beautiful."[12] This indicates that the characteristics of being hard-working and productive in the family and community are highly valued and form part of the criteria of being considered "beautiful" in the culture. An object which is highly valued in Wa society is the skull of a buffalo – this object symbolises assiduity, honour, honesty and wealth which are valuable characteristics in the culture.[13] Thus, the head of a buffalo becomes a symbol of Wa ethnicity. The Wa also favour the colour black in

---

[8] Shilin Duan, 佤族历史文化探秘 [*The Mystery of the Culture and History of the Wa*] (Kunming: Yunnan University Press, 2007), 3-4 (in Chinese).
[9] Duan, *The Mystery of the Culture and History of the Wa*, 3.
[10] Furong Zhao, 中国佤族文化 [*The Culture of the Wa in China*] (Beijing: Ethnic Publishing House, 2005), 204 (in Chinese).
[11] Zhao, *The Culture of the Wa in China*, 204.
[12] Shi, *The Cultural Aesthetics of the Wa*, 236.
[13] Zhao, *The Culture of the Wa in China*, 269.

general, and red combined with some white. The colour black is associated with meanings of honesty, honour, simplicity and things that are long-lasting, showing that their aesthetics are connected to their value and functions in their society and daily life.[14] This means that Wa aesthetics need to be understood not only in terms of what is attractive to the eyes but also in terms of functionality and problem-solving in their everyday lives.

Impact of Chinese Arts and Aesthetics

Reflecting contextually on Wa aesthetics, it is crucial to note the impact of wider Chinese culture and the cultural world of Yunnan and take into account the way in which their influence affects the appreciation of arts in relation to the Wa. Yunnan is known for its ethnic and cultural diversity and for most of the people groups who live there, the arts often have a clear focus and meaning and perform functions that are relevant to people's daily lives.[15] Some research shows that when the Wa lived with the Shan people, they were influenced by the Shan; when they lived amongst the Lahu people, their living habits were influenced by the Lahu[16] indicating that Wa people easily assimilate to the surrounding environment. However, those who live in remote areas usually keep traditional values in their costume, language and culture. There are differences as well: for example, the aesthetic concepts of Chinese arts often emphasise the emotions and feelings of the artist in relation to the object or scenery depicted.[17] Unlike, for example, Filipino and African styles of art, Chinese painting always keeps free space and makes use of this as either a white colour or sky or water.[18] Such an approach does *not* generally appear explicitly in Wa aesthetics.

Wider Reflections on Aesthetics

William Dyrness has also observed that in post-modern western culture, whilst a section of society no longer engages in religious practices, people engage in other kinds of social practices including engagement with art which helps them find meaning and transcendence in life. Therefore, interacting with art not only helps with the quest to derive meaning from human existence but can also become a feasible point of theological reference.[19] Viewed in this way, Dyrness' points connect with one of the central traits of the Wa culture's arts and their sense of the aesthetic. Seeing the beauty of art and experiencing and reflecting

---

[14] Shi, *The Cultural Aesthetics of the Wa*, 24.
[15] Wenxun Zhang, 滇文化与民族审美 [*The Culture and Folk Aesthetics of the Dian*] (Kunming: Yunnan University Press, 1992), 10 (in Chinese).
[16] Shi, *The Cultural Aesthetics of the Wa*, 7.
[17] See further William A. Dyrness, *Christian Art in Asia* (Amsterdam: Rodopi, 1979).
[18] Kathleen D. Nicholls, *Asian Arts and Christian Hope* (New Delhi: Select Books, 1983), 73.
[19] William A. Dyrness, *Poetic Theology: God and the Poetics of Everyday Life* (Grand Rapids, MI; Eerdmans, 2011), 5.

on God's creation as part of the story of everyday life matches the aesthetics of the Wa because they do not have a special thing called "art" or "high art" in their culture.

In the everyday discovery of such arts – through the use of colour and shape, form and beauty – not only can art reflect human creativity and human feelings but art can point us to the depth, breadth and height of God's creativity in the created world and help nudge people towards new directions so that they can explore God's goodness and character.[20] Thus it is through contextual and local art that people are pointed to different dimensions of everyday life and they experience God in a deeper way so that their spiritual life is deepened.

Suggesting Reading on Arts, Visual Arts and Christian Faith
Bustard, N., ed. *It Was Good: Making Art to the Glory of God*. Rev. and expanded ed. Baltimore, MD: Square Halo Books, 2007.   Dyrness, W. A. *Senses of the Soul: Art and the Visual in Christian Worship*. Art for Faith's Sake 1. Eugene, OR: Cascade Books, 2015.   Dyrness, W. A. *Visual Faith: Art, Theology, and Worship in Dialogue*. Grand Rapids, MI: Baker Academic, 2001.   Romaine, J. *Objects of Grace: Conversations on Creativity and Faith*. Baltimore, MD: Square Halo Books, 2002.

Theological Perspectives on the Arts in Mission

This section will explore further the relationship between theology and the arts. It will address the question of the theological role that the visual arts play in mission and spiritual formation and the importance of developing art that is contextually relevant. Like Dyrness and Sedmak (see below), who both acknowledge the significance of personal stories and experiences in theological reflection and spirituality, John Drane[21] articulates the idea that our own personal stories play a pivotal role in effective evangelism making a contribution that goes beyond both the individual stories of the Bible and "God's story," which he sees as underlying and giving coherence to the elements of the biblical account. Thus, the intersection of the three areas of God's story, Bible stories and our own personal stories is where effective evangelism takes place.[22] If that is true for evangelism, it would also be true in spiritual formation. When one is honest with oneself and serious about God's story and the stories in the Bible, at that point a person is ready to grow in terms of spiritual formation. Art that is culturally attuned and helps to make connections between God's story, the stories of the

---

[20] William A. Dyrness, *Visual Faith: Art, Theology, and Worship in Dialogue* (Grand Rapids, MI: Baker Academic, 2001), 99.

[21] John Drane, *Evangelism for a New Age: Creating Churches for the Next Century* (London: Marshall Pickering, 1994), 55-81.

[22] Drane, *Evangelism for a New Age*, 67.

Bible and our own personal experience – our own personal stories – can make a profound contribution to the way in which spiritual formation takes place and can be a focus for personal (internal) meditation and meaningful (outward) communication with God through prayer.

Contextualisation of Visual Art in Asia

Sawai Chinnawong is a Myanmar-born ethnic Mon artist who converted to Christianity from a Buddhist home in Thailand.[23] His paintings genuinely reflect his life and his cultural identity in a very fresh and creative manner and they engage deeply with the stories of the Bible, pointing beyond to God's story viewed in a very Asian manner. These paintings represent a place where God communicates effectively to his heart. His example suggests that missional artists need to make the stories of the Bible and the underlying message – God's story – relevant to our cultural contexts and our audiences so that they can more easily understand and better accept the ideas that are being communicated.[24] Also, it has been suggested by Dyrness that the role of art in Christian discipleship – especially the important role of the artist – is that of servanthood. He believes that if Christian artists strive to produce genuine and worthwhile art, the experience of engaging with such art can help lead people to God.[25] The work of an artist such as Chinnawong illustrates the way in which art that draws on Asian elements can powerfully draw people into a deeper understanding of Christian faith around the story of good news which is shared in the Bible. Dyrness' reflections on the unique and distinctive character of art[26] remind us of Nicholas Wolterstorff's words that "art does not provide us with the meaning of human existence. The gospel of Jesus Christ does that."[27] Dyrness has further suggested that visual arts can reflect theology, depict the incarnation of Jesus and help Christians in their glorification of the Triune God. However, in Asian settings visual arts which make a contribution to theology need to reflect contextual perspectives not just in terms of biblical and theological themes but also in relation to the arts themselves. The project "A Divine Journey" considers how the use of contextualised visual arts helps in the Christian spiritual formation of the Wa people within their Asian cultural setting.

---

[23] "Chinnawong, Sawai – VM – Sawai Chinnawong," Artway, accessed Aug 4, 2021, https://www.artway.eu/content.php?id=959&action=show&lang=en.

[24] Drane, *Evangelism for a New Age*, 77.

[25] Dyrness, *Visual Faith*, 144 and 151.

[26] Dyrness, *Visual Faith*, 99. Dyrness asks – "What makes art unique among other human activities?"

[27] Quoted in Tim Dean and David Porter, eds., *Art in Question*, The London Lectures in Contemporary Christianity: 1984 (Basingstoke: Marshall Pickering, 1987), 19.

Book Idea

He, Q. *Look toward the Heavens: The Art of He Qi*. New Haven, CT: OMSC, 2006.

This book introduces the artist He Qi and the rationale for his work. It looks at how he seeks to express his Christian faith through his art by drawing on a range of artistic styles and approaches (including those from other cultures). Nonetheless, He Qi seeks to show that Christian art in Asia does not have to retain a western "image." Rather, it needs to foster and reflect an Asian identity – this is beautifully illustrated by his paintings.

Contextualisation and "Little Theologies"

The importance of the local and contextual is also stressed in the writings of Clemens Sedmak. His proposal of doing "little theologies" is about developing a local theology appropriate to local cultural context and to particular circumstances in life.[28] He cites Koyama's statement favourably: "… we do not live in some general idea of history. We live in a certain locality, each locality has a history, culture and language."[29] Thus listening, seeing, learning and discovering the difference between times and places, cultures and people is important when implementing theology to a specific culture and making it relevant for a particular context. According to Sedmak, theology can take various forms, and painting is one of the forms that can show forth implicit theologies in certain contexts.[30] Sedmak's writing addresses the use of "image" as way of making "little theologies" more detailed and colourful. Both Sedmak and Dyrness appear to hold similar ideas, but approach them from different angles, to show the possibility of using art to draw people into an intimate relationship with God. Sedmak, in particular, clearly affirms that powerful messages can come from images that touch life and context in a way that is familiar and accessible to the viewer.[31] Regarding this point, McCullough explores representative examples of art and uses Makoto Fujimura's "The Four Holy Gospels"[32] as an example of how the visual arts can be a strong catalyst for spiritual growth and a source of inspiration to help us think theologically about our lives. Our daily life is the primary context where Christians experience God

---

[28] Clemens Sedmak, *Doing Local Theology: A Guide for Artisans of a New Humanity* (Maryknoll, NY: Orbis Books, 2002), 120.
[29] Kosuke Koyama, *Water Buffalo Theology* (Maryknoll, NY: Orbis Books, 1999), 32, quoted in Sedmak, *Doing Local Theology*, 124.
[30] Sedmak, *Doing Local Theology*, 3, 11, 12, and 124.
[31] Sedmak, *Doing Local Theology*, 146-48.
[32] James McCullough, *Sense and Spirituality: The Arts and Spiritual Formation* (Eugene, OR: Cascade Books, 2015), 73-87.

– in our community and through relationships with one another. It is in this everyday context that believers constitute their theology.

Underlying Sedmak's idea of theology is the fact that people need to seek intimate relationship with Jesus and communion with God in whatever context they find themselves – this involves listening carefully to God because the task of theology is to bring people closer to God.[33] Such a view helps us to understand our identity in the light of who God is. Hence, we see aesthetics and identity are connected. Woodward points out that identity is often bonded in national, racial, ethnic, regional and local ways,[34] but identity is often specific about shared belonging such as an ethnic group sharing the same history and geographic space and time. These perspectives help to reveal how ethnic aesthetics could be related to Wa culture and to the creation of a visual arts project for spiritual formation.

Further Reading on Christian Art in Asia
Dyrness, W. A. *Christian Art in Asia*. Amsterdam: Rodopi, 1979. Pongracz, P. C., V. Küster and J. W. Cook, eds. *The Christian Story: Five Asian Artists Today*. New York; London: Museum of Biblical Art; D. Giles, 2007. Takenaka, M., and G. Singh, eds. *Mission and Art*. Singapore: Christian Conference of Asia, 1994. Takenaka, M., and R. O'Grady. *The Bible through Asian Eyes*. Auckland: Pace Publishing, 1991. Takenaka, M., ed. *Christian Art in Asia*. Tokyo: Kyo Bun Kwan and the Christian Conference of Asia, 1975.

A Visual Arts Project for the Wa

In terms of geographical focus this visual arts project has a focus on the Wa people in the Yunnan province and has a contextual interest in Wa culture viewed in relation to the Christian faith – recognising that "Wa" is an umbrella term for over seventy different sub-groups. This art project, therefore, can only depict the Wa culture in a general sense.[35] The portfolio of visual art works entitled "A Divine Journey" consists of four paintings which deal with the life, ministry and resurrection of Jesus and have been produced as creative resources to inspire the Wa people to reflect more deeply on their journey with God. The project aims to use contextual visual arts to depict Bible passages. These pictures are used as resources to encourage Bible study and to stimulate contemplation of Christian

---

[33] Sedmak, *Doing Local Theology*, 6.
[34] Kathryn Woodward, *Identity and Difference*, Culture, Media and Identities 3 (London: Sage, 1997), 1-6.
[35] In terms of my understanding of Wa culture, I mainly draw on literature from Chinese scholars and researchers, in addition to my own reflections from the experience of working with them in their own areas.

themes through the inspiration of local arts. If they find it helpful, Wa Christians will be encouraged to create their own contextual visual materials into the future. As a result, the project is intended to be a catalyst for other local projects. There are two dimensions of this visual arts project that need to be addressed prior to a discussion of the art works themselves. The first is the contextual nature of the project showing how the visual arts connect to both Wa culture and Christian art. The second is the way in which the project connects to spiritual formation.

A Contextual Project – Drawing on Local Arts

The visual arts project "A Divine Journey" for the Wa people intends to show that the visual arts can be utilised to enhance spiritual formation for an ethnic minority people if done sympathetically and in line with local arts traditions. According to David Hesselgrave, one of the ways in which Christ can be communicated cross-culturally is through media, as these provide "ways of channelling the message."[36] Pictures produced through the visual arts (one form of medium) can be as communicative as words, and they have real and often unexploited potential in many cultures. Likewise, Langdon Gilkey reminds us that art makes us "see in new and different ways, below the surface and beyond the obvious. Art opens up the truth hidden and within the ordinary."[37] Such perspectives inspired the artist to produce visual art that could be an effective aid to encourage the Wa people in their spiritual formation and growth in Christian life. The degree of freedom to use visual arts in the church has fluctuated through the history of Christianity. One major division between art and the church occurred in the 16th century in the Protestant Reformation led by Martin Luther, and later John Calvin. The main cause of this iconoclasm was the misuse of art which led to corruption in the church, and the images implied exploitation and superstition that needed to be destroyed.[38] Nevertheless, art was reaffirmed by the newly revived evangelicals in the Victorian era and others.[39] The western church successfully contextualised Christianity to their world and Bible pictures showed European people and cultural settings which probably helped Europeans to accept the gospel by showing it in local cultural terms.

Following the recovery of art in the global church, a further question arises in the late 20th and early 21st century: "What would Asian Christian art look like?" This prompted Masao Takenaka to ponder a further question, "Do Asians see the

---

[36] David J. Hesselgrave, *Communicating Christ Cross-Culturally: An Introduction to Missionary Communication*, 2nd ed. (Grand Rapids, MI: Zondervan Academic, 1991), 537.

[37] Langdon B. Gilkey, "Can Art Fill the Vacuum?" in *Art, Creativity, and the Sacred: An Anthology in Religion and Art*, ed. Diane Apostolos-Cappadona (New York: Crossroad, 1984), 189-90.

[38] Dyrness, *Visual Faith*, 53-54.

[39] Hilary Brand and Adrienne Chaplin, *Art and Soul: Signposts for Christians in the Arts* (Carlisle; Downers Grove, IL: Piquant; IVP Academic, 2001), 32.

Bible in a particular way?" He responded to his own question with the following pertinent comments: "The Bible speaks universal words of life which are the same wherever they were read. However, the context in which those words are read, imagined and interpreted differs from one culture to another."[40] He realised that the situation we are in determines our perception; and the cultural habitat of our lives gives us a unique way of seeing the world. The message of Christianity should not be communicated in purely cerebral terms, without sensory and sensual aspects, allowing that art, by itself, may not provide all the spiritual connections that the human heart needs. Despite that, the arts can play a vital role in catching the attention of a generation using art forms that speak to the hearts and minds of a given cultural group.[41]

Further Reading on the Arts in Asia from Chinese Perspectives
He, Q. 基督教艺术纵横 [*Christian Art History and Today*]. Beijing: China Religious Culture Publisher, 2013. (In Chinese).
Lin, S. C. *Spaces of Mediation: Christian Art and Visual Culture in Taiwan.* Contact Zone Explorations in Intercultural Theology 24. Leipzig: Evangelische Verlagsanstalt, 2019.
The Life of Christ by Chinese Artists. Westminster: Society for the Propagation of the Gospel, 1939.

Contextualisation starts from a valid concern for the relationship between the Gospel and the receiving culture,[42] and remains a critical component of the effective communication of the Christian faith. Hwa Yung argues that contextualisation is rooted in the incarnation,[43] and its goal is to complement mission.[44] A common example of that would be the Bible pictures which show blond and light-complexioned people (including portrayals of Jesus) and such contextualisation probably helped Europeans to embrace the Gospel. This has demonstrated how powerful it can be when the contextualisation of art is used to approach and engage people. It has been asserted by Megumi Yoshida that the power of Christian art comes from the power of imaging: [45]

---

[40] Takenaka and O'Grady, *The Bible through Asian Eyes*, 7.

[41] Dyrness, *Visual Faith,* 22.

[42] Charles H. Kraft, ed., *Appropriate Christianity* (Pasadena, CA: William Carey Library, 2005), 4.

[43] Hwa Yung, *Mangoes or Bananas? The Quest for an Authentic Asian Christian Theology*, Regnum Studies in Mission (Oxford: Regnum Books, 1997), 62.

[44] Yung, *Mangoes or Bananas?* 61.

[45] Megumi Yoshida, "The Power of Imaging – Art as Love and Struggle as Beauty," *The Asia Journal of Theology* 22, no. 2 (Oct 2008): 287.

The power of art in Asian Christian arts depends on how deeply ego-consciousness descends into the psyche's depth to the ultimate universal stratum, and how profoundly one can see through the psyche's depth in order to stick to imaging.

Ego-consciousness and cultural identity are closely related. When cultural identity is recognised, the power of the image can be seen by the audience. Dyrness recognises that beauty is defined culturally and depends on values and experience.[46] The Wa's perspective on aesthetics is functional.[47] In fact, to many ethnic minority people, beauty means "goodness" and is supposed to be useful in daily life. There is no such thing as "pure beauty" without function. Therefore, even though dealing with an artistic object such as a painting, it should still serve a useful function in these cultures. As a creative visual resource, its function is to contribute to their spiritual maturity.

Spiritual Formation

Spiritual formation is essential for Christian growth in any culture. The Christian scriptures encourage us to pursue Christ-likeness and sanctification. This is an important goal of our Christian lives. Elaborating on the nature of "spiritual formation," Henri Nouwen has suggested that it represents an inward journey from the mind to the heart to find the Christ dwelling in us[48] which, through prayer, reunites us with God. The outward journey is the journey to find Christ's abode amongst us and in the world.[49] Nouwen underlines that in this gradual development of the mind and heart in our lives, it is important for Christians to grow in the areas of contemplative prayer and inclusive community leading to compassionate ministry.[50]

Spiritual Formation and the Arts

James McCullough resonates with Nouwen and Teague that this analogy of an inward and outward journey is helpful for developing an intimate relationship with God.[51] His book *Sense and Spirituality: The Arts and Spiritual Formation* explores the implications of how the arts can contribute to spiritual formation. By making connections between "the senses" – the aesthetic dimensions of life – and spiritual formation, McCullough sees the "the arts" as a kind of bridge that can help people deepen their spiritual lives. It is important, however, that

---

[46] Dyrness, *Visual Faith*, 70.

[47] Zhang, *The Culture and Folk Aesthetics of the Dian*, 10.

[48] Henri Nouwen, *Spiritual Formation: Following the Movements of the Spirit* (New York: HarperCollins, 2010), xix.

[49] Nouwen, *Spiritual Formation*, xvi and 130.

[50] Nouwen, *Spiritual Formation*, 5. See also others such as Teague, who have parallel ideas on what constitutes key aspects of spiritual formation: David Teague, *Godly Servants: Discipleship and Spiritual Formation for Missionaries* (N.p.: Mission Imprints, 2012), 9.

[51] McCullough, *Sense and Spirituality*, 11.

resources for spiritual formation are appropriate to the cultural context and help Christians in their own environments. Christian spiritual formation refers to an internal transformation towards being more Christ-like.[52] Spiritual formation in this project refers to the internal transformation which enables Wa Christians to obey Christ and engage at a deeper level in their relationship with God in their everyday life, by learning how to be rooted in scripture, Christ-centred and empowered by the Holy Spirit. By contextualising biblical stories and accounts of the life of Jesus in visual arts formats, this project intended to help the Wa people in their spiritual growth.

This kind of contextual project wants to show that visual arts can be utilised to enhance spiritual formation for ethnic minorities and the example of an art project for the Wa people shows the relevance of such art projects for smaller people groups who have relatively little Christian art of their own. The paintings visualise and reimagine the accounts of the life, death, and resurrection of Jesus Christ in John's gospel to create a set of paintings as creative resources for Christian spiritual formation for the Wa Christians. According to Romans 8:29 and 2 Corinthians 3:18, the aim of spiritual formation is to help Christians become more like Christ and have a deeper personal relationship with God. The aim of the project is to help Wa Christians to internalise in a creative way, their relationship with God through contextual visual resources. The process is enhanced by explanations, guidelines and reflective questions on the visual arts that accompany the paintings.

John's Gospel – A Spiritual Gospel for Spiritual Formation

John's gospel was chosen as a biblical starting point for several reasons. John's gospel is known as the "spiritual gospel" due to its spiritual themes, distinguishing it from the synoptic gospels. It illustrates Jesus' life in quite a unique perspective in symbolic ways.[53] It is also called a "book of signs" because the author had stated his purpose in the book in John 20:30-31. Thus, the author intended that the story of Jesus should lead to faith on the part of the listeners.[54] In John's gospel, important life events and stories that are relevant to the Wa culture, such as birth, weddings, daily conversations and death are featured. The birth of Jesus in John's gospel was described beyond his ancestors, beyond even Adam and Eve, back to the very beginning of the world and its creation.[55]

The four paintings in this arts project are intended to be a set of supplementary materials for Bible study of John's gospel for spiritual growth. They can be used

[52] McCullough, *Sense and Spirituality*, 9.
[53] L. Michael White, "The Gospel of John: The Spiritual Gospel," Frontline, accessed Sep 15, 2016, http://www.pbs.org/wgbh/pages/frontline/shows/religion/story/john.html.
[54] Larry Kreitzer, *The Gospel According to John*, Regent's Study Guides 1 (Oxford; Macon, GA: Regent's Park College; Smyth & Helwys, 1990), 4-7.
[55] David Pawson, *A Commentary on the Gospel of John* (Ashford: Anchor Recordings, 2012), 31.

to accompany a series of four separate Bible studies, for example, in a house-group setting with a leader giving guidance through an introduction and asking questions as the Bible study continues. Each painting is accompanied by a paragraph-length caption to guide the viewer's interpretation together with reflective questions and the intended purpose of each topic. The paintings are not designed simply to be looked at in an attitude of emotion-oriented free contemplation. Viewers of the paintings are expected to be guided by God's truth in their hearts through the enabling of the Holy Spirit whilst they look at the paintings – in this way the experience of viewing will contribute to spiritual formation. This contextualised visual creative resource aims to encourage and elicit discussion for the Wa Christians to pursue spiritual growth and develop a deeper relationship with God. The paintings are developed to facilitate understanding of the Bible with contextualised visual aids as resources to supplement Bible passages (for Bible study) and to inspire contemplation. It is hoped that Wa Christians would be encouraged to create their own contextualised visual materials in the future so that a local Christian art would continue to flourish.

Suggested Reading on Arts Ministry and Church
Begbie, J. S., ed. *Sounding the Depths: Theology through the Arts*. London: SCM Press, 2002.
Bond, F. *The Arts in Your Church: A Practical Guide*. Carlisle: Piquant, 2001.
McElroy, J. S. *Creative Church Handbook: Releasing the Power of the Arts in Your Congregation*. Downers Grove, IL: IVP, 2015.
Taylor, W. D. O., ed. *For the Beauty of the Church: Casting a Vision for the Arts*. Grand Rapids, MI: Baker Books, 2010.

A Visual Reconception Using Four Accounts of Jesus in John's Gospel

The main audience of this project is Wa Christians. Therefore, the focal point of the biblical message in each painting is expressed in a highly cultural way that relates to the Wa people. The reason that the artist chose the themes and accounts of Jesus in John's Gospel is that the Wa value celebrations in life and festivals. Therefore, weddings, funerals, births and daily interactions with people are all important in their culture. The artist called this series of paintings "A Divine Journey" because it reflects the process of spiritual growth as a journey with God. Unlike the synoptic gospels, John's Gospel has no description of the birth of Jesus. However, John 1:1 implies the "Word" is Jesus and his biography started from the very beginning when the Word was with God, which went far beyond his ancestors.[56] The artist intended to paint John 1:1 – the Word was with God in the beginning – as the birth, and it was also the beginning of the divine

---

[56] Pawson, *A Commentary on the Gospel of John*, 31.

journey of Jesus. Indeed, each step of Jesus' journey, from the manger to the cross, was made by the deliberate choice of obedience.[57] Each of the four paintings will now be described in turn.

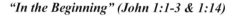

"In the Beginning" (John 1:1-3 & 1:14)

The first painting depicts "in the beginning, the Word was with God," and the Word become flesh on the earth. The word for "word" in the Wa language is *gumlox*, and the word for "God" is *Siyiex*. The two words were placed together in the centre of a whirlpool and became the focus of the painting as the starting point of all creation. The whirlpool creates a profound sense of the mystery of creation. There are various Wa cultural elements in the painting to embody the cultural identity of the Wa people. Another element is there to represent the

---

[57] Tony Horsfall, *Working from a Place of Rest: Jesus and the Key to Sustaining Ministry* (Abingdon: Bible Reading Fellowship, 2010), 41.

culture of the kingdom of God: a dove that symbolises the presence of the Holy Spirit and peace; and there is a set of footprints to illustrate Jesus' presence, Jesus' care, and our relationship with Jesus during our predicaments. Jesus was there since the creation.

Wa legend viewed the origin of human beings as coming from *Si Gongli* – in Wa language literally meaning a gourd or rock.[58] The gourd, rock and buffalo head together with their livelihoods (the root crops and the animals) are in the periphery of the painting to show they are all part of God's creation instead of being the ultimate source of blessings.

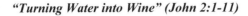

"Turning Water into Wine" (John 2:1-11)

---

[58] Duan, *The Mystery of the Culture and History of the Wa*, 176-77.

In the second painting, a particular type of container represents Wa traditional "watery-wine" used for their celebrations and hospitality. A thin bamboo or a straw is normally placed into those containers. The way they get the wine out is to take a first sip and then the wine will come out along the thin pipe. In the painting, the watery-wine is pouring out gently from the six traditional wine jars without the use of a straw. It denotes that God can use the Wa jars in a new way to pour out the miraculous blessings and joy of turning water into wine from above to his people as it is written in Acts 2:17.

Dancing is an important part of the Wa culture. To join the circle of blessing and wedding celebration, people come from different directions and places and the picture shows that it represents a journey of those people who come from different directions to join the circle. The painting illustrates how the Wa can be chosen by God as a valuable vase to channel Jesus' blessing and joy, not only to the Wa themselves but also to many other peoples. It carries a message of mission and reconciliation.

"The Conversation by the Well" (John 4:1-26)

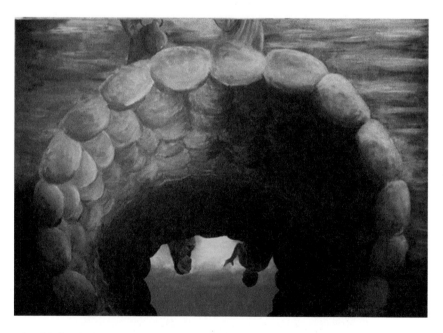

The third painting is about John 4:1-26. It depicts the time when Jesus was on his journey to Galilee and he intended to pass by Samaria. He was tired and took a rest by the well in Sychar. The painting intentionally left out the face of Jesus and the Samaritan woman, but in the reflection of the well, Jesus is shown as a Wa man and the Samaritan woman as a Wa woman to portray that Jesus dwells amongst them. When Jesus dwells amongst us, he should be reflected in us and in our lives in context.

The background of the well at the woman's side is a brownish colour to indicate the dryness and emptiness of her inner situation. By contrast, the background on Jesus' side is greener and looks like this because it is nourished with the living water from Jesus. He is the spring of life; whoever drinks the water from this spring will never be thirsty again. Not long ago, whilst the Wa people were still using water from the well in the villages, this scenario of chatting by the well would, apparently, not have been strange to them, although nowadays, many Wa families have tap water in their homes and have no need to fetch water from the well anymore. This ordinary activity can still help them to make associations with such familiar daily tasks in which they themselves can meet Jesus.

"From Humiliation to Glory" (John 19:16-30 & 20:1-9)

In the last painting, the empty wood that represents the "tomb" shows that Jesus was resurrected and overcame death. The glory and hope of his resurrection are depicted as being over the Wa mountainous area. The painting exhibits the relationship between the accounts of Jesus' death and resurrection and the Wa people themselves through the combination of the scene of Golgotha and the Wa village.

The composition of the painting can be viewed as being in three parts. The upper left part is the cross on Golgotha: it contrasts with the Wa village on the upper right part and relates the two different spaces and times together in the painting. The lower part is taken from John 20:1 when Mary Magdalene was the first person who discovered the empty tomb of Jesus. The Wa people traditionally did not use tombs or coffins, but placed the body in a piece of hollow tree trunk. Here, a Wa woman takes Magdalene's role to witness Jesus' victory of resurrection. Moreover, the power and glory of Jesus' resurrection is over the Wa land.

Reflections on "The Divine Journey"

In the portfolio for this visual arts project, the content of the paintings is mainly drawn from John's gospel and it demonstrates both cultural and spiritual elements. The cultural components are complex and would need a kind of artistic "decoding" for those who are not familiar with the culture. The colour spectrum – including hue, saturation and value – is used to reflect the atmosphere of mystery,[59] happiness,[60] and hope[61] within the message and the "journey." Since the Wa are robust, pragmatic and "wild," the brush strokes can express their ethnic traits. The paintings use different angles and perspectives to depict the story from a unique approach that prompts a new way of seeing it by the viewers. As McCullough claims, "arts address more than feelings, they deliver ideas, values, and perception as well."[62] Connecting these to the realm of the spiritual involves the work of theological aesthetics, which convey the ideas and thoughts. It also needs effort on the part of the viewers to listen to and study the painting carefully so that it impacts their lives.

Conclusion

Using symbols and artefacts from the Wa culture, and elements of the Bible to manifest the hope of Christian eschatology, this series of paintings divulges the divine journey of Jesus and invites the viewers to engage with Jesus in their own journey of faith as "a divine journey." Looking at these paintings forces the viewer to think and be honest with themselves. Jesus' image is not explicit but

---

[59] In the painting – "In the Beginning."
[60] In the painting – "Turning Water into Wine."
[61] In the painting – "From Humiliation to Glory."
[62] McCullough, *Sense and Spirituality*, 26.

the combination of the cultural images and the biblical messages can encourage the Wa people to meet Jesus in their daily context, which is the ultimate purpose of the paintings. The elements of journeying are expressed by a combination of the depiction of distance and varied visual components in the paintings which together offer new insights and perceptions. Echoing the divine journey of Jesus, the "Word became flesh" from heaven to earth, these help to reflect the journey of faith in a deeper way.

It is important for Christians, if they are to connect with local cultures through the arts, to spend time and energy in the research and investigation of local arts. Beyond this, artists need to step out in faith to use the visual arts for God's glory and reach out to people in every culture through the arts. God has revealed in his story in the Bible that he would like to draw people to himself and be reconciled with them through the death and sacrifice of Jesus on the cross for our sins and through his resurrection power made available in the Holy Spirit. God has given us the beauty of his creation including the gift of creating art. Therefore, we need to use this gift appropriately to encourage people to experience God in a deeper way. The Dutch art historian and critic Hans Rookmaaker has stated that:[63]

> God gave humanity the skill to make things beautiful, to make music, to write poems, to make sculpture, to decorate things. The artistic possibilities are there to be actualized, realized by us, and to be given a concrete form. God gave this to humankind and its meaning is exactly in its givenness. ... If in this way art has its own meaning as God's creation, it does not need justification. Its justification is its being a God-given possibility.

Such a proposition affirms the importance for Wa Christian artists to create art pieces themselves that will help them in their quest to engage with God. In the future, through the witness of the Wa, contextual arts and similar creative resources could continue to help promote maturity in spiritual life, not just for the Wa but for the neighbouring people groups who live around them.

Visual arts, like the paintings at the heart of this project, can elicit both reflection and contemplation in ways that are beneficial to spiritual life. This is especially true where the arts in question are contextually appropriate. Responses to this project have suggested that contextual art can help local Christians to see beyond their normal horizons and, in some senses, to grasp what had been hitherto unseen visions from God that stretch them in their quest for a deeper spiritual formation and draw them closer to God.[64] It is hoped that this project will help Wa Christians find creative ways to engage with scripture, and to establish their own theology by using contextualised visual arts. The project can also be a source of inspiration for others, as they consider making connections

---

[63] Hans R. Rookmaaker, *Art Needs No Justification* (Vancouver: Regent College Publishing, 2010), chap. 4.
[64] See Chiu, "A Visual Re-Conception," Appendix I – Sample Responses – "ID-25," 61-62.

between their own contexts and spiritual formation, through the medium of the visual arts.

Questions for Reflection/Discussion
1. The discussion of aesthetics starts to probe aspects of Wa culture and makes comparisons with aesthetics in other cultural contexts. What do you learn about Wa culture and arts? What thoughts does this stimulate about arts in other contexts known to you?
2. The section on theology and the arts draws on the work of Drane, Sedmak and Dyrness. What are some of the key points that they make? How might their ideas contribute to the way that contextual arts are created and designed?
3. "Painting is one of the forms that can show forth implicit theologies in certain contexts." How does the discussion on theology suggest ways of using "locality" to inform the creation of contextual arts that really connect with local people?
4. The choice of John's gospel relates to themes of everyday life: "In John's gospel, important life events and stories that are relevant to the Wa culture, such as birth, weddings, daily conversations and death are featured." In what ways do the pictures deal with key themes in John's gospel? How do the four pictures each contribute to aspects of spiritual formation?

5. Digital Media and Urban Youth Culture: Engaging Missionally with New Approaches to Storytelling
Anne M. Y. Soh

Anne Soh shows the interest in contemporary Singapore regarding stories told through two forms of electronic media – anime and K-drama. Using the categories of learner, user and producer, she explores ways in which missional artists can engage with the cultures of Japan and Korea, interact with the issues that surface from storytelling in these electronic media, and learn from the example of missional artists who create their own formats for cultural engagement shaped by Christian perspectives.

It is a typical weekday morning and I am seated on a subway train in Singapore filled with teenagers rushing to school. A student in front of me is in the middle of a basketball game, feeling the heat from the fierce competition. He goes "into the zone" and zooms across the court at lighting speed to score a basket. His face breaks into a grin whilst he savours the spectators' applause. The student on my left is talking to her dashing neighbour on the phone when a group of men suddenly jump out of a passing van, throw her into the vehicle, and drive off. Before she can scream for help, a piece of masking tape is plastered over her mouth.

The reader must have realised by now that my fellow passengers are not experiencing these situations in real life. They are merely absorbed in the scenes of an *anime*,[1] *Kuroko's Basketball*, and a Korean drama, *My Secret Terrius*,[2] respectively on their mobile phones (with headphones attached so they do not disturb other passengers). Such a scenario is common not only in Singapore, which has one of the fastest internet connection speeds in the world,[3] but also in urban settings all over Asia. A significant percentage of people, especially youth

---

[1] An *anime* is a graphic image or animation film from Japan. *Anime* has become an international word so will subsequently be referred to simply as anime.
[2] References to all anime and Korean dramas mentioned are given in the Filmography.
[3] Simon Kemp, "Digital 2020: Global Digital Overview," DataReportal (Jan 30, 2020), accessed Jan 24, 2021, https://datareportal.com/reports/digital-2020-global-digital-overview, slides 50 & 52.

and young adults,[4] are glued to their phones, consuming a wide variety of media, in particular online videos,[5] at all hours of the day. Across Asia, the number of mobile phones connected to the internet exceeds the total population and around 60% of people have access to the internet.[6] It is therefore not surprising to find several Asian countries listed amongst the top 20 countries with the highest percentage of internet users who watch online videos.[7] These videos can be downloaded or streamed on numerous video-hosting websites such as YouTube, and video-on-demand (VOD) apps such as Netflix, often for free but sometimes for a small, hence affordable, subscription fee.[8] Out of all the different video genres found online, anime and Korean drama (K-drama) are amongst the most popular in Asia. There are even dedicated VOD platforms for each genre,[9] for example Crunchyroll[10] and Viu.[11] It is thus useful to consider how these two genres could be tapped for mission in order to reach the urban youth of Asia.[12]

Development and Impact of Each Genre

Anime

Anime, or Japanese animation, has developed significantly since it first gained international attention in the 1960s. The most common format is the anime series

---

[4] Irene Tham, "Nine in 10 young viewers watch shows online," *The Straits Times* (Jul 15, 2016), accessed Jan 30, 2021, https://www.straitstimes.com/singapore/nine-in-10-young-viewers-watch-shows-online.

[5] Out of the world's 10 most popular video streaming services, seven are based in Asia – iQiyi, Tencent Video, Youku, Viu, Alt Balaji, Eros Now, Iflix. Martin Armstrong, "The World's Most Popular Video Streaming Services," Statista (Feb 5, 2020), accessed Aug 10, 2020, https://www.statista.com/chart/20701/video-streaming-services-with-most-subscribers-global-fipp/.

[6] Kemp, "Digital 2020: Global Digital Overview," slides 180 & 34.

[7] These are Saudi Arabia (#1), Turkey (#2), China (#3), The Philippines (#7), India (#9), Indonesia (#14), South Korea (#16), and Japan (#17). "Percentage of internet users who watch online video content on any device as of January 2018, by country," Statista (Jan 26, 2021), accessed Sep 24, 2021, https://www.statista.com/statistics/272835/share-of-internet-users-who-watch-online-videos/.

[8] Half of the top 10 highest-earning mobile apps in the world in 2019 are video apps – Netflix (#2), Tencent Video (#3), iQiyi (#4), YouTube (#5), and Youku (#9). Three out of these five apps originate from Asia (namely China) – Tencent Video, iQiyi, and Youku. Kemp, "Digital 2020: Global Digital Overview," slide 204.

[9] Siddhant Jain, "Top 20 Online VOD Platforms in Asia [Updated 2021]," VdoCipher (Jul 25, 2018), accessed Oct 8, 2021, https://www.vdocipher.com/blog/2018/07/asia-vod-platforms/.

[10] Crunchyroll, accessed Aug 10, 2020, https://www.crunchyroll.com/.

[11] Viu, accessed Aug 10, 2020, https://www.viu.com/.

[12] Although there are other hugely popular genres such as Bollywood films and Chinese drama from China, Hong Kong and Taiwan, this investigation will focus on two genres (anime and K-drama) as they are the most popular amongst Asian youth.

which comprises multiple episodes each lasting around 20 to 30 minutes. Some popular anime may run for many years, such as *Pokémon* which is into its 24th season[13] since it began in 1997. A well-received series such as *Neon Genesis Evangelion* may lead producers to release a movie which either summarises the story (*Neon Genesis Evangelion: Death and Rebirth*) or concludes it (*The End of Evangelion*), although there are also successful standalone movies such as *My Neighbor Totoro*, which has become an internationally-recognised classic. Traditionally, many anime productions were inspired by *manga*, but the influence of anime has increased and in recent years, *manga* stories are also based on anime.[14]

Digital technology, especially the internet, has also facilitated the distribution of anime and contributed to a dramatic increase in its worldwide popularity.[15] The impact of anime reaches far beyond the screen. There are countless selfie-camera phone apps that edit self-portraits,[16] and YouTube videos that teach make-up techniques[17] to help fans look like anime characters. Entire industries are built on "cross-media story-telling"[18] where anime narratives are conveyed through various media including video and computer games (for example, *Astro Boy*, and the augmented reality phone game *Pokémon Go* that took the world by storm), toys, and even AI-operated holograms.[19] There are virtual anime pop idols known as VOCALOIDs,[20] such as Hatsune Miku, who hold live concerts, whilst some popular anime stories are translated into stage musicals. Large-scale

[13] "Explore Seasons," Pokemon.com, accessed Sep 24, 2021, https://www.pokemon.com/us/pokemon-episodes/pokemon-tv-seasons/.
[14] *Manga* describes Japanese comic books or graphic novels. Leo Reyna, "15 Manga Series Based on Anime You Might Not Know About," Ranker (Apr 11, 2018), accessed Aug 10, 2020, https://www.ranker.com/list/best-manga-based-on-anime/leo-reyna.
[15] Thomas Lamarre, *The Anime Machine: A Media Theory of Animation* (Minneapolis, MN: University of Minnesota Press, 2009), ix.
[16] A search for apps on Google Play with the phrase "anime selfie" generated 250 results. Google Play, accessed Aug 10, 2020, https://play.google.com/store/search?q=anime%20selfie&c=apps&hl=en.
[17] YouTube, accessed Aug 10, 2020, https://www.youtube.com/results?search_query=anime+makeup+ tutorial.
[18] Alba Torrents, "Technological Specificity, Transduction, and Identity in Media Mix," in *Japanese Media Cultures in Japan and Abroad: Transnational Consumption of Manga, Anime, and Media-Mixes*, ed. Manuel Hernández-Pérez (Basel: MDPI, 2019), 85.
[19] "An Anime Hologram Assistant That Lives in Your Room and Controls Your Devices," *Grape Japan* (Jan 21, 2016), accessed Aug 10, 2020, https://grapee.jp/en/53655.
[20] "VOCALOIDs," Fandom, accessed Aug 10, 2020, https://vocaloid.fandom.com/wiki/VOCALOIDs.

events such as anime and "cosplay"[21] conventions are frequently held all over the world. Anime characters are often featured in advertising campaigns.[22]

Korean Drama

In the year of writing, the online world was abuzz with news and commentaries on the first-ever foreign language film to win the Best Picture award in the Oscars – a Korean film, *Parasite*. Meanwhile, international K-drama fans were binge-watching *Crash Landing on You* after learning of its phenomenal ratings in Korea.[23] K-drama productions are usually either feature-length films or series made up of 12 to 24 hour-long episodes. There are also extended series such as *Jewel in the Palace* which could run for over 100 episodes. However, there is a growing trend of single-episode drama specials such as *Come to Me Like a Star*, or mini-series such as *Hymn of Death* with anything from two to eight episodes, as well as web series[24] such as *A-Teen*, which are published exclusively online and more flexible in terms of the number and length of episodes (although they tend to be less than 30 minutes long).

K-drama started gaining popularity throughout Asia in the late 1990s and contributed to the rise of the Korean Wave (*Hallyu*), which spread across the world within a decade.[25] With the easy availability of K-drama online, viewers are now able to watch almost any series at any time from anywhere. The impact of K-drama on other industries is wide-ranging. Popular actors endorse multifarious products from cars to cosmetics and clothes, whilst product placements in popular K-drama series often lead to business booms.[26] Some web series are even intentionally produced to advertise various products or brands, such as *7 First Kisses* and *Soul Plate* which promote a duty-free shop and Korean cuisine, respectively. Korean tourism has also benefitted from *Hallyu*[27] as

---

[21] "Cosplay" refers to role playing of characters from anime, *manga* and video games, with elaborate make-up, costumes, accessories and props.

[22] Takashi Muto, "Harnessing the Power of Anime as an Outstanding Marketing Solution," Dentsu, accessed Aug 11, 2020,
https://www.dentsu.co.jp/en/news/ideas/harnessing_the_power_of_anime.html.

[23] Krissy Aguilar, "'Crash Landing On You' topples 'Goblin' as highest-rated drama in channel's history," *The Jakarta Post* (Feb 18, 2020), accessed Aug 11, 2020,
https://www.thejakartapost.com/life/2020/02/18/crash-landing-on-you-topples-goblin-as-highest-rated-drama-in-channels-history.html.

[24] Nakky, "Korean Web Dramas," MyDramaList (Feb 16, 2020), accessed Aug 11, 2020, https://mydramalist.com/list/O3odrv04.

[25] Doobo Shim, "The Growth of Korean Cultural Industries and the Korean Wave," in *East Asian Pop Culture: Analysing the Korean Wave,* eds. Beng Huat Chua and Koichi Iwabuchi (Hong Kong: Hong Kong University Press, 2008), 25; 27.

[26] Chung-un Cho, "'Descendants of the Sun' buoys Korean economy," *The Korea Herald* (Mar 31, 2016), accessed Aug 11, 2020,
http://www01.koreaherald.com/view.php?ud=20160331000660.

[27] Pao-Li Chang and Hyojung Lee, "The Korean Wave: Determinants and Its Impacts on Trade and FDI," *Singapore Management University* (May 9, 2017), accessed Aug 11,

throngs of K-drama fans make pilgrimages to visit Korean landmarks made famous by their favourite K-drama.

Powerplay: Stories, Talkies and the Internet

Stories

The success of anime/K-drama owes much to the inherent power of storytelling to grip and "move the whole person – the emotions and senses as well as the intellect."[28] Stories have long been used to educate the young, whilst nowadays in storytelling marketing, an emotive rendering of a personal story can convince viewers to buy into the narrative.[29] In oral traditions, stories have connected parents with their offspring, families with communities, and succeeding generations with the ones before. Jesus used parables to teach and counsel, for "a story gets at aspects of the truth that are beyond the power of didactic teaching."[30] In fact, nearly 75% of the Bible is made up of stories.[31] Storytelling is also a key feature in Asian cultures. Various storytelling genres have been used to narrate literary works, such as the Indian epic *Ramayana*, as well as to teach history, for example through the Japanese *kōdan*. Stories are often sung, such as the Korean *pansori*, but sometimes dramatised too, as in the Indonesian *wayang kulit* and the Chinese *xiqu*.

Talkies

Another factor behind the success of anime/K-drama is the advances in technology, particularly television and film, where visual and sound effects, image, voice, and music come together "to actively engage viewers both emotionally and intellectually by immersing them, visually and aurally, in an onscreen experience."[32]

2020, https://economics.smu.edu.sg/sites/economics.smu.edu.sg/files/economics/Events/SNJTW2017/Hyojung%20Lee.pdf, 19.

[28] Charles Colson and Nancy Pearcey, *How Now Shall We Live?* (London: Marshall Pickering, 1999), 440.

[29] Bel Booker, "12 Top Storytelling Marketing Examples: How Brands Tell Stories," Attest (Sep 19, 2019), accessed Aug 13, 2020, https://www.askattest.com/blog/marketing/12-top-storytelling-marketing-examples.

[30] Colson and Pearcey, *How Now Shall We Live?* 440.

[31] Colin Harbinson, "Restoring the Arts to the Church: The Role of Creativity in the Expression of Truth," Colin Harbinson, accessed Aug 11, 2020, https://www.colinharbinson.com/teaching/resthearts.html.

[32] Sheila Curran Bernard, *Documentary Storytelling: Creative Nonfiction on Screen*, 4th ed. (Abingdon and New York: Focal Press, 2016), chap. 1, Kindle.

The Internet

With the advent of the internet and the ability to stream or download videos, viewers now hold the power in their fingertips to decide where and when to engage with anime/K-drama online. Along with the pervasiveness of social media, especially amongst urban youth, it only takes one swipe or a tap to share their favourite videos with others, resulting in viral circulation of anime/K-drama online. Furthermore, anime/K-drama fans are connecting across physical borders through online communities based on their common interests.[33] They derive a sense of identity and belonging in these virtual communities, and perpetuate the sharing and spreading of popular videos. Christian communicators have long known that 70% of the world's population are oral communicators and storytelling is a powerful way to reach them. However, we now need strategies to reach "people whose orality is tied to electronic media," the ones who "get most of the important information in their lives through stories and music coming through radio, television, film, internet and other electronic means."[34] Urban youth, often referred to as "digital natives,"[35] clearly fall into this category. In this chapter, we will look at how we can connect in a missional way with this group effectively through digital media such as online videos including anime/K-drama.

Learner

One practical way that anime/K-drama can inform missional artists is for those engaging with Japan/Korea to learn about Japanese/Korean cultures, respectively, through viewing relevant programmes. Apart from visible aspects of Japanese/Korean cultures such as language, food, customs, and artistic traditions that can be learned from watching anime/K-drama, "it is through the personalities and lifestyles of the characters featured … that young people around the world are exposed to, and may come to know, the soul and culture"[36]

---

[33] Castells suggests that people are enmeshed in a global network connected beyond time and space where "citizenship does not equate with nationality," and begin to establish an "invisible national boundary" based on common languages/interest rather than geography. Manuel Castells, *The Power of Identity*, The Information Age: Economy, Society, and Culture 2, 2nd ed. (West Sussex: Wiley-Blackwell, 2010), 54-55.

[34] Lausanne Movement, "Making Disciples of Oral Learners," Lausanne Occasional Paper, no. 54 (2004), accessed Aug 11, 2020, https://www.lausanne.org/content/lop/making-disciples-oral-learners-lop-54.

[35] Marc Prensky, "Digital Natives, Digital Immigrants Part 1," *On the Horizon* 9, no. 5 (2001): 1-6, accessed Aug 11, 2020, https://doi.org/10.1108/10748120110424816.

[36] Sugiura Tsutomu, "Japan's Creative Industries: Culture as a Source of Soft Power in the Industrial Sector," in *Soft Power Superpowers: Cultural and National Assets of Japan and the United States*, eds. Yasushi Watanabe and David L. McConnell (London and New York: Routledge, 2008), 134.

of these countries. Through close analyses of the storylines in anime/K-drama, we can catch a glimpse of the hearts and minds of Japanese/Korean people, including their spirituality and worldviews such as concepts of death and the afterlife, and their understanding of Christianity.

Culture and the People's Psyche

Animism is deeply-rooted in Japanese culture, so much so that Yoneyama, an academic of Japanese origin, opines that the animistic elements in Miyazaki's works such as the Oscar-winning *Spirited Away*, "resonate with something we have inherited from our ancestors."[37] Most anime stories are imbibed by a high level of spirituality, magic and supernatural powers, which are often employed to exert control over others including nature, as in *Weathering with You*. The Japanese are also "famous for embracing anything and everything foreign,"[38] from the western icon of a broom-flying witch in *Kiki's Delivery Service* to Christian symbols in the *Evangelion* series. *Evangelion* assistant director, Tsurumaki, admitted that these were appropriated because they would "look cool."[39] Missional artists engaging with Japan would do well to consider how such pluralism[40] and the desire for power and control impact the Japanese people's willingness to submit to "no other gods"[41] but the one true God.

The importance of Confucian ancestral worship to the Koreans is woven into K-drama. For instance, in *The Greatest Marriage*, the male protagonist's family conducts elaborate memorial rites eleven times a year to honour four generations of ancestors, and they expect his wife to continue the tradition. There are also countless portrayals of Korean shamanistic beliefs in the afterlife (*Come Back Mister*), supernatural beings (*Guardian: The Lonely and Great God*), fortune-telling (*Lucky Romance*), and magical powers (*Queen of the Ring*). Christian traditions have also been "shamanized,"[42] for example in depictions of angelic beings (*Angel's Last Mission: Love*), and Catholic folk religious elements (*The*

---

[37] Shoko Yoneyama, "Animating the Life-World: Animism by Film Director Miyazaki Hayao," in *Animism in Contemporary Japan: Voices for the Anthropocene from Post-Fukushima Japan* (Abingdon and New York: Routledge, 2019), chap. 4, Kindle.

[38] Adam Barkman, "Anime, Manga and Christianity: A Comprehensive Analysis," *Journal for the Study of Religions and Ideologies* 9, no. 27 (Winter 2010): 26, accessed Aug 11, 2020, https://www.academia.edu/30207502/_Anime_Manga_and_Christianity_A_Comprehensive_Analysis.

[39] Jason Morehead, "A Deep Dive Into Hideaki Anno's Mind-blowing, Groundbreaking *Neon Genesis Evangelion*," *Opus* (Jun 17, 2019), accessed Aug 11, 2020, https://opuszine.us/posts/neon-genesis-evangelion-hideaki-anno-deep-dive.

[40] Barkman, "Anime, Manga and Christianity," 26-29.

[41] Ex. 20:3.

[42] Seung Min Hong, "Uncomfortable Proximity: Perception of Christianity as a Cultural Villain in South Korea," *International Journal of Communication* 10 (2016): 4536, accessed Aug 11, 2020, https://ijoc.org/index.php/ijoc/article/viewFile/4505/1783.

Guest). Although nearly 20% of the population professed to be Protestants in 2015 (and around 8% Roman Catholic),[43] missional artists should bear in mind how religious syncretism can impact the Korean Christian narrative.

Book Idea

Noble, A. *Disruptive Witness: Speaking Truth in a Distracted Age*. Downers Grove, IL: IVP Books, 2018.

Modern life and media break through into our lives creating distraction and turning us from deeper realities. Using the language of "barriers" and drawing on the idea of the "buffered self," this book suggests how we can move beyond these "disruptions." It pushes us to think afresh about the good news of the gospel and create new patterns that will transform our personal lives, our churches and, ultimately, our engagement with the world around us.

Historico-Political Backgrounds

Wars feature prominently in anime, as can be seen in the internationally-renowned series about inter-galactic wars (*Mobile Suit Gundam*), ninja wars (*Naruto*), and virtual reality battles (*Sword Art Online*). *Princess Mononoke*, a highly-acclaimed film by Miyazaki, is about the war between humans and nature. However, it was Miyazaki's Ghibli Studio co-founder, Takahata, who began the trend of anti-war films set in World War II with *Grave of the Fireflies*. Nevertheless, just like all the other anti-war films that have been made so far, there is no explicit mention of the atrocities committed by Japan across Asia. The closest ever to admitting any wrongdoing can only be found in *Rail of the Star*, which is about a Japanese family living in Korea during the Japanese occupation. Even then, it merely hints at the oppression of Koreans. It is precisely due to this reluctance to acknowledge and apologise for its complicity in the war that some Asian countries, especially Korea, still harbour "anti-Japanism."[44] In K-drama, however, numerous portrayals of Japanese brutality are seen, such as in *The Battleship Island*, *The Last Princess*, and *Chicago Typewriter*. These "historical narratives disseminated by public media probably have greater impact on the public than those taught in schools and universities,"[45]

---

[43] "Religion," Korea.net, accessed Aug 11, 2020,
http://www.korea.net/AboutKorea/Korean-Life/Religion.
[44] Leo T. S. Ching, *Anti-Japan: The Politics of Sentiment in Postcolonial East Asia* (Durham, NC and London: Duke University Press, 2019), 2.
[45] Peter Duus, "Introduction: History Wars in Postwar East Asia, 1945–2014," in *'History Wars' and Reconciliation in Japan and Korea: The Roles of Historians, Artists and Activists*, ed. Michael Lewis (New York: Palgrave Macmillan, 2017), 2.

hence reinforcing and perpetuating anti-Japanese sentiment even amongst the younger generation including Korean Christians.[46] The criticism against *Mr Sunshine* for justifying the cruelty of a pro-Japan character towards the Koreans[47] reveals the level of antagonism that still exists towards Japan. There is a real need for sensitive and compassionate ministries of reconciliation, in addition to existing dialogue amongst Christian leaders,[48] to bring about reconciliation within the body of Christ and beyond. Conversely, the narratives of North–South relations in K-drama are much more positive, where North and South Koreans are often portrayed as brothers (*Underground Rendezvous*), team-mates (*As One*), friends (*Joint Security Area*), and even lovers *(Crash Landing on You)* yearning for reconciliation and unification. There are some stories that put North Korea in a bad light (*Doctor Stranger*), but they are few and far between. Therefore, when interacting with South Koreans, one should be mindful to critique North Korean culture in a measured way.

Socio-Ethical Issues

Viewers can glean from anime/K-drama various socio-ethical issues in Japan/Korea, especially those caused by urbanisation, such as overcrowding and high housing costs (*Weathering with You*; *Come to Me Like a Star*), aging population (*Roujin Z*; *Dazzling*), human trafficking (*Now and Then, Here and There*; *Midnight Runners*), corruption (*One Piece*; *The Fiery Priest*), hierarchy and social stratification (*Food Wars!*; *Ms Hammurabi*), and the rich–poor divide (*Arakawa under the Bridge*; *Parasite*). Some of the issues addressed in anime/K-drama that most directly concern the urban youth of Japan/Korea are examined in what follows.

A major concern faced by Japanese youth is how anime's "virtually generated images can easily demonstrate sexually deviant scenarios," and "shape individuals' sexual norms."[49] For instance, *Sailor Moon* has been popular for decades amongst young children who gradually become desensitised to the

---

[46] Ingrina Shieh, "Japanese and Korean Students Find Reconciliation," InterVarsity (Jan 22, 2007), accessed Aug 12, 2020, https://intervarsity.org/news/japanese-and-korean-students-find-reconciliation.

[47] Jin-hai Park, "'Mr. Sunshine' embroiled in history distortion dispute," *The Korea Times* (Aug 21, 2018), accessed Aug 12, 2020,
http://www.koreatimes.co.kr/www/nation/2018/08/688_252685.html.

[48] "Journeying Across Divides Toward Reconciliation," The Christian Forum for Reconciliation in Northeast Asia, accessed Aug 12, 2020,
https://neareconciliation.com/78-2/.

[49] Mutsumi Ogaki, "Theoretical Explanations of Jyoshi Kousei Business ("JK Business") in Japan," *Dignity: A Journal of Analysis of Exploitation and Violence* 3, iss. 1, article 11 (2018): 6, accessed Aug 12, 2020,
https://doi.org/10.23860/dignity.2018.03.01.11.

highly-sexualised images and themes.[50] Since then, objectification of women through "fanservice,"[51] including that of young girls in *lolicon* and *moe*[52] characters (Shiro from *No Game No Life*; Mikuru Asahina from *The Melancholy of Haruhi Suzumiya*), has become commonplace, whilst *hentai*[53] and *yaoi*,[54] and even themes such as incest[55] have been normalised. Whilst adult-rated Korean films contain overt depictions of themes such as lesbian relationships (*The Handmaiden*) and teacher–student affairs (*Innocent Thing*), the mainstream K-drama audience remains relatively conservative, judging by the criticism *Backstreet Rookie* received for being "way too dirty."[56] Nonetheless, a survey of web dramas, which revolve mostly around high school crushes and college romances, reveals that pre-marital sex (*Love Playlist*), one-night stands (*Ending Again*), and cohabitation (*Flower Ever After*) have become acceptable and even expected behaviour amongst young people. Although homosexuality is still controversial in Korea,[57] cross-dressing is an oft-used plot device, as in *Coffee Prince* where the unknowing male protagonist kisses his supposedly male employee after deciding that love triumphs over his personal reservations about same-sex relationships. This kind of subtle messaging is progressively shifting attitudes, especially amongst the young, by legitimising same-sex attraction.[58]

Another set of challenges common to both Japanese and Korean youth has to do with the pressures of school. There is intense rivalry to perform not only in academics where ranking counts for everything (*Classroom of the Elite*; *School 2017*), but also in extra-curricular activities such as sports (*Kuroko's Basketball*; *No Breathing*), and music (*Forest of Piano*; *Page Turner*), where the expectation

---

[50] Nicole D'Andria, "Sailor Moon: 15 Ways It Was Censored In America," *ScreenRant* (Feb 27, 2017), accessed Aug 12, 2020, https://screenrant.com/sailor-moon-censored-in-america/.

[51] "Fanservice" refers to titillating images or scenes that are inconsequential to the plot.

[52] *Lolicon* and *moe* refer to underaged and youthful characters, respectively, which arouse heightened feelings of affection and excitement (usually of a sexual nature).

[53] Pornographic *manga* or anime.

[54] Also known as Boys' Love, it features male same-sex relationships.

[55] Christy Rebecca Sally Gibbs, "Breaking Binaries: Transgressing Sexualities in Japanese Animation" (PhD thesis, University of Waikato, Hamilton, New Zealand, 2012), accessed Oct 6, 2021, https://hdl.handle.net/10289/6746, 292.

[56] "'Way too dirty': Netizens fume over sexual tones in K-drama Backstreet Rookie," *CNA Lifestyle* (Jul 4, 2021), accessed Sep 24, 2021, https://cnalifestyle.channelnewsasia.com/trending/backstreet-rookie-ji-chang-wook-kim-yoo-jung-12877548.

[57] Julia Hollingsworth, "In the camp world of K-pop, it's hard for stars to be gay," *CNN* (Jan 27, 2020), accessed Aug 12, 2020, https://edition.cnn.com/2020/01/25/asia/k-pop-gay-star-intl-hnk/index.html.

[58] In 2019, 79% of 18- to 29-year-old Koreans said homosexuality should be accepted by society, compared with only 23% of those 50 and older. Jacob Poushter and Nicholas Kent, "The Global Divide on Homosexuality Persists," Pew Research Center (Jun 25, 2020), accessed Aug 12, 2020, https://www.pewresearch.org/global/2020/06/25/global-divide-on-homosexuality-persists/.

is to win every competition. The high level of stress created is a major contributing factor for other related problems – bullying, depression, self-harm and suicide – which feature prominently in many anime/K-drama such as *Colorful, Orange, Jungle Fish 2*, and *Cheer Up!* Suicide, in particular, is of national concern in Japan/Korea as the suicide rates in both countries are amongst the highest in Asia and the world.[59] The heavy demands from society not only affect students detrimentally, but teachers (*Sayonara, Zetsubou-Sensei*) and parents (*Sky Castle*) too. There are other coping mechanisms amongst students to manage the pressures they face, for instance, playing computer games or turning to social media. However, these can spiral very quickly into various addictions in gaming, internet use, and even anime itself.[60] Symptoms range from hiding in internet cafes to play games instead of studying for examinations (*A-Teen*), to *otaku*[61] having difficulty in relating with others (*Wotakoi: Love Is Hard for Otaku*), *hikikomori*[62] who withdraw completely from society (*And You Thought There Is Never a Girl Online?*), and cyberbullying on social media (*Rascal Does Not Dream of Bunny Girl Senpai*; *Social Phobia*). Despite the fact that anime, and to a certain extent K-drama, often contain "disturbing … and sexually explicit content," they can offer us "a thought-provoking experience"[63] and enable us to understand some of the reasons behind the brokenness of Japanese/Korean youth. Having a godly appreciation of their needs will empower Christians to minister to them more efficaciously.

Further Reading on Making Sense of & Responding to Popular Culture
Asay, P. *Burning Bush 2.0: How Pop Culture Replaced the Prophet.* Nashville, TN: Abingdon Press, 2015.
Strange, D. *Plugged In: Connecting Your Faith with What You Watch, Read, and Play*. Epsom: The Good Book Company, 2019.

---

[59] Korea has the fourth highest suicide rate in the world, and Korea and Japan are the first and second highest in East Asia, respectively. "Suicide Rate By Country 2021," World Population Review, accessed Sep 24, 2021, https://worldpopulationreview.com/country-rankings/suicide-rate-by-country.

[60] Chris Kincaid, "Are You Addicted to Anime?" *Japan Powered* (May 21, 2017), accessed Aug 13, 2020, https://www.japanpowered.com/otaku-culture/are-you-addicted-to-anime.

[61] Someone whose life is absorbed in anime and *manga*.

[62] Although it originated from Japan, the *hikikomori* phenomenon, where social recluses shut themselves in their rooms or homes and withdraw completely from society, has since spread to other Asian countries including Korea. John Chee Meng Wong *et al.*, "Hikikomori Phenomenon in East Asia: Regional Perspectives, Challenges, and Opportunities for Social Health Agencies," *Front. Psychiatry* 10 (2019): 512, accessed Sep 25, 2021, https://doi.org/10.3389/fpsyt.2019.00512.

[63] Jason Morehead, "Unpacking Anime's Thematic and Spiritual Depth," *Christian Research Journal* 37, no. 6 (2014): 2, accessed Aug 13, 2020, http://www.equip.org/PDF/JAF5376.pdf.

Turnau, T. *Popologetics: Popular Culture in Christian Perspective.* Phillipsburg, NJ: P&R Publishing, 2012.

User

This section draws on the category of "everyday theologians"[64] and considers three roles that can be informed by such a stance – cultural analysts, "popologists"[65] and witnesses. These represent a sequence from cultural analysis, through engagement – where critique leads to discussion and response – and then on to witness, where Christian perspectives on life are shared as good news. A subsequent section ("Producer") explores the role of missional artists in the creation of their own media products.

The urban youth of Asia are immersed in an endless stream of distraction and "information glut"[66] in the form of online media. One of the negative implications of this is that there are no control mechanisms, resulting in the breakdown of moral and spiritual categories. To them, Christ is "just another character or plot point"[67] amongst the smorgasbord of anime/K-drama storylines. Furthermore, the nature of onscreen media is such that it discourages active participation by the viewer, and does not give them the "right of reply."[68] Hence, missional artists need to consider how they can engage with "cultural works" such as anime/K-dramas "that evoke some of the hidden realities of life … to challenge someone to see the gospel afresh," and break them out of their "consumerist stupor."[69] It needs to be kept in mind that "the best stories show us … our psyches and our very souls. Stories are, by their very nature, spiritual."[70] Therefore, as "everyday theologians," missional artists need to cultivate "cultural literacy" so as to appropriate popular culture and be an "agent of redemptive change," through "reading culture" critically and learning to "write culture … as an active participant."[71]

---

[64] Kevin J. Vanhoozer, "What Is Everyday Theology? How and Why Christians Should Read Culture," in *Everyday Theology: How to Read Cultural Texts and Interpret Trends*, eds. Kevin J. Vanhoozer, Charles A. Anderson and Michael J. Sleasman (Grand Rapids, MI: Baker Academic, 2007), 46.
[65] "Popologists" are those who engage in "popologetics." Ted Turnau, *Popologetics: Popular Culture in Christian Perspective* (Phillipsburg, NJ: P&R Publishing, 2012), 238.
[66] Neil Postman, *Amusing Ourselves to Death: Public Discourse in the Age of Show Business*, 20th anniv. ed. (London: Penguin Books, 2006), chap. 5, Kindle.
[67] Alan Noble, *Disruptive Witness: Speaking Truth in a Distracted Age* (Downers Grove, IL: IVP Books, 2018), 5.
[68] Postman, *Amusing Ourselves to Death*, chap. 5.
[69] Noble, *Disruptive Witness*, 174; 180.
[70] Paul Asay, *Burning Bush 2.0: How Pop Culture Replaced the Prophet* (Nashville, TN: Abingdon Press, 2015), x.
[71] Vanhoozer, "What Is Everyday Theology?" 56; 18.

Understand the Times – Cultural Analysts

First and foremost, there is a need to understand the anime/K-drama scene in order to speak the "lingo" of anime/K-drama fans. There is much online chatter associated with anime/K-drama on genre-specific forums (Anime Forums;[72] OneHallyu[73]), as well as generic ones (Reddit[74]). Discussions cover a wide range of topics including anime/K-drama plots, characters, soundtracks, and even the love lives of K-drama actors in real life. Whilst K-drama fans follow their favourite actors' social media posts avidly,[75] both anime and K-drama fans also follow bloggers (*Wrong Every Time*;[76] *Dramabeans*[77]), and vloggers (Mother's Basement;[78] Jesica Ahlberg[79]), who post reviews or commentaries of anime/K-drama. There are close associations between anime, *manga* and computer games. It has been noted that anime and Japanese popular culture have "created intimate objects and texts" that are part of young people's everyday lives, and have formed a "shared time and space where one can reference another via common texts."[80] A similar phenomenon is occurring with K-drama and Korean popular culture, especially since K-pop idols often crossover into acting.[81] Instead of adding to the entertainment fodder online, cultural analysts must understand the times like "the sons of Issachar"[82] and point out the "dissonance between our fallen world and God's glorious blueprint,"[83] whether through making social commentaries or asking existential questions that will interrupt the flow of never-ending distractions and make people pause to think.

---

[72] Anime Forums, accessed Aug 13, 2020, https://animeforums.net/.

[73] OneHallyu, accessed Aug 13, 2020, https://onehallyu.com/.

[74] "r/Anime," Reddit, accessed Aug 13, 2020, https://www.reddit.com/r/anime/; "r/KDRAMA," Reddit, accessed Aug 13, 2020, https://www.reddit.com/r/KDRAMA/.

[75] Laure, "Top 23 Most Followed Korean Actresses On Instagram & 70 Other Actresses' Instagram," *Kpopmap* (Oct 12, 2021), accessed Oct 29, 2021, https://www.kpopmap.com/top-19-most-followed-korean-actresses-on-instagram-others-70-actresses-instagram/.

[76] *Wrong Every Time*, accessed Aug 13, 2020, http://wrongeverytime.com/.

[77] *Dramabeans*, accessed Aug 13, 2020, https://www.dramabeans.com/.

[78] Mother's Basement, YouTube, accessed Aug 13, 2020, https://www.youtube.com/c/mothersbasement.

[79] Jesica Ahlberg, YouTube, accessed Aug 13, 2020, https://www.youtube.com/c/JesicaAhlberg.

[80] Ching, *Anti-Japan*, 134-35.

[81] Emlyn Travis, "25 Popular Korean Actors Who Originally Started Their Careers As K-Pop Idols," *BuzzFeed* (Mar 19, 2021), accessed Oct 7, 2021, https://www.buzzfeed.com/emlyntravis/k-pop-idols-who-are-also-actors.

[82] 1 Chron. 12:32.

[83] Asay, *Burning Bush 2.0*, x.

Engage the In-Group – "Popologists"

Aspiring "popologists" can engage anime/K-drama fans in conversation by physically meeting up with them. The Level Up Game Nights[84] ministry team organises get-togethers in the Philippines for anime fans and gamers to talk about anime and games, where they also share about their faith with participants. They have set up booths at anime conventions to interact with attendees and publicise their events. There are Christians who join anime rock bands that perform at various events, whilst some "cosplay" and chat with people who ask to take photos with them. Christian psychologists and counsellors could also speak on mental health issues at anime conventions.[85] Christian fans of K-drama actors who join fan clubs and attend fan meets or signing events would get to connect with other fans. Places where fans congregate, including movie premieres and concerts, could become spaces for engagement. *Her Private Life* shows many examples of how fans bond with one another, both in person and online. Additionally, Christians who work in the anime/K-drama industries are strategically positioned to infuse their faith into productions[86] as well as be witnesses for God when relating with colleagues and fans (like Park Bo-Gum[87]). These are just some of the many ways that "popologists" could use a common interest in anime/K-drama as the bridge to link up with pre-believers.

Further Reading on Christian Analysis of Culture
Crouch, A. *Culture Making: Recovering Our Creative Calling.* Downers Grove, IL: IVP Books, 2013.
Smith, J. K. A. *How (Not) to Be Secular: Reading Charles Taylor.* Grand Rapids, MI: Eerdmans, 2014.
Vanhoozer, K. J., C. A. Anderson and M. J. Sleasman, eds. *Everyday Theology: How to Read Cultural Texts and Interpret Trends.* Grand Rapids, MI: Baker Academic, 2007.

Concurrently, such engagement with anime/K-drama fans can also happen virtually. Some possibilities include writing or posting from a Christian

---

[84] Level Up Game Nights, Facebook, accessed Aug 13, 2020, https://www.facebook.com/lugamenights/.
[85] Personal Development Institute, "Elizabeth Speaks on Anti-Bullying Panel at Ninja-Con," LA Teen Therapist (Feb 15, 2018), accessed Aug 13, 2020, https://lateentherapist.com/elizabeth-speaks-on-anti-bullying-panel-at-ninja-con/.
[86] Casey Covel, "Interview: Kenneth Bright Jr. – Creator of Christian Anime, Prince Adventures," *Geeks under Grace* (Jul 26, 2015), accessed Aug 13, 2020, https://geeksundergrace.com/anime-cosplay/interview-kenneth-bright-jr-creator-of-christian-anime-prince-adventures/.
[87] A Christian actor, the tagline on Park's Twitter page is, "with God all things are possible." 박보검 @BOGUMMY, Twitter, accessed Aug 13, 2020, https://twitter.com/BOGUMMY.

perspective about anime/K-drama in blogs (*Beneath the Tangles*;[88] *Faith, Worship, Arts*[89]), vlogs (MVPerry[90]), social media (Christian Anime Group[91]), websites (YMI[92]), and online magazines (*Thir.st*[93]). Discussion forums and comments on online videos or posts are other channels to connect intentionally with anime/K-drama fans. Many share openly about personal struggles when identifying with anime/K-drama stories that mirror their own. Some may talk about how they are suffering from depression[94] or confess suicidal thoughts.[95] In particular, such virtual means of contact could enable Christians to minister to *hikikomori*, many of whom are anime/K-drama fans, as their doors are literally closed to conventional face-to-face outreach methods.

Proclaim Good News – Witnesses

Urban youth across Asia face similar challenges to the Japanese/Korean youth depicted in anime/K-drama – especially issues associated with academic pressure.[96] Those who support and engage with young people facing the stress of competition and related problems such as bullying, depression, self-harm and suicide, could encourage them by referring to anime/K-drama with positive messages. In *Silver Spoon* and *A-Teen 2*, for instance, some of the high school student characters choose alternative pathways to pursue their dreams, showing how one does not need to conform to societal definitions of success. *Free! – Iwatobi Swim Club*, *Your Lie in April*, *Thumping Spike*, and *Naeil's Cantabile* emphasise the importance of friendship and enjoyment of activities such as sports and music, instead of focusing on rivalry and competition. *A Silent Voice* and *Student A* both show how it is possible for victims of bullying to overcome depression and suicidal tendencies, and be reconciled with the perpetrators.

---

[88] *Beneath the Tangles*, accessed Aug 13, 2020, https://beneaththetangles.com/.

[89] Anne Soh, "k drama," *Faith, Worship, Arts*, accessed Aug 13, 2020, https://faithworshiparts.blogspot.com/search/label/k%20drama.

[90] MVPerry, YouTube, accessed Aug 13, 2020, https://www.youtube.com/c/MVPerry.

[91] Christian Anime Group (CAG), Facebook, accessed Aug 13, 2020, https://www.facebook.com/groups/1098367070549427/.

[92] Rebecca Lim, "4 Essential Life Lessons from Start-Up," YMI (Dec 21, 2020), accessed Jan 24, 2021, https://ymi.today/2020/12/4-essential-life-lessons-from-start-up/.

[93] Siqi Wong, "It's Okay to Not Be Okay: For all the drama with our parents, there is a love that never dies," *Thir.st* (Jul 17, 2020), accessed Aug 13, 2020, https://thir.st/blog/its-okay-to-not-be-okay-for-all-the-drama-with-our-parents-there-is-a-love-that-never-dies/.

[94] "Depression," MyAnimeList, accessed Aug 13, 2020, https://myanimelist.net/forum/?topicid=1256463.

[95] "Suicide," Soompi, accessed Aug 13, 2020, https://forums.soompi.com/topic/72426-suicide/page/30/.

[96] Louise Moon, "Inside Asia's pressure-cooker exam system, which region has it the worst?" *South China Morning Post* (Jun 9, 2018), accessed Aug 13, 2020, https://www.scmp.com/news/china/society/article/2149978/inside-asias-pressure-cooker-exam-sytem-which-region-has-it-worst.

Rascal Does Not Dream of Bunny Girl Senpai and *The World of My 17* tell of how teenage school girls suffering from low self-esteem due to poor body image grow to accept themselves and the way they look through the support of friends. Finding and using relatable anime/K-drama like these when reaching out to youth could bring hope to the hopeless and help to lead young people to break away from the psychological chains that bind them.

Furthermore, others can be pointed to God through discussion of anime/K-drama plots and characters, and by helping them to see "God's fingerprints."[97] Conversations could be sparked about existential questions such as: "Why is there suffering in the world?" In both *Your Name* and *Weathering with You* by Shinkai, the characters try to mitigate the impact of natural disasters, which is a reflection of Japan's real-life struggles.[98] The male leads in *The Time* and *Uncontrollably Fond* are both dying from terminal illnesses in the prime of life. Suffering is something human beings cannot escape from, due to the consequences of sin. However, Christian witnesses could testify as to how God has chosen to share in human suffering through His "redemptive suffering for the world,"[99] and that one day, people can be entirely free from suffering.[100] In many time-travelling anime/K-dramas, characters go back to the past to prevent the deaths of loved ones (*Erased*; *Somehow 18*), or to correct their former mistakes (*The Girl Who Leapt through Time*; *One More Time*). These easily lead into conversations about power and control – how in real life individuals do not have the ability to change the past; ultimately, only God has overcome the grave,[101] and life and death are in His hands.[102] When considering the multitudinous Christ-like figures in anime/K-drama (*Evangelion*;[103] *Memories of the Alhambra*[104]), it emerges that most of them are lacking in some way and usually motivated by selfish reasons. Only in Jesus do humans find the perfect, selfless sacrifice and receive complete redemption.[105]

---

[97] Asay, *Burning Bush 2.0*, 184.

[98] For further reflections on the place of art and faith in the Japanese context of suffering, see Makoto Fujimura, *Silence and Beauty: Hidden Faith Born of Suffering* (Downers Grove, IL: IVP Books, 2016).

[99] Atsuyoshi Fujiwara, *Theology of Culture in a Japanese Context: A Believers' Church Perspective*, Princeton Theological Monograph Series 179 (Eugene, OR: Pickwick Publications, 2012), xviii.

[100] Rev. 21:4.

[101] 1 Cor. 15:55-57.

[102] 1 Sam. 2:6.

[103] "Kaoru as Jesus; Evangelion as Christianity," EvaGeeks.org Forum, accessed Aug 13, 2020, https://forum.evageeks.org/thread/5759/Kaoru-as-JesusEvangelion-as-Christianity/.

[104] Anne Soh, "'Memories of the Alhambra' – augmented reality and the spiritual realm [SPOILER ALERT!]," *Faith, Worship, Arts* (Feb 25, 2020), accessed Aug 13, 2020, https://faithworshiparts.blogspot.com/2020/02/memories-of-alhambra-augmented-reality.html.

[105] Heb. 10:14.

Christians can derive meaningful discussions from almost any anime/K-drama by asking focused questions such as, "What's the story?", "Where are we?", "What is good and true and beautiful here?", "What is false and evil and perverse here, and how can I subvert it?", and "How does the gospel apply?"[106] Asay offers more conversation starters in *Burning Bush 2.0*[107] that could also help witnesses to engage with others so as to share the gospel through anime/K-drama. God spoke through stories in Biblical times. He continues to speak to people today, believers and pre-believers alike, via stories told through anime/K-drama and other online media. It is the task of missional artists to find the traces that God has imprinted in stories that are being told and dialogue with sensitivity, in order to "challenge the distracted, secular age"[108] and help others "feel the solicitations of the spiritual."[109]

Producer

With advances in technology and the internet, it is not only convenient to view online videos, it has become very easy for anyone to create and upload their own videos without the need for sophisticated equipment or skills. Even a mobile phone-wielding hunter living in the "remote parts of the wilderness" is able to produce a video montage of "his hunting exploits" with "a local song in the background."[110] Fan-made videos (FMV) of anime/K-drama are popular and easily available online with viewers actively seeking online content that is produced by ordinary people just like them.[111] The online space "where the cultural action is" thus becomes the "most current marketplace,"[112] and missional artists must seek to fill it with redemptive stories in order to challenge and shift cultural perspectives.

---

[106] Turnau, *Popologetics*, 313-14.

[107] Asay, *Burning Bush 2.0*, 192-93.

[108] Alan Noble, "How Stories Unsettle Our Secular Age," *The Gospel Coalition* (Feb 4, 2019), accessed Aug 13, 2020, https://www.thegospelcoalition.org/article/stories-unsettle-secular-age/.

[109] Charles Taylor, *A Secular Age* (Cambridge, MA and London: The Belknap Press of Harvard University Press, 2007), 360.

[110] Keith Williams, ""Mobilizing" the Story of His Glory (Part 1)," *Orality Journal* 2, no. 2 (2013): 96, accessed Jul 2, 2020, https://orality.net/wp-content/uploads/2015/11/V2N2-Orality-Journal.pdf.

[111] "APAC online viewers prefer free content," WARC (Nov 22, 2016), accessed Jan 24, 2021, https://www.warc.com/newsandopinion/news/apac_online_viewers_prefer_free_content/37784.

[112] Calvin Seerveld, *Rainbows for the Fallen World: Aesthetic Life and Artistic Task* (Toronto, Ontario: Toronto Tuppence Press, 1980), 36.

Redemptive Storytelling

Stories have the potential to challenge falsehoods without making "negative assaults on the beliefs of the audience" so that they will "feel comfortable in sharing these materials with others."[113] Instead of being directly antagonistic towards the lies inherent in viewers' cultural values and beliefs, through the use of allegory and symbols, missional artists can give "a metaphoric promise of life and hope at the gracious rule of Jesus Christ on earth,"[114] especially in contexts where explicitly Christian discourse may not be well-received. Narratives can speak into deep yearnings for love, truth, meaning or purpose, and offer glimpses of something altogether more positive. Redemptive storytelling has the power to disrupt the audience's "conception of the world by revealing and validating eternity hidden in their hearts."[115] Missional artists should take care that their storylines are neither contrived nor formulaic. Life is not a bed of roses just because one has become a Christian. When stories project hope whilst being authentic and "firmly aware of the brokenness within which we live and build, suffer, expect, laugh and cry,"[116] they will become vessels to change the hearers and "heal our wounded souls."[117]

Suggested Reading on Storytelling
Bernard, S. C. *Documentary Storytelling: Creative Nonfiction on Screen.* 4th ed. Abingdon and New York: Focal Press, 2016. Kindle.
Booker, C. *The Seven Basic Plots: Why We Tell Stories.* London and New York: Continuum, 2004.
Mead, G. *Coming Home to Story: Storytelling beyond Happily Ever After.* London and Philadelphia: Jessica Kingsley Publishers, 2017.
Simmons, A. *The Story Factor: Inspiration, Influence, and Persuasion through the Art of Storytelling.* New York: Basic Books, 2001.

---

[113] Keith Williams and Leith Gray, "The Little Phone That Could: Mobile-Empowered Ministry," *International Journal of Frontier Missiology* 27, no. 3 (Fall 2010): 142, accessed Sep 20, 2021, https://ijfm.org/PDFs_IJFM/27_3_PDFs/mobile_williams.pdf.

[114] Calvin Seerveld, *Bearing Fresh Olive Leaves: Alternative Steps in Understanding Art* (Carlisle: Piquant, 2000), 112.

[115] Alan Noble, "The Disruptive Witness of Art," *The Gospel Coalition* (Oct 21, 2017), accessed Aug 13, 2020, https://www.thegospelcoalition.org/article/the-disruptive-witness-of-art/.

[116] Seerveld, *Bearing Fresh Olive Leaves*, 112.

[117] Geoff Mead, *Coming Home to Story: Storytelling beyond Happily Ever After* (London and Philadelphia: Jessica Kingsley Publishers, 2017), 3.

Case Studies

1) TrueLove.Is

TrueLove.Is is an online ministry of 3:16 Church[118] in Singapore that aims to provide stories and resources about LGBTQ issues for Christians. This is done through sharing personal stories that touch the heart, studies and articles that convince the head, and reaching out a hand to support those who are struggling with their sexuality and gender identity. The stories are presented in documentary-story style with partial re-enactments woven into each person's retelling of their own story. From an initial team of three people in 2014 it has now grown to become a parachurch ministry comprising an executive committee, scriptwriters, directors, a cinematography team, a video editing team, and a writing team that responds to online comments. TrueLove.Is explores the nature of identity in relation to sexuality by telling authentic and relatable stories which send a message of hope despite facing considerable pressures.[119] Volunteers staff a helpline for those seeking support for their struggles with sexual brokenness. TrueLove.Is videos are posted on their website,[120] YouTube channel,[121] and social media pages. These have been watched by over three million viewers from all over the world, and the pastors have been invited to speak about the ministry to more than 100 groups, including Bible colleges, in Singapore, Taiwan, Japan, Australia, and Malaysia.

The TrueLove.Is videos exemplify the need for good storytelling even in non-fiction genres such as the documentary-story. They can "bring viewers on a journey, immerse them in new worlds and explore universal themes," as well as "compel viewers to consider and even care about topics and subjects they might previously have overlooked."[122] Young people seem to favour shorter video formats including the web drama and anime series which generally range from 10 to 30 minutes per episode. Similarly, TrueLove.Is videos are within 11 minutes in length. The ministry has gathered Christians across churches in Singapore with stories to tell, or who have specific skills, to work together. Missional artists should be ready to collaborate with those from different churches and organisations in order to tap relevant expertise that is available and, more importantly, to reflect the unity of the church.

---

[118] Based on a phone interview with Pastor Norman Ng from 3:16 Church, Creative Director of TrueLove.Is, on Feb 18, 2020.
[119] "#WeExist," TrueLove.Is, accessed Aug 13, 2020, https://truelove.is/weexist/.
[120] TrueLove.Is, accessed Aug 13, 2020, https://truelove.is/.
[121] Truelove.is, YouTube, accessed Aug 13, 2020,
https://www.youtube.com/c/trueloveis.
[122] Bernard, *Documentary Storytelling*, chap. 1.

2) Pearl Ganta

Ganta is an independent filmmaker from India.[123] She joined a Christian film project as a production assistant and discovered that media could be a powerful tool for sharing the Christian faith when she noticed many pre-believers calling a hotline to find out more about Christianity after watching the film. Subsequently, she took up relevant courses, joined CBN India, and helped to pioneer several programmes including *700 Club India*.[124] In 2002, she founded her own production company, took up commercial and humanitarian projects, and began to train children to produce videos of Bible stories. In the KidsHub[125] ministry that has spread to Africa, many children, some of them from other religious backgrounds, received Christ whilst studying the Bible to script their videos, and some went on to train and disciple others.[126] Ganta has also mentored younger Christians, including a substantial number of women, who work in the secular media industry. She encourages them to be role models for their non-Christian colleagues, and incorporate biblical values in their productions. When she first stepped into the industry, the church viewed media as "evil" and many questioned her decision to leave Christian ministry for such a worldly occupation. She has seen the impact made by those who are willing to be salt and light in the secular field, and some secular companies have acknowledged the quality of Christian productions by copying the stories and other elements in their own work.

Ganta emphasises the importance of both sharpening skills in video production, and developing knowledge and understanding of the Bible, so that the stories told will glorify God. Missional artists must be intentional in showing the transformation of people featured in the stories, and consider how the audience may be transformed after the viewing experience. Along with praying for God's inspiration, wisdom and guidance, Ganta also suggests gathering a team of prayer supporters, as video production is a spiritual undertaking and there will be opposition. With God's help, videos can reach people and places that are normally inaccessible to the Christian message, just like the man living in a remote mountainous area who became a Christian after watching one of her programmes and went on to plant a church in his village of 200 people.

---

[123] Based on a Skype interview with Pearl Ganta on Jul 23, 2018.

[124] CBN India is involved in ministry through internet, media and television. "Ten Years Later, Gospel Flourishes in India," The Christian Broadcasting Network, accessed Aug 13, 2020, https://www1.cbn.com/700club/ten-years-later-gospel-flourishes-india.

[125] KidsHubTV, accessed Aug 13, 2020, https://kidshubtv.com/.

[126] Some children-produced videos, and those produced by her company, can be viewed on her Vimeo channel. Pearl Ganta, Vimeo, accessed Aug 13, 2020, https://vimeo.com/pearlganta.

3) CGNTV

Christian Global Network Television (CGNTV)[127] is a satellite TV broadcast network established in 2005 by Onnuri Community Church, Seoul, to provide Christian resources for Korean missionaries and diaspora worldwide, and to bring the gospel to the remotest parts of the world through customised media content. Since then, additional stations have been set up in a few other countries such as Indonesia, Japan, and Taiwan to produce targeted programmes for specific people groups in local languages. CGNTV programmes are also published on various online platforms (Facebook; Naver TV;[128] YouTube). These include sermons, worship recordings, and daily devotionals for children, youth, and adults, as well as variety shows and documentaries that often feature celebrities who are Christians (*Reason to Travel*). Beyond producing video programmes, CGNTV was also involved in the *Love Sonata* movement which tapped on the popularity of *Hallyu* in Japan to draw Japanese audiences to evangelistic rallies where Korean stars performed and shared their testimonies.[129]

More recently, CGNTV has also started to produce K-drama series injected with biblical perspectives on pertinent issues. In a results-driven culture prevalent in Korea (and most of Asia), the male lead in the web series *Church Oppa's QT Romance*[130] realises that God loves him as he is, regardless of his achievements or lack thereof. The young adults in the mini-sitcom series *Heart-Pounding Macarons* learn the meaning of true Christ-like love in the midst of dating whilst a newlywed couple discovers the pitfalls of materialism. Set in a community that celebrates the elderly and those with special needs, the mini-series *Go Go Song* presents a scenario common in most Asian cultures – that of the absent father – and offers healing for its female lead as well as for viewers. Some episodes from CGNTV's *Mini Human Documentary* series, which tells the stories of ordinary Christians who live out the gospel through tackling societal problems such as poverty and homelessness, have become viral. This has led to a spin-off series *King of Enlightenment* that focuses on redemptive stories of juvenile delinquents. A new YouTube channel (ButsoHandsUp)[131] has even been created to release content by Joseph Butso, who was featured in the series.

---

[127] About CGNTV, accessed Sep 9, 2021, http://eng.cgntv.net/.

[128] Naver TV, accessed Sep 9, 2021, https://tv.naver.com/.

[129] Eiko Takamizawa, "A Missiological Analysis of the "Love Sonata" Project in Japan," *Torch Trinity Journal* 11, no. 1 (2008): 149, accessed Sep 9, 2021, http://www.ttgst.ac.kr/upload/ttgst_resources13/20124-238.pdf.

[130] *Oppa* is a term of endearment used by females which means "older brother" in Korean – with a range of subtle connotations and difficult to translate, such terms are often transliterated into English.

[131] 붓소핸섭-ButsoHandsUp, YouTube, accessed Sep 9, 2021, https://www.youtube.com/channel/UCsD4qHGC9SxK2567sg3V8oQ.

The success of CGNTV videos lies in several factors such as the spotlight on well-known personalities (Yoon Eun-Hye;[132] Joseph Butso[133]), professional production standards, bite-sized lengths,[134] and subtitles in other languages.[135] More importantly, they introduce counter-cultural narratives about issues that concern young people, hence initiating conversations that begin to transform culture and open hearts to the gospel.

Practical Advice for Missional Artists Using Contemporary Media

The work of video producers should be of credible quality to attract and retain a following. Beyond picking up necessary skills and techniques to begin, there is a need to keep polishing one's craft. There are many relevant resources available both online and offline: those offered by Mobile Ministry Forum[136] cover both ministry and technical considerations. Beyond refining music, animation and video production skills, books and courses on storytelling and script-writing can help inform the artistic process.[137] Artists need to keep up-to-date with current trends and the latest apps, so they can tap those that would help to best reach their target group (for example, Instagram and TikTok for younger audiences), and explore the use of cutting-edge technology such as augmented reality.[138]

---

[132] Yoon, leading actress in *Go Go Song* of which the first episode has reached nearly 4 million views online, first gained stardom as a K-pop idol after her debut in 1999. Subsequently, she took on leading roles in several popular drama series including *Coffee Prince*.

[133] Before being featured in *Mini Human Documentary,* Butso was already an internet sensation due to his appearance on the public music game show *I Can See Your Voice 3*.

[134] *Go Go Song* consists of only two hour-long episodes whilst *Church Oppa's QT Romance*, *Heart-Pounding Macarons*, *Mini Human Documentary*, and *King of Enlightenment* episodes range from three to twelve minutes each.

[135] The subtitled versions of *Go Go Song* on YouTube have much higher viewership than the one without subtitles – the versions with English and Indonesian subtitles have more than 1 million views each whereas the one without subtitles has been viewed less than 0.25 million times. CGNTV, "[Full] K-Drama 'Go Go Song' (Yoon EunHye, Ji IlJoo) Ep1 @CGNTV 드라마 '고고송' 1화 [영어자막]," YouTube, accessed Sep 25, 2021, https://youtu.be/9K_Cp19iV9o; CGNTV Indonesia, "[K-Drama] Go Go Song Episode 1(Yoon EunHye, Ji IlJoo)," YouTube, accessed Sep 25, 2021, https://youtu.be/GyXI7Sy3YFc; CGNTV, "[Full] CGNTV 드라마 '고고송' 1화(윤은혜,지일주)@ K-Drama 'Go Go Song' Ep1(Yoon EunHye,Ji IlJoo)," YouTube, accessed Sep 25, 2021, https://youtu.be/q_USgc8xX9E.

[136] Mobile Ministry Forum, accessed Aug 13, 2020, https://mobileministryforum.org/.

[137] See Robert McKee, "The Legendary Story Seminar," McKee Seminars, accessed Aug 13, 2020, https://mckeestory.com/seminars/story/ and "Suggested Reading on Storytelling" (above).

[138] Kyle O'Brien, "Coca-Cola embraces augmented reality with interactive experience," *The Drum* (Sep 10, 2019), accessed Aug 13, 2020,

Consider cross-posting videos on multiple platforms for a wider reach. Videos should be formatted appropriately, so they are optimised for streaming and/or downloading on any device. Timed releases of trailers and previews help stir up interest and build anticipation, whilst publicity posts on social media could "generate a lot of secondary internet buzz, ... creating a relatively long-lasting positive ripple effect."[139]

In the pursuit of increasing reach online, keep in mind the original purpose and intent of sharing meaningful, life-changing stories. Engaging stories are more than *mere* entertainment, unlike much secular content where "the overarching presumption is that it is there for our amusement and pleasure."[140] Specify the target audience of each video, do the necessary research to understand their culture, beliefs and needs, and find or write stories that would speak into these needs (Moving Works[141]). Some stories may be found in the personal testimonies of celebrities who are Christians (7Media[142]), in which case their popularity could help to draw a bigger audience.

Churches and mission organisations should encourage Christians with interest and aptitude in arts and media to further their studies in relevant disciplines so they can become creators of media themselves. They can support and promote online video ministries, and teach their members to apply biblical truths to daily life and culture. They can plan strategies to connect with audiences to follow-up on their viewing experience, and journey with them in their spiritual discovery to fulfil our calling to make disciples of all nations.[143] They can encourage missional artists to extend their work through contextualising (IndigiTube[144]), or by translating into different languages (BibleProject,[145] Superbook[146]). Through

---

https://www.thedrum.com/news/2019/09/10/coca-cola-embraces-augmented-reality-with-interactive-experience.

[139] Virág Molnár, "Reframing Public Space through Digital Mobilization: Flash Mobs and Contemporary Urban Youth Culture," *Space and Culture* 17, no. 1 (2014): 51-52, accessed Sep 25, 2021, https://doi.org/10.1177/1206331212452368.

[140] Postman, *Amusing Ourselves to Death*, chap. 8.

[141] The Moving Works ministry produces culturally relevant videos for specific countries in each country's language and context. Moving Works, accessed Aug 13, 2020, https://movingworks.org/.

[142] 7Media is a media ministry that reaches out to the Japanese people. Some of their videos feature the personal testimonies of sports personalities who are popular in Japan. 7Media, "THE FOUR Sports," YouTube, accessed Aug 13, 2020, https://www.youtube.com/playlist?list=PL6Xxh8CN5jLvs1RGNMY_ros5G9W8v26M4

[143] Matt. 28:19.

[144] In the videos hosted by IndigiTube, the language, music, dances, attire/costumes, and animation styles are contextualised for specific people groups. IndigiTube, accessed Aug 13, 2020, http://www.indigitube.tv/.

[145] "The story of the Bible in your language," BibleProject, accessed Aug 13, 2020, https://bibleproject.com/languages/.

[146] Superbook, YouTube, accessed Aug 13, 2020, https://www.youtube.com/c/SuperbookTV/channels.

such efforts, "Christians who understand biblical truth and have the courage to live it out can indeed redeem a culture, or even create one."[147]

Conclusion

Through interactions with Christian youth and young adults who are anime/K-drama fans, it appears that many church leaders hold the attitude that anime corrupts minds whilst K-drama is a waste of time. Certainly, popular culture not only influences the secular world but even "the Christian community is prey to the unbelieving, God-damning artistic culture." Before this becomes the norm, missional artists have to offer a "redemptive, imaginatively rich alternative."[148] Therefore, younger members should be taught not to isolate themselves from popular culture but rather, to go into the world as Jesus did and engage redemptively with the culture, thus becoming a positive influence for other young people. Instead of being dominated by popular culture, they should be challenged to move from what Castells called a "resistance identity" to a "project identity."[149] A project identity is formed when people build a new identity that redefines their position in society and, by doing so, seek the transformation of overall social structures. Missional artists can bring about social change through the use of information technology and electronic media to influence the way people think.[150] Rather than shun anime/K-drama, missional artists should consider how to equip Christians to understand these genres, by learning how to discern and filter out anime/K-drama of poor quality whilst retaining the gems. Missional artists themselves must embark on a personal redemptive journey, pray and be led by the Holy Spirit, and be grounded in the Word and cultural literacy, so they can understand the times and know what to do. Only when we raise our prophetic voice as learners, users (whether as cultural analysts, "popologists" or witnesses), and producers of anime/K-drama can we then engage with others who are immersed in popular culture, so as to redeem and transform the wider culture.

---

[147] Colson and Pearcey, *How Now Shall We Live?* 477.

[148] Seerveld, *Rainbows for the Fallen World*, 35 – both quotes.

[149] Resistance identity is generated by people who are in devalued and/or stigmatised positions/conditions, by building trenches of resistance and survival on the basis of principles different from, or opposed to, those permeating the institutions. Castells, *The Power of Identity*, 8.

[150] Castells, *The Power of Identity*, 425.

Questions for Reflection/Discussion
1. In what ways can readers learn from the use and prominence of stories in the two forms of anime and K-drama?
2. The "learner" section suggests three key categories for learning more about Japanese and Korean cultures: "culture and the people's psyche," "historico-political backgrounds," and "socio-ethical issues." How might such a frame advance your own understanding of these or other cultures?
3. The section on "user" looks at three different kinds of response: cultural analysts, "popologists" and witnesses – which of these are you most drawn to, and why?
4. How might the case studies from the section on "producer" inspire you on your own "missional artist" journey?

6. Intercultural Worship:
A Contemporary Understanding of Church and Worship in the Global Age
Ian Collinge

Ian Collinge aims to show that "intercultural worship" is now the most constructive and nuanced way of describing the kind of worship that can be adopted by culturally diverse congregations. He considers the relationship between intercultural churches and worship in a range of key areas, such as culture and cultural diversity, emphasising the role of intercultural listening and experimentation. He moves towards a definition of intercultural worship and surveys, with critique, a series of concrete approaches.

The time has come for intercultural worship. In an increasingly globalised and interconnected world, no longer is the vision of God's people "from every nation, tribe, people and language" worshipping God together simply a future to be anticipated. It is a possibility in the present. Sandra Maria Van Opstal insightfully calls this, "The Next Worship."[1] Population movements from rural to urban settings and migrations from one country to another mean that societies are becoming more diverse culturally and linguistically. This signals a mandate to the church, especially the urban church, to be "one" – but with greater cultural diversity. The Intercultural Church Plants network believes that:[2]

> … the church of the future will be an intercultural church because our cities will be more and more colorful and therefore we would like to plant churches that explicitly reach out to different ethnicities.

In this chapter, the character of the intercultural church and its worship will be explored in relation to cosmopolitan cities, with particular interest in Asian peoples.[3]

---

[1] Sandra Maria Van Opstal, *The Next Worship: Glorifying God in a Diverse World* (Downers Grove, IL: IVP Books, 2016). She raises the questions: "What is the future of worship in our changing church? What spaces and places of worship does this global millennial generation of leaders need to create?" (49).
[2] Intercultural Church Plants EU, accessed Aug 13, 2020, https://www.icpnetwork.eu.
[3] Given the global diversity of peoples in cosmopolitan cities, examples will be drawn more widely than Asia, as appropriate.

Book Idea

Van Opstal, S. M. *The Next Worship: Glorifying God in a Diverse World.* Downers Grove, IL: IVP Books, 2016.

One of the clearest books on intercultural worship; a readable route map for worship in a culturally diverse world which is very well researched. Opstal is an experienced, widely informed and anthropologically astute worship leader of Hispanic background. She challenges church leaders to empower their members from different cultures, saying, "Leading worship in relevant, dynamic ways for the future of a diverse church depends on our ability to share leadership."[4] The book's appendices also provide some very usable practical tools.

Intercultural Worship and the Changing Asian Context

The Asian context and Asian diaspora communities are fertile ground for intercultural worship. However, the predominant pattern in Asia is monocultural[5] worship and derives from models laid down by missionaries and denominational leaders of the 19th and 20th centuries. Jacob Joseph[6] writes of the Indian context:

> Although India is multicultural, Christian worship is mono cultural (sic) in most contexts. Most of our rural churches are mono-cultural with some diversity which is usually ignored by church leaders. For example, in the context of a Hindi speaking region, if a Garhwali is present usually his presence is ignored because he or she can understand Hindi as well. On the other hand, in urban contexts multicultural worship is a need but often ignored. Instead of developing multicultural worship most of the churches in larger cities like Bangalore, Delhi and Mumbai tend to start independent worship services for each language group at different times on a Sunday.

Elsewhere in the Indian subcontinent, the context of my own fieldwork as an ethnomusicologist in the 1990s, was also a monocultural setting where I researched the music of an ethnic minority and worshipped with Christians amongst them. The language and customs were of one particular language group.[7] However, in this post-modern era, there are two new dynamics that shape

---

[4] Opstal, *The Next Worship*, 80.
[5] "Monocultural" refers to a single culture and ethnicity. The standard spelling is unhyphenated, see "monocultural," Collins, accessed Sep 16, 2020, https://www.collinsdictionary.com/dictionary/english/monocultural.
[6] Jacob Joseph, "Multicultural Worship in India," unpublished document attached to personal email communication, Jan 10, 2019.
[7] Tibetans in Nepal.

the life of the church. Firstly, migration often provokes a heightened need to express ethnic culture in a new place. As Jacob Joseph emphasises, many form ethnolinguistic congregations in response to this need. Although this benefits the first generation of migrants, it is often problematic for their children and grandchildren, for whom church can become an ethnic island and many fall away from church or seek an alternative church, where their background and language are largely ignored. This reflects a second dynamic – a more fluid cultural environment where many are more fluent in a language of wider communication than their parental language and their ethnicity may not be their primary cultural influence. Rather, the language, values and icons of the people with whom they interact, locally and globally, may exert greater influence. The result for such people is that their lived cultural experience can develop separately from their ethnicity.

In fact, "culture has been separated from geography," according to John S. Leonard.[8] On the one hand, those who emigrate from their homelands never have to leave their culture, like some Asians in ethnic communities in Britain or Koreans in parts of the USA. On the other, people can now identify with cultures from countries they have never lived in, such as a French woman interacting linguistically and socially with Koreans in north-west France.[9] A new paradigm beckons. One solution for the church in these situations is intercultural worship, which brings together worshippers of diverse backgrounds, whatever their perceived sense of ethnic identity – without losing sight of cultural diversity. Such worship also demonstrates Christ's love in action in Christian worship. Jesus said, "By this everyone will know that you are my disciples, if you love one another" (John 13:35). In what follows, we will explore what loving one another may mean for designing Christian worship.

Intercultural Worship Starts by Listening Well

Intercultural churches intentionally create a space for believers to worship together on an *equal* basis. Of course, embracing true equality takes humility on behalf of everyone involved, but is this not what Christ-followers are called to do?[10]

---

[8] John S. Leonard, "The Church Between Cultures: Rethinking the Church in Light of Globalization of Immigration," Westminster Theological Seminary (Jan 1, 2004), accessed Nov 6, 2021,
https://students.wts.edu/resources/westminsterspeaks/2004/01/01/The_Church_Between _Cultures_Rethinking_the_Church_in_Light_of_Globalization_of_Immigration.html.
[9] In 2017, the editor and his wife met a young French woman in the Loire-Atlantique who was interested in Korean culture, spoke Korean well, and attended Korean church events but, apart from one short visit, had never lived in Korea.
[10] Phil. 2:3-4.

Do nothing out of selfish ambition or vain conceit. Rather, in humility value others above yourselves, not looking to your own interests but each of you to the interests of the others.

In order to look to "the interests of others," the apostle Paul exhorts worshippers to "accept one another, then, just as Christ accepted you, in order to bring praise to God" (Romans 15:7) and to "please our neighbours for their good, to build them up" (Romans 15:2). Such mutual acceptance and honouring of the other is itself an act of worship – it will "bring praise to God." But how do we know what will help another to worship? What does this require in a multicultural community, where we understand less about others than we may think? To fully "value," "accept" or "please" another involves entering into an open and ongoing conversation that aims to understand at a heart level (beyond words).

The key principle is this: intercultural worship arises out of "intercultural communication" between worshippers of different cultures.[11] It includes what communication specialists call "loving,"[12] "active,"[13] "deep,"[14] "compassionate,"[15] or "humble" listening.[16] Such listening starts by openly acknowledging our own cultural ignorance, so that we can humbly learn from and "value others above" ourselves. As Christ-followers, it involves sharing stories of faith and biblical perspectives on worship, as well as learning songs and other expressions of worship from one another.[17] It begins behind the scenes but can then overflow into public acts of worship where all are honoured. As Paul says:[18]

---

[11] Practitioners Davis and Lerner counsel being curious and asking questions. Josh Davis and Nikki Lerner, *Worship Together in Your Church as in Heaven* (Nashville, TN: Abingdon Press, 2015), 51-52.

[12] "SYIS Online Courses," International Training Partners, accessed Sep 14, 2020, http://itpartners.org/online/description/.

[13] "Active listening as an essential intercultural skill," The London School of International Communication (Mar 22, 2017), accessed Sep 16, 2020, https://www.londonschool.com/lsic/resources/blog/active-listening-essential-intercultural-skill/.

[14] "The Art of Deep Listening," Roger K. Allen, accessed Aug 2, 2021, https://www.rogerkallen.com/the-art-of-deep-listening/.

[15] Lori Halverson-Wente and Mark Halverson-Wente, "6. Listening," *Developing Intercultural Communication Competence*, accessed Sep 17, 2020, https://mlpp.pressbooks.pub/interculturalcommunicationcompetence/chapter/listening/.

[16] Ram Charan, "The Discipline of Listening," *Harvard Business Review* (Jun 21, 2012), accessed Aug 2, 2021, https://hbr.org/2012/06/the-discipline-of-listening.

[17] Opstal, *The Next Worship*, 80. "It begins with an environment of mutual learning and collaboration."

[18] 1 Cor. 14:26 (NIV) and Col. 3:16 (ESV).

> When you come together, each of you has a hymn, or a word of instruction, a revelation, a tongue or an interpretation. Everything must be done so that the church may be built up.

> Let the word of Christ dwell in you richly, teaching and admonishing one another in all wisdom, singing psalms and hymns and spiritual songs, with thankfulness in your hearts to God.

In other words, intercultural worship includes spoken and sung contributions from worshippers who, as in Paul's day, represent diverse language groups with their unique emphases, poetic traditions, melodic styles and other forms of expression. These biblical principles of learning how to value others imply a journey towards more genuine equality in corporate worship and demonstrate that intercultural worship goes well beyond "multicultural" song choices. It is fundamentally about Christ-honouring relationships.

Intercultural Worship Magnifies God

Working in multicultural cities in Europe where migrants from Asia and Africa have sought sanctuary, Rieneke Visser leads the Songs2Serve worship ministry of the European network, Intercultural Church Plants. She clarifies her aim as, "helping intercultural communities to worship God in unified diversity."[19] She cites John Piper's view that:[20]

> … the beauty and power of praise that will come to the Lord from the diversity of the nations are greater than the beauty and power that would come to him if the chorus of the redeemed were culturally uniform.

Intercultural worship, then, "magnifies the glory of God" in ways that reflect the creator's love of abundant diversity. As such, it is a rarely noticed Cinderella in much of the world church, a hidden beauty yet to have her time. The Christian scriptures point to culturally diverse worship in the celebrations of the age to come. They suggest that this is how worship is meant to be now, "on earth as it is in heaven." The rest of this chapter is an attempt to lay some foundations and chart a course so that intercultural worship can become a reality for those who want to worship Christ together in our global age.

---

[19] Songs2Serve Europe, accessed Nov 13, 2021, https://ilstream.info/nick/7-PcO6AOaOXTucEbRpt9aQ.html. The aim of Songs2Serve is: "Diversity in worshipping together magnifies the glory of God," as stated in "God With Us – Hymns, songs, music," Churches Together in Britain and Ireland (Dec 11, 20200, accessed Nov 13, 2021, https://ctbi.org.uk/god-with-us-hymns-songs-music/.

[20] John Piper, "Why Christians Love Diversity," Desiring God (Mar 31, 2016), accessed Aug 2, 2021, https://www.desiringgod.org/articles/why-christians-love-diversity, quoted in "About Songs2Serve EU," Songs2Serve, accessed Nov 14, 2021, https://songs2serve.eu/about.

Further Reading on Intercultural Worship
Black, K. *Culturally-Conscious Worship*. St. Louis, MO: Chalice Press, 2000.
Davis, J., and N. Lerner. *Worship Together in Your Church as in Heaven*. Nashville, TN: Abingdon Press, 2015.
Hawn, C. M. *Gather into One: Praying and Singing Globally*. Calvin Institute of Christian Worship Liturgical Studies. Grand Rapids, MI and Cambridge, UK: Eerdmans, 2003.
Krabill, J. R., F. Fortunato, R. P. Harris and B. Schrag, eds. *Worship and Mission for the Global Church: An Ethnodoxology Handbook*. Pasadena, CA: William Carey Library, 2013. [Chapters 132-36].
Milne, B. *Dynamic Diversity: The New Humanity Church for Today and Tomorrow*. Nottingham: IVP, 2006.
Root, J. *Worship in a Multi-Ethnic Society*. Grove Worship 236. Cambridge, UK: Grove Books, 2018.

Intercultural Worship – Clarifying Terms

The term "intercultural worship" requires explanation. The complexity of the concepts involved is reflected in the confusing variety of terms used, such as "multi-ethnic," "multiracial," "cross-cultural,"[21] "diverse," "culturally-conscious"[22] and "liturgical plurality."[23] This analysis will tease out different elements in turn. For our purposes in this chapter,[24] "***worship***" refers to corporate expressions used in Christian "services of worship," whatever their context and liturgical style. "***Culture***" can be defined as follows:[25]

> Culture is a fuzzy set of basic assumptions and values, orientations to life, beliefs, policies, procedures and behavioural conventions that are shared by a group of people, and that influence (but do not determine) each member's behaviour and his/her interpretations of the 'meaning' of other people's behaviour.

Firstly, the "fuzziness" of the term "culture" is helpful to discussions on worship, because it is fluid. It is not fixed in the past but is constantly being recreated in the present, whilst relating to the past. Furthermore, in today's

---

[21] Of these terms, "cross-cultural" requires a hyphen; "multiracial" and "multi-ethnic" do not. However, in this author's view, "multi-ethnic" needs a hyphen to separate adjacent vowels ("i" + "e").

[22] Kathy Black, *Culturally-Conscious Worship* (St. Louis, MO: Chalice Press, 2000).

[23] C. Michael Hawn, *Gather into One: Praying and Singing Globally*, Calvin Institute of Christian Worship Liturgical Studies (Grand Rapids, MI and Cambridge, UK: Eerdmans, 2003), 9-17.

[24] Recognising that "worship" has a broader application (e.g. a "lifestyle of worship," Rom. 12:1; Deut. 6:13) and narrower reference (personal devotional expressions, e.g. Ps. 95:6).

[25] Helen Spencer-Oatey, ed., *Culturally Speaking: Culture, Communication and Politeness Theory*, 2nd ed. (London and New York: Continuum, 2008), 3.

world, churches need to talk about race and ethnicity in order to expose underlying prejudices and clear the way for interactions on level ground. However, without such conversations, exaggerated attention given to race and ethnicity in "multiracial" or "multi-ethnic" worship can result in tokenism in worship – which ethnomusicologists call, "essentialised narratives."[26] Such "racialised stereotyping" of human beings can be deeply offensive – and hence counterproductive to intercultural worship. Secondly, because culture is fluid, intercultural worship can express itself in two main ways. The more obvious is to learn and celebrate the heritage of each worshipper. The other is to create new, shared worship expressions from diverse backgrounds, what some call a "third culture," as Kathy Black[27] explains:

> By all sharing their cultures, their histories and faith journeys, as well as the ways they traditionally praise God and the ways that God inspires them through certain songs and prayer forms, a "third" culture emerges out of shared memories that blends elements from each of the cultures present.

As an ethnodoxologist[28] working for many years in culturally diverse church contexts, I previously preferred the term "multicultural"[29] but have come to see that all "multi-" terms risk focusing too much on the more conspicuous *externals* of ethnicities, languages, skin colours, types of music and liturgical expressions, rather than the interaction *between* humans when they come together. Conversations about these outward factors are vital. However, worship that is truly "intercultural" is not firstly about *forms* but about the depth of true fellowship (*koinonia*) between culture groups and the degree to which each is free to express their unique voice. This dialogue needs to be both "cross-cultural" and "intercultural":[30] "***cross-cultural***" refers to a *comparison* between cultures, whilst "***intercultural***" requires *interaction* (see the work of Susan Fries,[31] Paula

---

[26] "Essentialise": to "portray or explain (a particular type of person or thing) in terms of one or more stereotypical or supposedly intrinsic traits." "essentialize," Lexico, accessed Sep 16, 2020, https://www.lexico.com/definition/essentialize.

[27] Black, *Culturally-Conscious Worship*, 90.

[28] About ethnodoxology, see Ian Collinge, "A Kaleidoscope of Doxology: Exploring Ethnodoxology and Theology," *Doon Theological Journal* 8, no. 1, part 1 (Mar 2011): 37-57.

[29] For reasons that are well expressed by Malcolm Patten in his book *Leading a Multicultural Church* (London: SPCK, 2016), 8-10.

[30] Susan Fries points out that, "In French the only possible adjective for this field is "intercultural," whereas in English we have both "intercultural" and "cross-cultural"." See Susan Fries, "Cultural, Multicultural, Cross-Cultural, Intercultural: A Moderator's Proposal," TESOL-France, accessed Sep 15, 2020, https://www.tesol-france.org/uploaded_files/files/susan-fries.pdf, 2.

[31] Fries, "Cultural, Multicultural, Cross-Cultural, Intercultural."

Schriefer[32] and Mari D. González.)[33] Of salience to our topic, "intercultural communication" is "what happens when two (or more) culturally-different groups come together, interact and communicate."[34] Interest in this chapter is mainly in "what happens" regarding worship when cultures interact.

Searching Questions (to Promote Intercultural Worship Communication)

The term "liturgical plurality" is used by Michael Hawn.[35] This term itself unfortunately still foregrounds plurality. Nonetheless, Hawn's comments are probing and we can reframe them as questions to aid discussion between cultures and develop worship diversity.

- Is our desire for multicultural worship diversity for diversity's sake ("ethno-tourism")?
  - We note that this can easily lead to cultural appropriation.[36]
- In our desire for inclusion, are we in danger of denying our own faith heritage and are we adequately and honestly examining our own practices?
  - Hawn suggests that each should "lay one's own heritage alongside another's and to critique each."[37]
- Is there a diversity of voices or simply a synthesis of styles that makes everything sound the same?
  - Opstal likens the latter to "smothering" a salad with the same dressing.[38] In my experience, churches need both diversity (to honour individuals) and synthesis (to bring them together).[39] However, Hawn is rightly concerned that cultural particularities may be lost within a generic style.

---

[32] Paula Schriefer, "What's the difference between multicultural, intercultural, and cross-cultural communication?" Spring Institute (Apr 18, 2016), accessed Oct 22, 2021, https://springinstitute.org/whats-difference-multicultural-intercultural-cross-cultural-communication/.
[33] Mari D. González, "Cross-Cultural vs. Intercultural," IXMATI Communications (Feb 3, 2011), accessed Sep 15, 2020, https://ixmaticommunications.com/2011/02/03/cross-cultural-vs-intercultural.
[34] González, "Cross-Cultural vs. Intercultural."
[35] Hawn, *Gather into One,* 13-17.
[36] Cultural appropriation has been defined as, "The unacknowledged or inappropriate adoption of the customs, practices, ideas, etc. of one people or society by members of another and typically more dominant people or society." See: "cultural appropriation," Lexico, accessed Sep 16, 2020, https://www.lexico.com/definition/cultural_appropriation.
[37] Hawn, *Gather into One,* 15-16.
[38] Opstal, *The Next Worship*, 105-107.
[39] To balance Hawn's and Opstal's concerns, Lerner and Black suggest churches develop their own sound, which is necessarily a unique synthesis. See Nikki Lerner, "Multicultural Worship," in *Multicultural Ministry Handbook: Connecting Creatively to a Diverse World*, eds. David A. Anderson and Margarita R. Cabellon (Downers Grove, IL: IVP Books, 2010), 97; Black, *Culturally-Conscious Worship*, 90.

- Is our liturgical plurality both "countercultural" (opposing cultural idolatries) and "cross-cultural" (embracing the culturally other)?[40]
- Are we giving "a voice to the voiceless," enabling cultures not present to be represented in song and prayer?
  o This question is also relevant to monocultural congregations.
- Is our liturgical plurality simply a variety show or is it an appetiser for the vision of the eternal city, where "the glory and honour of the nations" (Revelation 21:26) is a notable part of its beauty?
  o As Hawn affirms, all true intercultural worship is, in essence, eschatological.[41]

The issues Hawn raises are applicable not only to cosmopolitan cities in the global north but the church in Asia (and the global south more widely) when facing intercultural encounters and the dominant presence of globalised worship resources from the global north. Hawn also explores this global–regional tension in the work of Loh I-To, the Asian ethnomusicological hymnologist who desires to be "fully Christian" and "fully Asian."[42] Loh says, "I frequently tell my Asian students and colleagues that modernization does not equal Westernization. If you copy others all the time, then you lose yourself."[43] Loh's work is "a theological endeavor designed to help Asian Christians find their cultural voice in the context of Christian liturgy."[44] His collection of music for worship[45] in a church that lives between its Asian setting and the global church draws extensively on his musical learning as well as his concern that Asian liturgy and music should reflect Asian aesthetic values. An example of how this might work in practice in an intercultural Asian theological college in Singapore is given by Warren R. Beattie.[46] Beattie notes that such worship needs to address liturgical styles, language barriers, styles and traditions of music and the impact of culture on a

---

[40] Hawn here references "The Nairobi Statement on Worship and Culture (1996)" – a Lutheran document. Hawn, *Gather into One,* 14.

[41] Hawn, *Gather into One,* 16.

[42] Loh seeks to encourage other Asian Christians to embrace this challenge. See also I-To Loh [Michael N. C. Poon, ed.], *In Search for Asian Sounds and Symbols in Worship* (Singapore: Trinity Theological College, 2012), and Swee Hong Lim, *Giving Voice to Asian Christians: An Appraisal of the Pioneering Work of I-To Loh in the Area of Congregational Song* (Saarbrücken: Verlag Dr Müller, 2008).

[43] Loh, "Contextualization versus Globalization: A Glimpse of Sounds and Symbols in Asian Worship," 125-39.

[44] Hawn, *Gather into One,* 73-82.

[45] Most notably, Christian Conference of Asia, *Sound the Bamboo: CCA Hymnal 2000* (Tainan: Taiwan Presbyterian Church Press, 2000). The volume includes indigenous hymnody from China, Taiwan, Korea, Indonesia, Japan, Pakistan, Philippines and other Asian cultures, each with their unique scales, melodic structure, ornamentation and accompaniment styles.

[46] Warren R. Beattie, "Creating a Community for Contextual Learning," in *Ministry Across Cultures: Sharing the Christian Faith in Asia*, Regnum Studies in Mission, ed. Warren R. Beattie (Oxford: Regnum Books, 2016), 126-28.

range of factors from the use of physical space to interpersonal interactions. The article concludes with a number of practical changes through which this Asian college sought to embrace members from various cultures in its worship, especially the more marginalised. Beattie's approach exemplifies "intercultural involvement," one of three key approaches to intercultural worship to be explored later.

Further Resources on Asian Hymnody
Batastini, R. J., exec. producer, *Christian Music from Asia for the World: The Legacy of I-To Loh*. DVD. Chicago, IL: GIA, 2014. Christian Conference of Asia. *Sound the Bamboo: CCA Hymnal 2000*. Tainan: Taiwan Presbyterian Church Press, 2000.[47] Loh, I. T. *Hymnal Companion to Sound the Bamboo: Asian Hymns in Their Cultural and Liturgical Contexts*. Chicago, IL: GIA, 2011. Loh, I. T., M. Y. T. Gan and J. Laoyan-Mosomos, eds. *Let the Asian Church Rejoice*. Singapore: Methodist School of Music and Trinity Theological College, 2015.

Intercultural Worship Defined

In the light of these discussions, we can see that the term "intercultural" is especially appropriate to describe the fuller, biblical vision for worship in a church that takes seriously the complex cultural sensibilities of its members. "Intercultural" is made up of "inter-" (between) and "cultural" (of cultures), emphasising "interaction." Hence, to summarise, in much of the discussion so far, "intercultural worship" can be defined as:

> Expressions of corporate worship that flow from humble and creative relationships between culturally diverse followers of Jesus and that help them connect with God more profoundly and one another more equally.

In other words, "intercultural" emphasises *process* before *product*. Indeed, many of the pitfalls and criticisms of "multicultural worship"[48] – a term that simply describes "multiple" cultures in worship – can be overcome if worship comes out of genuine dialogue,[49] experimentation and intercultural sharing in

---

[47] For an edition easily available in the global north see: Christian Conference of Asia, *Sound the Bamboo*.

[48] Such as awkwardness, tokenism, cultural appropriation, racial privilege, cultural superiority, and so on. Also, see Constance M. Cherry, *The Worship Architect: A Blueprint for Designing Culturally Relevant and Biblically Faithful Services* (Grand Rapids, MI: Baker Academic, 2010), 172-74.

[49] For example, church leaders in a culturally diverse church in the global north (Leeds, England) called together representatives from minority ethnic groups to form a "diversity group," in order to explore what a truly intercultural church, including worship, might look like. This conversation has been their starting point.

liturgy creation. Another writer who finds that "intercultural" best describes the contemporary need is the missionary musician, Joyce Scott, who has worked widely in the global south. She uses the term "intercultural" music[50] to refer to:

> … groups of people from different races and cultural backgrounds, or with differing music styles, worshipping together in the same service, in a way that enables each group to enjoy feeling at home at some point in the singing … It is not assimilation but accommodation.

For Scott, this term includes ideas of acceptance, despite cultural differences, and the capacity for all to be at home[51] and accommodated. Such openness requires a true welcome towards all on equal terms rather than integration into some kind of implicit cultural hierarchy. Her interest is in the way that such hospitality extends to corporate worship in culturally diverse contexts which allows for expressions of worship that include the whole Christian community.

Further Resources on Hymnody for Intercultural Worship
Bell, J. L. *One Is the Body: Songs of Unity and Diversity*. Glasgow: Wild Goose Publications, 2002.
Donaldson, A., ed. *Hosanna! Ecumenical Songs for Justice and Peace*. Geneva: World Council of Churches, 2016.
Farlee, R. B., ed. *Leading the Church's Song*. Minneapolis, MN: Augsburg Fortress, 1998. [Includes a chapter on Asia].
Hawn, C. M. *Halle, Halle: We Sing the World Round (Teacher's Edition)*. Garland, TX: Choristers Guild, 1999.
Weaver, G., ed. *In Every Corner Sing: Songs of God's World*. Salisbury, Wiltshire: RSCM, 2008.

Six Approaches to Cultural Diversity in Worship

The preceding survey shows that cultural settings, personal and cultural identity, understandings of worship, and the combination of factors present in particular situations all have an impact on how worship is shaped and led. Each church needs to chart its own path. As Davis and Lerner[52] point out:

---

[50] Joyce Scott, *Tuning in to a Different Song: Using a Music Bridge to Cross Cultural Differences* (Pretoria: University of Pretoria Institute for Missiological and Ecumenical Research, 2000), 11.

[51] Note the mention by Andrew Walls of the church as "A Place to Feel at Home" in relation to his "indigenizing principle." See Walls, *The Missionary Movement in Christian History*, 7.

[52] Davis and Lerner, *Worship Together in Your Church as in Heaven*, 171-72.

> There is no perfect model for multicultural worship. All have benefits and challenges ... Also there is no way your church can look exactly like a model ... God is doing new things, and we need to respond in new ways.

Cosmopolitan, multicultural cities that have experienced recent waves of migration may have very different resources and needs from urban centres where multiple ethnicities have co-existed fairly separately over a few centuries, as in parts of the Malaysian peninsula. This multitude of contexts and histories is reflected in various forms of multicultural church: bicultural congregations; congregations with one cultural majority and some other cultures; congregations with no one cultural majority group; "nesting" churches that provide homes for congregations of different cultures; new multicultural church plants; and churches being developed in changing neighbourhoods.[53]

The chart presented below[54] profiles six approaches by churches to the presence of cultural diversity in worship. Crucially, it illustrates some key differences between "monocultural," "multicultural" and "intercultural" worship. In each case, these approaches show how Christian communities wrestle with the issue of intercultural worship and seek to worship God in ways that reflect their particular context and levels of ethnic diversity.

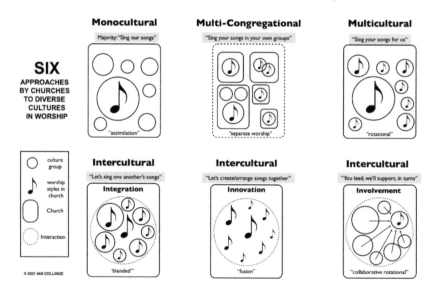

---

[53] I am indebted to the Presbyterian Church USA for these distinctions: "The Multicultural Church," Presentation (2011) by Grace Presbytery. (The website has since been updated and this report is no longer accessible).

[54] Improved version of an earlier presentation: Ian Collinge, "Moving from Monocultural to Multicultural Worship," in *Worship and Mission for the Global Church: An Ethnodoxology Handbook*, ed. James R. Krabill, Frank Fortunato, Robin P. Harris and Brian Schrag (Pasadena, CA: William Carey Library, 2013), 438-42.

1) Monocultural Inheritance –
One Culture's Worship Style in a Multicultural Church

The "monocultural" approach describes a church with a dominant culture, several other cultural groups and one main music style (represented by the single musical note symbol).[55] Worship expressions are "inherited" from the majority culture's practices. In essence, the church invites everyone to assimilate[56] and "sing our songs." As highlighted above, many multi-ethnic churches fall into this category. No changes are made to represent other cultures, on the basis that this is too difficult or will not unify people. Assumptions are easily made that attendees appreciate existing worship patterns. However, unity without diversity risks becoming uniformity, whether in a liturgical tradition, hymn culture or contemporary worship genres.

Multilingual Worship in Kerala (India)

How can such churches move towards a more inclusive approach? A simple first step is to sing in more of the languages of the congregation. In South India, Jacob Joseph led worship in a multicultural church with Malayalam, Tamil, English and Hindi speakers. He selected songs that existed in all languages excluding English, one of which lacked a Tamil translation. He relates what happened next:[57]

> … when we finished the Malayalam version of the song a man from the congregation instantly translated the chorus of the song into Tamil and started singing. It was powerful and I could see that people were enjoying it so much. That was a powerful sign that multicultural worship is something that needs to be taught in Indian churches.

Worship in Northern England (UK) – Embracing Minority Groups

Churches can go further. The following example comes from my experience as an elder in a homogenous white British church in the multicultural town of Oldham, Greater Manchester. This started as a monocultural congregation; then people from the global south and west Asia began attending. The first step involved welcoming a drummer from Sierra Leone to play his *djembe*, instantly adding his own sound to existing songs. Next, he and other immigrants taught their own songs. In doing this, we learned that it was vital for wider acceptance to translate some non-English songs into the common language (English) and select those songs that the church could more readily embrace. As a result, the

---

[55] This applies equally to a single congregation or distinct congregations within a larger church.
[56] Black says, the "majority culture is welcoming of persons from other cultures but those persons are expected to assimilate into the already existing worship." Black, *Culturally-Conscious Worship*, 92.
[57] Joseph, "Multicultural Worship in India."

church grew and began to attract people of diverse cultures. Worship was becoming "multicultural" – but it was not fully "intercultural." We then held conversations where we asked questions such as: "What are your preferred ways to worship God?" and "What English songs do you find more difficult?" The answers were revealing. These intercultural exchanges required a deepening level of relationship for honest answers to emerge.[58] We sought to know what each person's preferred worship expression was; in all cases we noticed a greater joy, energy and volume when we sang their culture's songs. For those from Asia and Africa, this was often shown in intensified emotions or bodily movements. Sometimes worship included poetry they brought. Such examples demonstrate it is possible to start moving from a monocultural to a multilingual approach and include a few items from other cultures;[59] these are initial steps to more intercultural expressions. They also highlight the role that understanding minority culture members' feelings plays in this journey.

2) Multi-Congregational Independence – Separate Worship

The "multi-congregational"[60] approach describes a church made up of distinct ethnolinguistic worship services, usually with their own leaders, where they meet for separate worship. Each group is monocultural (or bicultural) in its worship and the wider church's message is: "Sing your songs in your own groups." This is a common response to the presence of multiple language groups and is prevalent in Asia, as Joseph described above. In places with immigrant communities, this offers advantages for first and second generation immigrants, allowing for evangelism and discipleship. John Root writes of his multicultural context in London that, "diversity is served by offering worship in people's heart language and which reflects their culture."[61] As mentioned before, this approach, sadly, can reinforce cultural insularity and distance parents from their children. Therefore, steps to become more intercultural include:

- fellowships joining together periodically, with shared leadership, translation and worship representing the different cultures, where each group takes a lead in worship on an equal basis, or in preparing a joint contribution;
- each fellowship using more of its members' languages in their separate services of worship;
- young people being consulted about worship, seriously listened to, with leaders willing to embrace new ideas, including blended worship;

---

[58] People from deferential cultures can feel that it shows a lack of respect to the church leaders to express disapproval.
[59] Opstal calls this "acknowledgement;" Opstal, *The Next Worship*, 103-105.
[60] Also spelled without a hyphen: "multicongregational."
[61] John Root, *Worship in a Multi-Ethnic Society*, Grove Worship 236 (Cambridge, UK: Grove Books, 2018), 6.

- a possible, eventual transition to regular combined services, with weekly language-based groups to meet needs previously met in distinct fellowships.

In this way worship can move from multiple monocultural groups towards experiences that draw together the whole Christian community.

Worship in Reading (UK) – A Bicultural British and Nepali Church

Global north and south come together in Anderson Baptist Church, Reading, England. Half of its congregation are Nepali speakers.[62] They are an inspiring example of a church that does all it can to build interculturalism into all they do. For some time, they operated on a multi-congregational model but they held deliberate conversations about coming together for worship. This church certainly listens deeply and has an intentional intercultural strategy. They continue to hold separate Nepali-language services but they also meet and share fellowship together. Senior pastor Rev. Judith Wheatley[63] writes,

> From the outset Anderson decided it wanted to be a church where everyone was an equal, not easy when there is a natural deference from one culture to another … It has preached on Galatians 3 on numerous occasions, emphasising that neither 'Jew nor Greek' also meant 'neither English nor Nepali.'

This church highlights a persevering and sacrificial intentionality. Wheatley[64] continues,

> As the church developed its pattern for worshipping together, it recognised the need to include Nepali language into its services to be inclusive. This started with the Lord's Prayer and a few songs that were easy to learn. Different scripts, musical styles, and having non-readers in the congregation means this is always a challenge, but the church has persevered.

3) Multicultural Inclusion – Inviting Cultural Groups to Lead Songs

The "multicultural" approach (that some call "rotational")[65] emphasises "inclusion" by inviting members of different cultures to "sing your own songs for us," maybe on a rota or in an occasional international service. The emphasis here is on mutual acceptance through participation. Culture insiders lead the

---

[62] See Judith Wheatley, "Anderson Baptist Church, Reading," *Baptists Together* (Spring 2018): 19-20, accessed Aug 3, 2021,
https://www.baptist.org.uk/Articles/513632/Baptists_Together_magazine.aspx. [Volume entitled "Many Cultures: One Church."]
[63] Wheatley, "Anderson Baptist Church, Reading," 19.
[64] Wheatley, "Anderson Baptist Church, Reading," 19.
[65] Davis and Lerner, *Worship Together in Your Church as in Heaven*, 173-77. It has superficial similarities to the "collaborative rotational" model of Opstal, *The Next Worship*, 107-108.

songs. They are native speakers of those languages and demonstrate their passion for Jesus with their distinct styles. Whilst this seems a simple solution, a significant disadvantage is that if it is only cultural insiders who lead the songs, they need to be extremely careful not to alienate others – by virtue of the language they find easy (but others may not) and cultural assumptions they may not explain. If this persists, some church members may absent themselves from those services. Where these issues are not addressed, the church may become disillusioned and give up on their multicultural worship project.

Worship in East London (UK)

In one multi-ethnic church in East London, the author observed that a four-week cycle included worship-leading by South Asian members, other global south members (from African and Caribbean communities) and white British members. He visited this church when a Sierra Leonean was leading an African team in song. The latter announced that he would incorporate an Indian song, even though this was not his language. When the author enquired about his thinking afterwards, the worship leader admitted that he wanted church members to feel that they could join in songs not in their own style and language, so he wanted to demonstrate that this was possible. In doing so, he was reaching for a solution: a more intercultural approach.

Multiculturalism in a Hillsong Church in Sydney (Australia)

To be more "inclusive," some multi-ethnic churches hold occasional international services or special events centred on specific cultures. In 2016, the Hillsong Hills Campus in Sydney, Australia, held various celebrations.[66] Asians were given prominence on several occasions.[67] Each time, the church reached out to members from these backgrounds to affirm their presence in their church. However, if this is limited to special events but regular worship services remain monocultural, this raises questions about how genuine the church's attempt at multiculturalism is and whether certain cultures are being exoticised or assimilated. Positively, however, this church looks for their services to include translation, including several Asian languages.

---

[66] Hillsong Team, "Why Do We Have a Multicultural Ministry?" Hillsong Collected (Jan 31, 2017), accessed Sep 15, 2020,
https://hillsong.com/collected/blog/2017/01/why-do-we-have-a-multicultural-ministry/#.XDx8o_zgpJ9.
[67] For example, an Indian Independence event, a Korean night, and a Filipino Christmas party.

4) *Intercultural Integration – Maximising Accessibility and Participation*

The "integration" approach (also called "blended"[68] or "convergent")[69] brings together culturally diverse people and music. This multicultural congregation says, "Let's sing one another's songs in ways we can all participate." This approach is truly "intercultural" in that it entails genuine learning from one another. For example, musicians practise songs from a range of cultures, learning the words and styles as they are able. It is also adaptive: they decide how much of any language is appropriate for their community, and, where needed, add a translated set of lyrics in the common language. Two watchwords of this approach are: "participation" and "accessibility."

The church's existing language and musical style usually provide the framework. For the same song, one church may use a more choral approach,[70] whilst a praise band will fit the song to available instruments and voices.[71] This adaptation has the advantage of helping a church move forward into intercultural worship with their current musical talent. Groups with the capacity to replicate culturally-specific stylistic elements such as rhythms, instruments and vocal styles will be able to present musical genres more fully.[72]

Worship in West London (UK)

Rev. David Wise describes integrated worship in Greenford, London. Singing a Hindi song, "*Amrit Vani Teri,*" many sit on the floor and all repeat phrases after the leader:[73]

> … this is neither India nor an Asian congregation …; this is Sunday morning in a West London Baptist church. However, all is not how you may have pictured this … The English worship leader does not speak Hindi (… her pronunciation is very good), the [tanpura] drone sound is coming from a mobile phone app and, although

---

[68] "Blended" emphasises generational diversity but some adapt this to cultural diversity. Cherry, *The Worship Architect*, 244; Opstal, *The Next Worship*, 105-107; Davis and Lerner, *Worship Together in Your Church as in Heaven*, 178-80; Black, *Culturally-Conscious Worship*, 95-97.
[69] "Convergence" does not require cultural diversity but its applications are clear. Cherry, *The Worship Architect*, 243-57; Bruce Milne, *Dynamic Diversity: The New Humanity Church for Today and Tomorrow* (Nottingham: IVP, 2006), 112-13.
[70] Songbooks such as Geoff Weaver, ed., *In Every Corner Sing: Songs of God's World* (Salisbury, Wiltshire: RSCM, 2008); John L. Bell, *One Is the Body: Songs of Unity and Diversity* (Glasgow: Wild Goose Publications, 2002).
[71] See Songs2Serve and "Language Selection Songs Playlist," Arts Release, accessed Sep 15, 2020, https://artsrelease.org/en/resources/language-selection-songs-playlist.
[72] C. Michael Hawn, *Halle, Halle: We Sing the World Round (Teacher's Edition)* (Garland, TX: Choristers Guild, 1999). See also, *Sound the Bamboo* which includes indications of musical style.
[73] David Wise, "Multi-Ethnic Worship," *Ministry Today* 63 (Apr 2015), accessed Aug 15, 2020, https://www.ministrytoday.org.uk/magazine/issues/63/482/.

there are around twenty Asians in the congregation, most of the adults present were born in Africa or the Caribbean.

On another occasion, a visitor from the global south was deeply touched at the way in which his language was embraced in worship.[74]

> In the congregation was a visiting pastor, now living in the UK, but he was born and grew up in Nigeria. With tears in his eyes, he related that until today he had never worshipped God in his first language, he could not express how welcome he felt, not just by this congregation, but by God accepting him as a Yoruba.

By using the music of diverse cultures, this church taps into the music of different members. Worshippers often find that they are "strangely warmed" as they learn new ways to worship God themselves, even when singing in another language.

5) Intercultural Innovation – Maximising Collaborative Creativity

The "innovative" approach (often with elements of "fusion"[75]) describes a church or group able to write home-grown songs or arrange songs together, using various styles and languages. More common is a multilingual approach, such as Taizé.[76] The Taizé songs include Chinese, Korean and Japanese words for certain well-known sung chants. Other songwriters focus on language and stylistic diversity, such as Evan Rogers from South Africa,[77] Muyiwa in England[78] and Dan Adler in the USA.[79] Each has produced songs with an eye to embrace global south communities.

Worship in a Multicultural Worship Community (Clarkston, Georgia, USA)

One community that gives special attention to this innovative approach is Proskuneo Ministries, based in Clarkston, Georgia, where "60 languages are spoken within 1.4 square miles."[80] Korean Americans Jaewoo and Joy Kim play

---

[74] Wise, "Multi-Ethnic Worship."

[75] Davis and Lerner, *Worship Together in Your Church as in Heaven*, 180-81.

[76] Taizé music – see "Songs," Taizé, accessed Sep 15, 2020,
https://www.taize.fr/en_rubrique2603.html.

[77] For music by Evan Rogers, see, "hEvan Songs," SoundCloud, accessed Sep 15, 2020,
https://soundcloud.com/hevans-songs. Also see Aaron Lewendon, "Worship music:
How should we sing?" Eden.co.uk (Apr 11, 2012), accessed Sep 15, 2020,
https://www.eden.co.uk/blog/worship-music-how-should-we-sing-p1481.

[78] "Albums," Muyiwa, accessed Oct 16, 2021, https://muyiwa.co.uk/albums/.

[79] Heart of the City, accessed Sep 15, 2020, https://www.heartofthecity.org/home.

[80] Joy Hyunsook Kim, "Diaspora Musicians and Creative Collaboration in a
Multicultural Community: A Case Study in Ethnodoxology," (MA thesis, Graduate
Institute of Applied Linguistics, Dallas International University, Dallas, TX, 2018), 77-
78.

a central role in this community. Appropriately, therefore, several songs include Korean language. In this melting pot of cultures, collaborative intercultural innovation results in new fusion forms of music. Proskuneo Ministries have produced a range of interculturally innovative resources, including an album called "1" (ONE), which they describe as:[81]

> … all about unity and diversity in the Body of Christ. This album offers sounds of modern rock, Middle Eastern, Latin, funk, and gospel music with melodies … in Korean, Arabic, English, Spanish, and French …. These songs were written by community, in community, and for community.

Proskuneo beautifully illustrates the emergence of a "third culture" catalysed by the synergy coming from real-life interactions between bicultural worshippers from a range of cultures.

6) Intercultural Involvement –
Cultural Members Help Shape Whole Services (with Others)

"Intercultural involvement" describes Opstal's "collaborative rotation" model.[82] In my experience, this is the least common approach probably because it is the most ambitious. It demonstrates a deep intercultural vision, where leaders give power to particular cultural groups to shape every aspect of a service and host the worship event. Those of other cultures are also intimately involved. In effect, they say, "you lead, we'll support, in turns." The whole service is planned to give prominence to the hosting culture. Opstal[83] adds,

> The strength of this model is that it can move people beyond the music to the experience and story of different communities through teaching, prayers, rituals and testimony. Worship retains the authenticity of original style and form. Every community is given an opportunity to lead …. Collaborative rotation allows for full empowerment of the hosting community in expressing deeper cultural values.

Whilst this approach may be demanding to design and difficult to sustain on a weekly basis,[84] it is one that can be used for special events, such as in the examples above of the college in Singapore or Hillsong (Sydney). As noted in relation to Hillsong, there was a conscious decision to include and affirm the contribution of Asian members in the church. Filipino community leader Grace Garcia says a multicultural church helps us learn more about God,[85]

---

[81] Proskuneo Ministries, accessed Aug 2, 2021, https://proskuneo.org/.

[82] Opstal, *The Next Worship*, 107.

[83] Opstal, *The Next Worship*, 108.

[84] Opstal remarks that musicians "may experience fatigue constantly learning new music;" Opstal, *The Next Worship*, 108.

[85] Hillsong Team, "Why Do We Have a Multicultural Ministry?"

… you can learn from other cultures and apply it to your own culture. The benefit of diversity is you see the beauty of God's creation; God created all of these cultures. It goes to show the gospel isn't just for one ethnic background – white, black – it's for everyone and it shows we're reaching out to all.

Furthermore, it makes people feel more accepted. Of the Latino night, one student said: "I came from the land of tacos and mariachi, Mexico, and I hadn't felt the warmth of familiarity for months. But when I heard those songs, the melodies comforted my homesick heart." The great inspiration of this approach is the purposeful intercultural listening involved in event design and the deepening appreciation between cultures that can result.

Combining Intercultural Integration, Innovation and Involvement

In the above discussion about various strategies for intercultural worship, six approaches have been described. In reality, these are rarely isolated from each other. Each church can experiment with their particular mixture of people, ideas and resources. In fact, a truly intercultural approach can probably only arise from a synthesis of "integration" of existing diverse cultural elements, "innovation" of new ones, and "involvement" by each culture on its own terms (see diagram below). Each allows for different facets of intercultural dialogue and therefore the combination is much more likely to result in a healthy, new worship vocabulary and atmosphere, accepted by more and more participants, where each person's voice is heard more distinctly at times and, at others, there is a unique sense of blended togetherness.

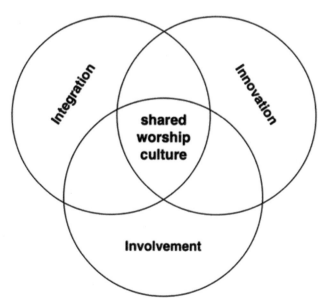

Coda: The Importance of Intercultural Worship

In the foregoing introduction to concepts, issues, terminologies and approaches, the intention has been to identify what makes for a worship that represents all the worshippers present and not just the leading group. It has been emphasised that intercultural worship expressions arise from intercultural interaction (both listening and experimentation) between humans in their real and multiple identities, where no prior assumptions about style are made by others and members of different cultures are not only consulted but are involved in song choices and service design. Along the way, there has been an encounter with several churches in Asia, and those with Asian diaspora members (often with others from the global south), who illustrate various journeys into intercultural worship. Each looks different. However, the new shared worship culture that emerges often includes a mix of intercultural integration, innovation and involvement.

The chapter has also shown clear examples of the impact of intercultural worship and how language and music from a person's home culture frequently evoke deep emotions that heighten their sense of human and divine embrace. The Tamil man spontaneously translated a Malayalam song. The Mexican student and Sierra Leonean pastor used words such as, "warmth," "comfort," "welcomed," and "accepted" to convey their feelings. The Nigerian pastor spoke with tears.[86] This reminds us of Paul's emphasis on "valuing," "accepting" and finding out what will "please" others, in order to "bring praise to God".

Therefore, for a church to take the effort to enter into the worship expressions of its members from various cultures, or of groups it seeks to reach, is an act of (sometimes sacrificial) love. It refuses tokenism, since it emphasises people. In this loving atmosphere, congregations can take the time they need to develop their sound, their approach and their potential. They illustrate Paul's body analogy, where the "eye cannot say to the hand, 'I don't need you!'" (1 Corinthians 12:21). Rather, worshippers begin to sense their need of culturally-other fellow worshippers and may feel something vital is missing without them. In other words, intercultural worship has the potential to transform culturally distinct worshippers into a demonstration of the living, unified, diverse body of Christ, where "each part does its own work" (Ephesians 4:16) to the glory of God.

---

[86] The author has seen that such emotions are common responses to songs in worshippers' own languages and styles when the Resonance multicultural worship bands of Arts Release ministry lead culturally-conscious worship, especially in Asia (mainly Singapore) and Europe. See "Music and Worship," Arts Release, accessed Oct 22, 2020, https://artsrelease.org/en/music-worship.

Questions for Reflection/Discussion
1. In your experience of churches where several ethnolinguistic groups worship together in the same service, what are the proportions of each cultural group and to what extent are their languages, music styles and cultural expressions equally represented in each part of the service? Does this reflect the diversity seen in 1 Corinthians 12:13 & 21; 1 Corinthians 14:26; Colossians 3:11 & 16; Revelation 7:9 and Revelation 21:26?
2. Considering the emphasis of this chapter on communication (active listening and creative experimentation) between culturally different individuals and groups, describe what listening skills and what forms of experimentation could be helpful for congregations that you know.
3. Which parts of the definition of intercultural worship stand out for you individually, in relation to your personal experience of Christian worship amongst believers of diverse backgrounds? Definition – *"Expressions of corporate worship that flow from humble and creative relationships between culturally diverse followers of Jesus and that help them connect with God more profoundly and one another more equally."*
4. Of the six approaches described in the second part of this chapter, which best describes churches you know? (It may be a combination.) If their approaches are not intercultural, is some form of intercultural worship desirable and, if so, what steps could be taken towards it? Are some of the examples described applicable to that end?

Part III

Nurturing the Arts and Artists in Local Contexts

7. Faith and Arts:
Emerging Local Engagement in Central Asia
Julie Taylor

Central Asia has changed dramatically since 1991. Mindful of the multi-layered contexts shaped by Islamic, Russian and western influences, this chapter presents narratives of non-Orthodox Christians in their engagement with faith. Special attention is given to the ways in which expressive and communicative arts are enabling the reimagining, shaping and sharing of beliefs as increasingly self-determined reflections of local identities today.

Map of the Five Republics of Central Asia

Map created by Freeworldmaps.net (Copyright)

Introduction

With the dissolution of the Soviet Union in 1991, the context of "Central Asia" was given opportunity to redefine itself as five independent republics, each with the potential of determining new pathways beyond Russianisation[1] and other historical influences. Missional awareness of this region has been documented up until the early 2000s, but since then, the closure of doors to most external faith agencies has clouded the picture and many non-local theological students perceive Central Asia to present insurmountable challenges. Ignoring such conceptions, a small, regionalised and persistent evangelical church is determining its path, regardless of limited access to Scriptural teaching, fellowship with other believers, or global missional approaches. To say that "post-Soviet space has been a blank spot from the perspective of the universal Church"[2] does little justice to the courage of those who have managed to maintain sparks of faith in the face of sustained persecution and relative isolation.

Central Asia is undeniably rich in arts, and a brief overview of the region reveals artistry functioning in multiple, interlocking capacities, whether as illuminations of faith, as tools in the hands of political players or as conceptualisations of identity. In considering how such interplay relates to the non-Orthodox evangelical church of today, the author has been assisted by local narratives and external sources,[3] recognising they present mere glimpses drawn from five increasingly divergent nations. This chapter seeks to identify a few of the ways in which arts are contributing to the imagining and resilience of the evangelical church within Central Asia, the need to affirm *local* Christian identity, and how this relates to Christian identity shared from outside. It is hoped that this brief account will spur readers to consider how faith, together with the creativeness of the arts, can surmount even the most challenging of situations.

The foci here are the five nations of Kazakhstan, Uzbekistan, Turkmenistan, Tajikistan and Kyrgyzstan, collectively designated as Central Asia.[4] Their total population in 2021 is just over 74 million[5] with more than 100 ethnic groups, and the main belief systems comprise Islam (ranging from 72% to 96% depending on country and source, the majority being Sunni Muslim) and

---

[1] Russianisation (rather than Russification) is used here to indicate the spread of Russian language, culture, and people into non-Russian cultures that has not necessarily resulted in assimilation of Russian identity as evidenced in Russification. They could be described as different stages of the same process.
[2] Mykhailo Cherenkov and William Yoder, "The Changing Face of Church and Mission in Eurasia (with William Yoder's Response to Mykhailo Cherenkov)," Occasional Papers on Religion in Eastern Europe 36, iss. 3, article 6 (May 2016): 50.
[3] Interviews with people from Central Asia have taken place in person, through internet meetings and by email. Only initials are used for most names.
[4] Other countries are sometimes included under "Central Asia," but these five are linked by historical events of the 19th and 20th centuries into post-Soviet times.
[5] DataReportal, accessed May 15, 2021, https://datareportal.com. Country figures are likely to be estimated.

Christianity (some surveys limit this to Orthodox, ranging from 0.75% to 12.15%). Many Protestants in Central Asia refer to themselves as "evangelicals," but may also speak of being followers of *Masih* (Messiah) or followers of *Isa* (Jesus). Their numbers are estimated to be low, ranging from less than 0.01% to 0.7%.[6]

Historical Overview

Although definitive dates are difficult to ascertain, Christianity was established in Persia during the Parthian Empire (247 BCE–224 CE), attributing its origins to the Apostles, but also benefitting from an influx of Christian traders from Antioch and Edessa. This early church was known as the Church of the East, or "the Holy Apostolic Catholic Church." Its primary liturgical language was Syriac (a dialect of Aramaic), but extant texts show the church sought to reach those with limited or no knowledge of Syriac through some use of local languages such as Persian, Sogdian and Old Uyghur.[7] The Church of the East then spread into Central Asia during the subsequent Sasanian Empire (224–651 CE), extending to the Altai mountains in the north-east. Other Christian churches such as the Syrian Orthodox, Melkites and Nestorians also emerged during this period.

Arrival of Christianity and Other Faiths[8] – Related Artistic Elements

It was Nestorianism that eventually reached China in 625 CE via the Silk Road trade routes,[9] but the Chinese were particularly drawn to the exotic range of arts brought by merchants from an ancient Persian-speaking region known as Sogdiana that spanned the countries known as Uzbekistan and Tajikistan today.

---

[6] Pew-Templeton Global Religious Futures Project, accessed May 14, 2021, http://www.globalreligiousfutures.org/countries. This lists Orthodox and all Christian denominations under "Christians," with individual figures for each of Buddhists, folk religions, Hindus, Jews and "other." For further comparisons see – Operation World, accessed May 14, 2021, https://operationworld.org/locations/.

[7] Mark Dickens, "Syriac Christianity in Central Asia," in *The Syriac World*, Routledge Worlds, ed. Daniel King (Abingdon and New York: Routledge, 2019): 583-624.

[8] These include the establishment of the Russian Orthodox Church, Orthodox (or classical) Islam and folk (or popular) Islam. The latter incorporates elements of Qur'anic teaching with pre-Islamic practices that may involve pilgrimages to tombs of ancestors, or to natural sites such as springs or caves believed to help cure illnesses. Other local traditions exist in funerals and weddings, having been handed down through families and serving to strengthen communal solidarity. See T. Jeremy Gunn, "Shaping an Islamic Identity: Religion, Islamism, and the State in Central Asia," *Sociology of Religion* 64, no. 3 (2003): 389-410.

[9] The Silk Road stretched from Antioch and Tyre in the west to the port of Hangzhou in eastern China. See route map "Mongol Empire A.D. 1294" at "The Mongol and the Ottoman Empires," Ottoman and Mongol Empires, accessed May 4, 2021, https://sites.google.com/site/ottomanandmongolsempire/.

The Sogdians were skilled in luxury silk-making and metalworking, along with figural wall paintings depicting stories and epic narratives. A form of dance known as the "Sogdian whirl" was highly popular, and many examples of decorated stone and pottery survive to this day.[10] The trade routes also brought groups of nomadic bards and camel herders who specialised in improvised poetry, songs and dramatic recitations from many parts of the continent, with some of the more famous performers still commemorated in the form of street names in Uzbekistan today. Musical instruments were also spreading across the continent, such as the stringed *rabab*, *dutar*, *tambur*, *dombra/komuz*, *kamancheh* and *gijak*; the *ney* (flute), *doira* (frame drum) and *chang* (zither). These and many regional variants continue to be played today.

In the latter part of the 600s, Arabs began pushing north and by the early 700s had conquered a region constituting today's Iran, Afghanistan, southern Turkmenistan and southern Uzbekistan. They brought Islam as well as a further rich array of artistic practices: illuminated manuscripts, calligraphy, architecture, mosaics, goldwork and textiles. By 751, important centres of classical Islamic learning and art had been established in the cities of Samarkand and Bukhara (Uzbekistan), but in contrast, many of the nomadic pastoralists of the rural steppes either chose to retain Christianity, seeing the biblical Hebrew practices as similar to their own lifestyles, or else retained their own folk traditions.[11]

Along with repression from Arab Muslims lasting from the mid-800s until the end of the first millennium, Christians were purged from China in the 980s, primarily for failing to relate or contextualise to Chinese life, but also due to the decline of the Tang dynasty, "on which the [Christian] church had too long relied for its patronage and protection."[12] The entire Asian continent was politically disintegrating until 1200 when the warrior Genghis Khan launched the Mongol invasions that eventually conquered vast swathes of Asia. The history of the resulting Mongol dynasty is lengthy and complex, stretching from 1211 when Genghis invaded northern China, to 1467 when his last successor died one hundred years into the Ming dynasty. Christianity was not new to the Mongols, many of whom had converted in the 7th century through contact with the Church of the East,[13] but successive warlords held differing attitudes towards belief

---

[10] Judith A. Lerner and Thomas Wide, "Who Were the Sogdians, and Why Do They Matter?" The Sogdians: Influencers on the Silk Roads, accessed Jul 19, 2021, https://sogdians.si.edu/introduction/. In addition to depictions of the "Sogdian whirl," the menu on this site leads to many examples of Sogdian artistic practices.

[11] Jack Weatherford, *Genghis Khan and the Making of the Modern World* (New York: Three Rivers Press, 2004), 29.

[12] Samuel Hugh Moffett, *A History of Christianity in Asia 1: Beginnings to 1500*, American Society of Missiology, 2nd rev. and corrected ed. (Maryknoll, NY: Orbis Books, 1998), 313.

[13] Weatherford, *Genghis Khan and the Making of the Modern World*, 28.

systems of their time.[14] Genghis himself was known to dialogue at length with Christians, Buddhists and Muslims, but when the Turko-Mongol warlord Timur the Great came to power in 1360,[15] he subjected Christianity to a period of savage destruction that once again almost entirely eradicated its presence from Central Asia. In strange contrast, and dreaming of an Islamic caliphate even though the Mongol Empire was weakening, Timur surrounded himself with beautiful wall tapestries and carpets, polychromic tile decorations, stained glass, ceramics and jade carvings, now referred to as Timurid Empire Art.

Despite the divided opinions amongst Islamic scholars on whether music and musical instruments were prohibited by Muhammad (see later comments on the Qur'an and Hadith), in reality many musical forms were practised, including dance (an essential element of Sufism). Trade routes and conquests invariably brought a musical synthesis of pre-Islamic styles, the Islamic urban classical *maqāmāt* (a system of melodic modes), and local folk art styles.[16] Today people still speak of artists such as Mashrab (1653–1711, a Sufi poet) and Saghyrbaiuly (1818–1889, a Kazakh *dombyra* player). A form of poetic synthesis also took place between Islam and Christianity, with the Qur'an adopting the antiphonal hymn structure known as *sogyāthā* (singular *soghītha*)[17] as was used in the early Syriac Christian church. *Sogyāthā* are still sung as antiphonal hymns in some Eastern Orthodox churches today, accommodating to the presence of Christian Turks and Mongols by alternating Syriac and Eastern Turkic strophes.

In 1368 the Chinese decided, for the second time in their history, to eradicate influences they perceived as increasingly foreign, this time involving the Mongols, the now Syriac Christian church, and recent arrivals, the Catholics.[18] Christianity did not reappear again in China until maritime trade routes brought the Jesuit China Missions in the 16th century. Meantime, from the 1300s through the 1800s, Russia was also expanding its empire, first eastward to the Pacific Ocean and then southward. By 1881 it had conquered most of Central Asia, widely establishing the Russian Orthodox Church with its striking gilded domes

---

[14] For a detailed account of this period, see Moffett, *A History of Christianity in Asia 1*, 471-88.

[15] Also known as Tamerlane, 1336-1405.

[16] See Amnon Shiloah, *Music in the World of Islam: A Socio-Cultural Study* (Detroit, MI: Wayne State University Press. 1995), 31-44, 102-103.

[17] *Soghītha* – a dialogic poetic construct designated for antiphonal singing by using alternating verses – see Robert Murray, *Symbols of Church and Kingdom: A Study in Early Syriac Tradition* (Cambridge: Cambridge University Press, 1975), 340. Also Jacob Fareed Imam, "The Annunciation to Mary as Retold in the Qurʾān" (MPhil thesis, University of Oxford, 2018).

[18] Franciscan friars arrived in Beijing in 1294.

and bell towers, vast biblical wall frescos (considered to be windows into heaven itself), and Byzantine icons with ornate metal riza.[19]

Migrant workers in Kazakhstan from the end of the 18th century included Protestant Christians (mostly Lutheran, Baptist, Mennonite or Adventist), who rapidly planted churches until Lenin's establishment of a communist, socialist and atheistic state from 1917 to 1924. This brought the spread of churches to a halt,[20] and thousands of Orthodox and evangelical leaders were executed or sent into exile whilst church buildings were destroyed. Lenin was succeeded by Stalin, under whom promotion of USSR nationalistic identity was strongly fostered, with state directives pressurising for mono-ethnic language use.[21] Whilst Christianity was never officially outlawed, citizens were encouraged to attend "anti-Christmas" and "anti-Easter" demonstrations.[22] Muslims were initially given more autonomy, but from 1926, their focus on intellectualism was stifled when socialist edicts forced the closure of mosques and Islamic schools. As a result, Islam became increasingly localised within societal contexts, "rendered synonymous with custom and tradition."[23]

Soviet Era (Pre-1991) – Strategic Use of "Nationalistic" Arts

It was during this time of Russian politico-cultural policies that a musical ethnographer called Aleksandr Zatayevich collected, transcribed and published numerous Kyrgyz/Kazakh folk songs from 1920 to his death in 1936.[24] The value of his collection was only appreciated post-independence as people sought to recommit to a sense of cultural belonging, but his work encouraged other musicologists to engage in documenting similar collections, such as Tansuǧ's bibliographic survey of Kyrgyz/Kazakh sources.[25] Although Zatayevich's primary interest was in the recording and continuance of cultural expressions, he was persuaded to adapt traditional Kazakh instruments for use in the large patriotic ensembles that became popular after World War I and which combined both traditional and western instruments. Due to the intimate sound qualities of traditional stringed instruments being subsumed in large ensembles, musicians

---

[19] *Riza* (Russian: "robe"), refers to a silver or gilded metal covering, sometimes filigreed or jewelled, intended to protect paintings of saints but leaving parts such as face and hands showing.

[20] The communist Union of Soviet Socialist Republics (USSR) was created in 1922.

[21] Jean During, "Power, Authority and Music in the Cultures of Inner Asia," *Ethnomusicology Forum* 14, no. 2 (2005): 146-48.

[22] Catherine Merridale, *Red Fortress: The Secret Heart of Russia's History* (London: Allen Lane, 2013), 304-305.

[23] Adeeb Khalid, *Islam after Communism: Religion and Politics in Central Asia* (Berkeley, CA: University of California Press, 2007), 82.

[24] Aleksandr Zatayevich, *1000 Songs of Kyrgyz/Kazakh People: Tunes and Melodies* (Orenburg: Kyrgyz State Publishing House, 1925).

[25] Feza Tansuǧ, "A Bibliographic Survey of Kazakh and Kyrgyz Literature on Music," *Yearbook for Traditional Music* 41 (2009): 199-220.

such as Zatayevich needed to reposition soundboards for greater volume, as well as creating more reliable tuning mechanisms and adding frets for a wider range of intervals.[26] This led to a debate over popularity versus authenticity.[27]

With similar intent to stir patriotism at the outbreak of World War II, Stalin now decided to promote the Russian Orthodox Church, but this politically-aided revival of Christianity proved short-lived. Suppression of the Church and anti-religious propaganda increased, seminaries were closed, and church leaders became subordinate to the state with efforts to "re-educate" them into atheism. Any Baptist, Adventist or Lutheran churches that had attained formal registration risked their leaders being "relocated" should they practise anything other than formal liturgy.[28] In 1936, the State Conservatory of Uzbekistan (Tashkent) was founded to counter not only a perceived loss of local cultural performance skills, but also to demonstrate knowledge of western "classical" repertoire to the world. The sounds of J. S. Bach's choral works mingled with Uzbek music, although to its credit, the Conservatory maintained the traditions of each system, such as using western musical notation for western music, and oral transmission from master to student for cultural genres.[29]

The Watershed of 1991

From the late 1980s, the last USSR head of state, Mikhail Gorbachev, relaxed anti-religious legislation and also introduced a period known as *glasnost* (Russian: "openness"). The growing social freedoms and political transparency enabled voices of dissent to manifest themselves in nationalist movements, swiftly accompanied by economic shortages and a backlash of youth against the Politburo. The result in 1991 was the collapse of the Soviet Union.

A Flux of Socio-Political and Cultural Norms

Theodore Levin, who had been a music student at the aforementioned State Conservatory of Uzbekistan from 1977, observed rapid de-Russianisation taking place, with Russian language disappearing from public signs, public announcements made in Uzbek, increasing promotions of western goods and a rise in general global awareness. This was accompanied by relaxations in

---

[26] Examples include the *qhijak* (a round-bodied spike fiddle used by Uzbeks and Turkmen) and the *saz* (a long-necked lute used amongst Tajik and Uzbek). For a video covering some of these changes, see The Juvanbur, "Master's Work – Mammadali Mamedov," YouTube, accessed May 5, 2021, https://youtu.be/U1o3Ym-b2UY.

[27] During, "Power, Authority and Music in the Cultures of Inner Asia," 148.

[28] Dimitry V. Pospielovsky, *Soviet Antireligious Campaigns and Persecutions*, A History of Soviet Atheism in Theory and Practice, and the Believer 2 (New York: St Martin's Press, 1988), 109-19.

[29] Theodore Levin, *The Hundred Thousand Fools of God: Musical Travels in Central Asia.* (Bloomington: Indiana University Press, 1996), 10-14, includes CD recordings.

hitherto strict Islam. Emerging from communism to democracy, all five republics of Central Asia were thrust into life as independent states in 1991, faced with redefining cultural freedom in their respective constitutions. In a spirit of "nativism," they reinstated many of their own languages, and encouraged a resurgence of local cultural traditions from pre-Soviet times such as weaving, embroidery, pottery making and cultural celebrations. Each of these republics has since been awarded UNESCO "Intangible Cultural Heritage" (ICH) status for one or more of their artistic practices,[30] the criteria being that they be viable living expressions, speaking to current societal values and actively transmitted to subsequent generations through festivals, contests or other activities.

A few such ICH examples include *askiya* (the art of wit, a form of verbal debating) in Uzbekistan, the *aitysh/aitys* contest centred on improvised oral poetry and practised in both Kazakhstan and Kyrgyzstan, and the *shashmaqom* musical genre that is common to both Uzbekistan and Tajikistan. The overlapping of ethnic clan systems over border demarcations has also resulted in some artistic practices occurring across all five republics, evident in the various genres employed to celebrate *Navruz*, the traditional New Year on March 21st. A question that remains unanswered is whether the governments of Central Asia have a sustainable plan for their local arts, other than the UNESCO ICH projects, for ensuring continuity of certain endangered traditions.[31]

Impact of the Influx of Missional Activity from Other Cultures

Establishing "religious freedom" has proved more elusive. Following independence, mission agencies rapidly entered Central Asia and many churches of varying denominations were re-established. Alongside this, high concentrations of Russian citizens in Kazakhstan after independence allowed Russian Orthodoxy and pro-Russian sentiments to remain dominant, whilst in other parts such as northern Turkmenistan, Islam prevailed.

Limits of Religious Freedom and Faiths under Pressure

The influx of foreignness eventually proved unsettling for all five national governments, and fearful of declining secular authority, a range of political

---

[30] For a definition, see Intangible Cultural Heritage, "Text of the Convention for the Safeguarding of the Intangible Cultural Heritage," UNESCO, accessed Jul 15, 2020, https://ich.unesco.org/en/convention. For lists of ICH awards, see Intangible Cultural Heritage, "Browse the Lists of Intangible Cultural Heritage and the Register of good safeguarding practices," UNESCO, accessed Jul 15, 2020,
https://ich.unesco.org/en/lists. UNESCO is the United Nations Educational, Scientific and Cultural Organization.

[31] Although much has changed since publication of this article, see Theodore Levin, "The Reterritorialization of Culture in the New Central Asian States: A Report from Uzbekistan," *Yearbook for Traditional Music* 25 (1993): 51-59.

strategic counter-moves were instigated.[32] These included promoting either Orthodox Christianity or Islam as concepts of nationhood or "traditionalism," and revising state constitutional laws on religious freedom and minority rights. Protestantism was discredited as foreign and thereby non-traditional. By circa 2007, the five states had closed their doors to external Christian agencies and banned proselytising as well as the practising of faith outside state-sanctioned structures.[33] All religious buildings and activities, whether Muslim, Orthodox, Catholic or Protestant, were then required to be registered, with teaching content checked by the authorities. In the case of Protestant churches, the content of hymnody was also scrutinised.

Emergence of the Unregistered Church Movement

Christians unable or unwilling to meet the strict registration requirements soon began to adopt a similar "underground" or house church model to that found in China and other parts of Asia, meeting in private homes for fellowship, prayer and sharing of God's word. Today, whilst acutely aware of ongoing restrictions and the need to be inconspicuous, some are finding ways to fellowship more openly:[34]

> Sometimes we picnic together as family or friends in a local park, quietly singing our cultural songs that everyone knows and enjoys, but with small changes of wording. For example, we have a *maqom*[35] melody from Uzbekistan that is very old and praises our kings, except our words are "We celebrate another King!" Passing Muslims will join in and even fellowship with us as they know these songs.

In Kyrgyzstan in 2014, a tightening of religious laws regulating worship has meant outsiders are no longer allowed to perform illusion, mime or story-telling in schools or public spaces. Until this time, foreign groups were able to obtain permission to enact stories containing gospel analogies, one popular example being the "*çay* (tea) story" where a drop of dirty water falling into a pot of tea was used to illustrate the far-reaching impact of the fall of humankind. People were drawn to the actors' use of local dress and receptacles, to musicians interacting with the storyline, and to the visual use of painted back-cloths setting each scene. Of significance was that the narrative in these plays (in a locally understood language) was provided by a puppet in a booth. Puppets of many

---

[32] For a more in-depth, regional account see Sébastien Peyrouse, "Why Do Central Asian Governments Fear Religion? A Consideration of Christian Movements," *Journal of Eurasian Studies* 1 (2010): 134-43.

[33] For an account of Orthodox and Muslim leaders pressurising Central Asian authorities to restrict missionary activity see Sébastien Peyrouse, "Christians in Central Asia, part 2," *East-West Church Ministry Report* 17, no. 4 (Fall 2009): 9-11, accessed Jun 8, 2021, https://www.eastwestreport.org/pdfs/ew17-4.pdf.

[34] Interviews with "NA" (Dec 2018) and "M" (Jun 2018).

[35] Uzbek spelling of *maqām* (the system of melodic modes noted above).

kinds have long been popular across Central Asia, and serve to balance local folklore alongside Russian and European influences. Their combined disembodiment and use of third-person commentary create a neutrality that enables a puppet to say things that people cannot.

A Paradigm Shift towards Self-Directed Missional Activities

Since many evangelical believers have few opportunities to meet together, there was an eager response when, in 2018, over forty evangelicals from across Central Asia were invited to gather at a local theological college in Moldova for two weeks. The majority were Muslim background believers but few had accessed any biblical training resources due to lack of internet access or security concerns. Those that did found materials primarily in Russian, and almost all the participants voiced an urgent need for biblical materials in their own local languages. However, contextualisation of art forms in order to bring clearer meaning to the scriptures was a very new concept, and a painful account of the consequences of not having considered this was shared by some amongst the group:[36]

> We are three (young) Christians from Uzbekistan, one of us a former professional dancer, and our house church asked us to move to Kabardino-Balkaria, a Russian republic located in the North Caucasus, for the purpose of undertaking mission. We lived there for three years, and attended a few local cultural celebration events but we did little to integrate with local communities or learn about their local arts, customs or values. We realise now that we assumed the same biblical resources and teaching methodology that had been helpful for us would be equally helpful for others. Since our choice of songs, dance and teaching had little impact, and feeling we were unable to gain people's trust, we returned home.

The paucity of trained Christian leadership reflects a combination of limited materials, legalisation, oppression, isolation and a lingering distrust. Although several Protestant theological colleges exist in Uzbekistan, Kazakhstan and Kyrgyzstan, evangelicals perceive graduates of these institutions as either "Russianised" or else overly westernised: "They have become a stumbling stone to the evangelical church due to their exposure to such values."[37] Added to this is inexperience, which Shamgunov, in his call for a more context-specific and missional model of theological education in Central Asia, refers to as the

---

[36] Interviews – as told by "I," "Z" and "A" (Jun 2018).

[37] Interviews – opinions expressed by "NA," "E" and "S" (Nov 2018). These are further supported by Insur Shamgunov, "Protestant Theological Education in Central Asia: Embattled but Resilient," *East–West Church Ministry Report* 17, no. 4 (Fall 2009): 5-8, accessed Jul 19, 2021, https://www.eastwestreport.org/pdfs/ew17-4.pdf.

"theory–practice divide."[38] In his research on four Protestant theological training institutions, he argues that theologically trained church leaders lack practical experience in contextualising their theological education for real-life ministerial situations, this being a failure of theological institutions to keep pace with the rapidly changing social needs in post-Soviet times.

This research, along with the Kabardino-Balkaria mission example, brings to mind Kosuke Koyama's recommendation that contextualisation for rooting the gospel effectively in a community is dependent on living and building relationships with them, and learning about their culture. Koyama points out that real conversations about theology need to happen on the "dirt floor" of daily life rather than more formalised settings.[39]

Amongst local Christians seeking to address this void in leadership, there is growing awareness that a more intentional and self-directed focus on outreach is needed. Examples are emerging of conversations based on cultural art forms, such as this example of hand-painted ceramic plates and bowls from the Uzbekistan Fergana valley region, using *Rishtan* and *Pakhta* designs.[40]

> We share the gospel via our cultural pottery, which is easy to access as these items are found in every Uzbek home. As Christians, we have assigned new meanings to the traditional patterns, starting with the central dot which represents a person's birth in Christ. Each of the circles that radiate towards the edges of the plate represent important events in a person's life, from their first steps to increasingly complex patterning that represents their interactions with others. The plates often incorporate designs of leaves and trees, representing paradise, and we use them to show God has a future and a hope for us. Before the potter begins to create such a dish, he must trample and knead the clay until all the air bubbles are removed. These bubbles signify the difficulties in our lives and that we should not give up trying to overcome them since God will help us. When a dish is fired, it changes from grey to bright colours, but the potter cannot predict which colours will emerge, or even if the dish will crack. Because of this, potters traditionally pray to a higher being before they fire the dishes, since if a plate emerges flawed, it must be thrown away. As Christians, we see this as God cutting away anything in our lives that is unfruitful.

Whether through pottery or any other form of communication, local evangelicals are seeking to convey messages in ways that are culturally sensitive and appeal to specific audiences. This in turn is causing in-country agencies to

---

[38] Insur Shamgunov, "Listening to the Voice of the Graduate: An Analysis of Professional Practice and Training for Ministry in Central Asia," (PhD thesis, University of Oxford, 2009), 274-75; footnote 71 on p. 284; and 51-53, "Theory–Practice Divide in Theological Education."

[39] Kosuke Koyama, *Water Buffalo Theology*, 25th anniv. ed., rev. and expanded (Maryknoll, NY: Orbis Books, 1999), 60.

[40] Interviews – recounted by "A," Uzbekistan (Jun 2018). The biblical reference is Jn. 15:1-2, the pruning of the vine.

rethink layout designs and illustrations used for scripture materials. In 2016, the first full Bible in the official language of Uzbekistan was published, the result of a partnership of Bible translation agencies in Central Asia.[41] As with the earlier New Testament in Uzbek, the full Bible used carefully chosen ornamental graphic designs on the cover and title pages in accordance with the local aesthetics for sacred texts.

The order in which materials are published is also reflecting value systems within local arts. For example, many Christians in Central Asia see similarities between the cultural setting of the book of Proverbs and their own backgrounds. Local proverbs are widely used, both written and in everyday speech, which is why the book of Proverbs was the first book to be released from the Uzbek Old Testament translation project. A standalone paperback edition of it was so popular that it went through four print runs in a decade, and the government's Committee on Religious Affairs asked the Bible Society of Uzbekistan to provide copies for all public libraries in the country. In 2020, The Gideons International published an Uzbek edition of the New Testament for distribution in the Russian Federation, significantly prefacing it with first the book of Proverbs, then Psalms.[42]

Also in Uzbekistan, a calendar was created in 2018 by local Christians for young Muslim women. It featured verses from Proverbs 31:10-31 describing the attributes of a perfect wife blessed by the Lord. In keeping with cultural expectations that women should be discreet and gracious, each month featured a woman with her face covered as required, but with close-ups of either her decorated hands, clothing or ornaments. These illustrations then drew people towards the accompanying proverb which was highlighted by means of local calligraphy, motifs and appropriate colours.[43]

Identity and Faith Discourse in Central Asia

Many of the examples in this chapter show evangelicals in Central Asia growing in awareness of how arts can intentionally heighten interconnections between local values of identity and the church. Participants of the Moldova event of 2018 came to three key realisations: that faith and arts could be in collaboration;[44] that worship could reflect their post-Soviet identities; and that arts could

---

[41] Amongst those involved in the Uzbek project were IBT (Institute for Bible Translation), UBS (United Bible Societies) and BSU (Bible Society of Uzbekistan). The IBT website lists materials available for download in each language group – see "Translation Projects," Institute for Bible Translation, accessed May 14, 2021, https://ibtrussia.org/en/projects.

[42] Interviews – email information provided by "AF" (Jun 2021).

[43] See chapter 3 of this book for the use of Proverbs in other cultural contexts.

[44] See Roberta R. King and Sooi Ling Tan, eds., *(un)Common Sounds: Songs of Peace and Reconciliation among Muslims and Christians*, Art for Faith's Sake (Eugene, OR: Cascade Books, 2014).

communicate scripture. "If we don't have living, prophetic words from *Isa* in our songs, our churches will become like a marketplace."[45] They started by re-evaluating their existing worship materials such as the Tajik songbook, printed pre-1991 and used in evangelical churches in Tajikistan. One of the Tajik church leaders from those meetings reported:[46]

> Less than 20 out of 226 songs in this book were written by Tajik authors who relate to our cultural song styles. And when I evaluated the themes, I found only three Christian messages represented in the entire songbook – be filled with joy; God provides; He is my shepherd. Our people are searching for knowledge; we need to create songs that share so much more from God's Word!

They also talked of the need for healing and reconciliation, and of ways they could see the arts being helpful in encouraging new believers facing social persecution, or helping common problems such as alcohol addiction.

Further Reading on the Arts and Multifaith Contexts
Dyrness, W. A. *Senses of Devotion: Interfaith Aesthetics in Buddhist and Muslim Communities*. Art for Faith's Sake 7. Eugene, OR: Cascade Books, 2013.
King, R. R. "Performing Witness: Loving Our Religious Neighbors through Musicking." In *The Arts as Witness in Multifaith Contexts*, edited by R. R. King and W. A. Dyrness, 39-68. Missiological Engagements. Downers Grove, IL: IVP Academic, 2019.

The same questions and searching for answers are also emerging amongst Muslims, along with growing disenchantment over the directions being taken by fundamental Islamists. Many have limited understanding of Qur'anic teaching as only Arabic versions can be used for recitation and not everyone understands Arabic sufficiently. Due to recent vernacular versions of the Qur'an being published in multiple languages for personal use,[47] readers are now able to form their own comparisons between Islam and Christianity, with some unexpected outcomes. "Once I read the Qur'an in my own language I realised I was lost."[48] This salient reminder of the need for clear, accurate, natural and acceptable translations is a guiding goal for agencies engaged in translating scripture into local languages.

---

[45] Interviews – comment by "R," a pastor from Kyrgyzstan (Jun 2018), referring to Jn. 2:13-16.

[46] Interviews – quote from "JJ," a Tajik local worker (Jun 2018).

[47] See "List of Translations of the Quran," Wikipedia, accessed Aug 26, 2021, https://en.wikipedia.org/wiki/List_of_translations_of_the_Quran.

[48] David Garrison, "Muslims turning to Christ – a global phenomenon," *Premier Christianity* (May 12, 2016), accessed Aug 26, 2021, https://www.premierchristianity.com/home/muslims-turning-to-christ-a-global-phenomenon/2056.article.

In addition to this, many citizens of Central Asia are, some thirty years later, still trying to separate their understandings of identity from Soviet and Communist Party ideology. Anti-Russian sentiment, particularly in Uzbekistan, is fuelled in part by persistent hardships plus memories of cultural suppression and Russian enculturation, and suspicions remain that all forms of Christianity are in some way shaped by Russia and therefore to be avoided.[49]

> Historically, Russians neglected national people groups such as my own, and stifled our identity. I studied in a Russian school and emerged with that same attitude toward my own people. The love for my culture and history came when I started to read the Old Testament and saw many parallels with our ways of life. I am also now seeing that like-minded brothers and sisters in our national church house groups love their culture and identify themselves with it. This is helping to win souls among our relatives and friends who still consider the ways of Orthodox Christians as a stumbling stone.

In post-Soviet times, the Orthodox Church has been promoted through national authorities as the "traditional religion," emphasising the immutability of its liturgical practice and indirectly serving to downplay democratic freedoms of social modernisation in the minds of Central Asians. "Orthodox discourse rarely conceals its dual purpose, to make society moral but also to destroy the illusion of the West."[50] Partnering this is a level of disillusionment fostered by perceptions that the independent states are failing to deliver promises of affluence and freedom so loudly proclaimed on independence. In Orthodox churches within Russia, there are reports of a recent rise in younger membership,[51] but although the interviewee below mentions "former Soviet Bloc," supportive demographic statistics cannot be found as yet for Central Asia.[52]

> Many of my [Christian] age-mates from the Soviet and former Soviet Bloc have now returned to the Orthodox faith. None of them, even my university friends who studied in the west, talk of the more contemporary types of worship. Instead they desire to connect to a deeper tradition, to the roots, to centuries of liturgical practice, to valuing expressions of worship that trace back to Byzantium.

---

[49] Interview with "NA," a member of a house church in Uzbekistan (Nov 2019).
[50] Peyrouse, "Why Do Central Asian Governments Fear Religion?"
[51] Statistics indicate that the number of younger Russians identifying themselves as Orthodox has risen 43% amongst ages 16-49, but they do not necessarily attend services. "Russians Return to Religion, But Not to Church," Pew Research Center (Feb 10, 2014), accessed May 17, 2021, https://www.pewforum.org/2014/02/10/russians-return-to-religion-but-not-to-church/.
[52] Interviews – email discussion with "AE," a Russian-American student studying in the USA (Nov 2018).

The evangelical church is not immune to so-called "worship wars" between young and old or globalisation and tradition, but the manner in which it seeks to find resolution is increasingly through the less direct nature of arts, seen as helpful in softening disagreements and restoring community by encouraging group participation. An example in Central Asia is a dance depicting a popular moral tale of a grandmother complaining that her grandchild needs to learn how to clean a house the "proper way." Showing mutual exasperation, the older lady uses a folk dance style to enact cleaning, whilst her grandchild insists on using contemporary dance movements. Eventually, they agree they should learn from each other, an acceptance of generational difference that is greatly enjoyed by onlookers and in a small way exemplifies how Central Asia is negotiating sentiments of co-existence. Using art forms such as this to enact solutions to challenging times attracts people from all faiths and walks of life who are in search of answers, and inter-faith barriers are often set aside when the arts are involved, since they present a unique opportunity to foster respect and dialogue.

Generational gaps are significant in Central Asia as many of those who endured decades of atheist propaganda during Soviet times now co-exist with an increasingly liberal post-1991 generation. Discussions on concepts of identity and memory, politics and education are common both in homes and amongst published scholars of this region.[53] Add to this the emergence of increasingly hybridised multilingual identities for whom translanguaging[54] and multilingualism are the new normal, and a strong correlation with arts emerges.[55] "Transmusicking" could be defined as people who are already familiar with multiple musical practices (or "multimusical"), choosing to use selective expressions that are meaningful to specific events, localities and social contexts rather than entirely switching into the music system of those contexts. This has been evidenced in the sharing of artistic genres and musical instruments across borders in Central Asia (reference earlier comments on UNESCO), and with

---

[53] Examples in these Routledge publication series, Central Asia Research Forum and Advances in Central Asian Studies include, respectively (i) Timur Dadabaev, *Identity and Memory in Post-Soviet Central Asia: Uzbekistan's Soviet Past* (London and New York: Routledge, 2016); (ii) David Radford, "Religious Conversion and Its Impact on Ethnic Identity in Post-Soviet Kyrgyzstan," in *Politics, Identity and Education in Central Asia: Post-Soviet Kyrgyzstan*, ed. Pınar Akçalı and Cennet Engin-Demir (London and New York: Routledge, 2013), 118-30.

[54] For definition, see Sangsok Son, "Translanguaging, Identity, and Education in Our Multilingual World," in *Language and Identity in a Multilingual Migrating World*, eds. J. Stephen Quakenbush and Gary F. Simons (Dallas, TX: SIL International Pike Center, 2019), 131, 135 – available online (free to download): http://leanpub.com/languageandidentity.

[55] SIL International's MUSE Initiative (Multilingualism, Urbanization, and Scripture Engagement) points to language communities becoming less linguistically homogenous. "What is the "heart language" in multilingual communities?" SIL International (Aug 2017), accessed May 3, 2021, https://www.sil.org/about/multilingual-communities.

growing access to global music, is resulting in multiple layers and blends of expressions that adjust to the context of each situation.

Believers are actively seeking opportunities to meet in less regulated locations and explore these convergences between regional and other song genres:[56]

> Myself and other house church members recently travelled to Tashkent to worship together. An older believer, a professional musician, had brought a traditional long necked lyre (*dutar*),[57] another had a frame drum with metal rings (*doira*), and there was also an accordion. The younger believers brought guitars, and at first it seemed as if finding common ground was unlikely. But then we decided to share our skills, try out different ideas and see what might emerge. Some chose folk tunes from their own cultures, adding messages about God, cultural dance, costumes and instruments and calling these "new national church melodies." They were very popular with our entire group and we all joined in, but those who created the songs knew little of the Bible and their words were expressing emotions rather than helping to convey scripture teaching. Someone from Kazakhstan with an Orthodox background set gospel messages to solo liturgical chant, and a group of younger people sang new songs to *estrada*[58] backing tracks on their phones. We learnt many things from each other, but the most important was that despite being from different generations, backgrounds and locations, we shared a common sense of purpose, unity and identity in our faith.

Further Reading on Music in Central Asia
Levin, T., S. Daukeyeva and E. Köchümkulova, eds. *The Music of Central Asia*. Bloomington: Indiana University Press, 2016. (Includes online recordings).   Shiloah, A. *Music in the World of Islam: A Socio-Cultural Study*. Detroit, MI: Wayne State University Press, 1995.

Examples of Faith Engagement through the Arts

Along with this growing cultural and generational symbiosis, negotiation between artistic idioms is now fronting a more fundamental question for Christians – that of dialoguing with Muslims on deeper truths in the Bible. In

[56] Interview with "M," a Uyghur house church leader now living in Kazakhstan (Jun 2018).

[57] A popular two-string instrument common to much of Central Asia.

[58] *Estrada* is a term that emerged in the early 1900s, referring to popular music that incorporates many influences including national genres. In recent writings it is described as "tradition-based" or "mainstream popular music," terms introduced by Federico Spinetti, "Tradition-Based Popular Music in Contemporary Tajikistan," and Kerstin Klenke, "Popular Music in Uzbekistan," in *The Music of Central Asia,* eds. Theodore Levin, Saida Daukeyeva and Elmira Köchümkulova (Bloomington: Indiana University Press, 2016), 586 and 556-58, respectively.

addition to the Torah, Islamic classical literature has many references to *masih* and *Isa* (Jesus),[59] which the poet Alisher Navoi (also Nava'i, 1441-1501) chose to represent as symbolic and metaphorical images in his *ghazals*.

The following example is from a collection entitled "*Badoyi ul-Bidoya*" ("The Rarity of the Beginning")[60] and translated from the Chagatai language:

> Like Jesus, she gives life with her ruby lips,
> And, like Joseph, she captivates our hearts with the beauty of her face.
> The smile of the sweet-lipped beauty dressed in yellow
> is like the Messiah hidden in the sun.
> My soul, like a bird, was trapped by the lady of Tarsus with the spirit of
>   the Messiah,
> like a bat in the corner of the dome in the chapel of angels.

Classical lyric poetry often uses parallelism, and in Navoi's writing, "lips" commonly symbolise divine words whose function is "to give life" or to animate love. The addition of ruby colouring indicates a depth to which these divine words will reach, and Joseph (Yusuf) symbolises mental and physical beauty. The yellow dress alludes to the sun, whilst the image of a bat "plays a special role in the interpretation of the personality of Masih, … with the will of the Highest, … a metaphor for the bird of the soul."[61] Since Muslims revere *Isa* as a prophet, Uzbek Christians see Navoi's poetry as an opportunity to draw them into dialogue. In addition to written poetry, recent videos have emerged in Kyrgyzstan of an entire sermon delivered as improvised poetry by a Christian pastor (now deceased). This was not the *aitys* genre (mentioned earlier), which

---

[59] The term *masih* or *masihiy* ("of the Messiah") is a qur'anic transliteration of the Hebrew term *meshiach* ("anointed one"), and in addition to *Isa*, is used as a title for Jesus by Muslims and Arabic-speaking Christians. For Muslims, *masih* is reduced to a unique honorific for Jesus, whilst Christians have infused the transliterated term with the biblical significance of *meshiach/christos* "the anointed one." Part of the debate concerning the literary works of Navoi is how he interpreted the terms *masih* and *Isa.*

[60] Navoi (1441-1501) was a man of multiple talents – musician, composer, painter, sculptor, dramatist and poet. His prolific writing subsequently earned him the nickname "Chaucer of the Turks" – see Barry Hoberman, "Chaucer of the Turks," *Saudi Aramco World* 36, no. 1 (1985): 24-27. He was unusual in preferring to write in the Turkic language of Chagatai (Chaghatay) instead of Persian or Arabic, but that language declined in use between the 17th and 19th centuries, replaced by modern Central Asian Turkic languages such as Uzbek, Kazakh and Kyrghyz. Navoi's *ghazals* (poetic odes) continue to be highly respected amongst Uzbeks today, incorporated in the traditions of *maqom* or art song with instrumental music. His handwritten works from the 15th century were published in 1987 as 20 volumes, and the example cited is a poem about "a lady of Tarsus" – see Alisher Navoi, "Badoyi ul-Bidoya," in *A Collection of Navoi's Completed Works 1* (Tashkent: Fan Publishing, 1987), 160 (editor unknown).

[61] U. U. Kobilov, "Interpretation of the Image of Masih in the Divan of Alisher Navoi "Badoyi ul-Bidoya" ("The Rarity of the Beginning")," *Theoretical and Applied Science* 72, no. 4 (2019): 44.

to this point has never been used for Christian themes, but the pastor recognising that improvised poetry is valued in his community and causes people to listen more intently to the message it conveys.

The themes of secular wisdom, common humanity and God as Creator are appreciated by both Muslims and Christians, and are often included in songs, dramas and local storytelling. However, Muslims dispute key elements of the biblical narrative that are not incorporated in the Qur'an, and finding a means to extend their understanding can be challenging. Those who become Christians will have experienced some form of comparative bridging between the Qur'an and Bible yet, post-conversion, they often speak of "cutting" or distancing themselves entirely from the Qur'an, thus closing potential means of dialogue between the two faiths. If from backgrounds of folk Islam, they are less likely to be concerned with the Islamic interpretations of "music" as found in the Hadith,[62] whilst others may describe themselves as having been an "atheist Muslim," only identifying with Islam to indicate their cultural background.[63] Pelkmans adds, "the description of Christian is often replaced by "follower of *Isa* [Jesus]," a practice which avoids some ethno-religious sensitivities and lends credence to the ideal of forming a world community of faith that transcends cultural and ethnic differences."

---

[62] The Hadith are a collection of sayings and deeds of the Prophet Muhammad along with other early Muslims, and are considered an authoritative source of revelation, second only to the Qur'an. They are believed to have emerged during the two centuries after Muhammad's death in 632 AD, after which they were collected in written form and codified. No direct mention of "music" exists in the Qur'an.

[63] Mathijs Pelkmans, "Introduction: Post-Soviet Space and the Unexpected Turns of Religious Life," in *Conversion after Socialism: Disruptions, Modernisms and Technologies of Faith in the Former Soviet Union*, ed. Mathijs Pelkmans (Oxford: Berghahn Books, 2009), 6-11.

Book Idea

King, R. R., and S. L. Tan, eds. *(un)Common Sounds: Songs of Peace and Reconciliation among Muslims and Christians*. Art for Faith's Sake. Eugene, OR: Cascade Books, 2014.

This book documents ways in which music-making of Christian and Islamic communities can interact and lead to greater understanding and empathy towards reconciliation. It begins with historical examples and theological reflections from both faiths, and at its heart is a discussion of the potential of music for cooperation, as well as peace and reconciliation in a range of contexts shared through case studies. It concludes by exploring how musical encounter can lead towards more enduring relationships.

Growth and Dispersal – Strategies of Contextualised Media

Options for printed materials in rural parts of Central Asia are minimal, and in the villages much happens orally, especially through storytelling.[64] Increasingly commonplace alongside oral preference are mobile phones and the internet, although the latter remains a long way from becoming fully available in many parts. In April 2021, DataReportal indicated 57% internet penetration in Central Asia,[65] with country-specific figures being Kazakhstan 82%, Uzbekistan 55%, Kyrgyzstan 50%, Turkmenistan 33% and Tajikistan 26%, but actual usage is far lower due to the cost of broadband, slow connections, government restrictions and censorship.[66] Political authorities exert tight control over external social media sites, but as of 2021, the Bible Society is officially registered in all countries of Central Asia with the exception of Turkmenistan, producing biblical materials in local languages, many of which are available online.

Despite the communicative limitations that Christians in Central Asia face, phones are considered a "cultural insider" for many, enabling personal interaction with the gospel and providing an easy way to share resources amongst

---

[64] From an unpublished EthnoArts Survey undertaken in 2018 by SIL in Eurasia, looking at artistic expressions in various language communities and how they are currently being used.

[65] See Simon Kemp, "6 in 10 People Around the World Now Use the Internet," DataReportal (Apr 26, 2021), accessed Jul 19, 2021, https://datareportal.com/reports/6-in-10-people-around-the-world-now-use-the-internet. Data on this site is constantly updated, providing statistics on how the internet is being used globally and by whom. Using "search" for each of the Central Asia countries reveals individual statistics. Note that offline mobile phone use is more difficult to ascertain.

[66] In Turkmenistan, for example, Turkmen Telekom, the only internet provider, is government-run, whilst Facebook, Twitter, YouTube, VKontakte (a Russian social media site) and numerous news websites have been blocked.

house church members. More importantly, they also enable local believers to create their own contextualised digital scripture products via apps and social media platforms. Local churches in Uzbekistan currently lack the means to make professional productions, but are recording and disseminating songs and other media as best they can via phones. Whereas the printing press was considered a historical watershed in enabling dissemination of faith-related materials, the use of mobile phones and digital media is equally significant in regions such as Central Asia.

The following short example demonstrates how a media app is building upon the arts in ways determined by local believers. Using either an offline or online phone device, users are able to create locally-produced audio-visual Bible stories within their own homes. Choosing from a collection of story boards within the app, users can translate and record a version in their own language, and may also directly record and insert their own songs, proverbs or poetry, merging all these into a new localised video or audio file. The finished product can then be distributed via Bluetooth or online via social media, to all types of devices. In short, this is a self-directed and simple media tool, which at the time of writing is being evaluated in one of the Central Asian countries.[67]

A second example is a production by an external film agency giving voice to communities in a story of family values and reconciliation, but with an unexpected ending.[68] Entirely filmed in a remote mountainous area of Tajikistan, its cast comprises local villagers going about their daily lives of subsistence farming and social interactions. Many nuances of their culture are captured, and as is fitting for a Muslim community, the film includes quotes from the Qur'an in addition to the use of local proverbs. Near the end, a series of flashbacks to earlier scenes are shown, each accompanied with a relevant verse from Matthew 5:3-10. The author watched this film whilst seated beside a Christian from that country, who, with tears in his eyes at the end, quietly said, "All of us must wrestle with such things. These are my people and my culture. Christ is speaking through this film."

Another external agency released three short scripture films in 2018 that incorporate scenes filmed in Uzbekistan along with other media, integrated with text from the Bible. Dissemination of these videos is difficult due to YouTube being blocked in Uzbekistan, but the idea of embodiment or putting people into the story has many benefits. In "The Bride's Ten Friends"[69] (Matthew 25:1-13),

---

[67] Populated with Bible story video templates, this free app is now deploying around the world. "Story Producer App," SIL International Media Services, accessed Aug 26, 2021, https://www.internationalmediaservices.org/story-producer.

[68] Produced by GemStone Media, an international film production company, "The Traveler" is available in many languages. For an English version, see GemStone Media, "The Traveler – English," Vimeo, accessed May 14, 2021, https://vimeo.com/327554260.

[69] Released by Create International, a communication ministry producing and distributing indigenous media resources globally – "Келиннинг ўнта дугонаси" [The

the process of production reportedly made a significant impact on the girls involved,[70] increasing their understanding even if they were already familiar with the parable. The use of drama, along with traditional Uzbek clothing, music, customs and local artefacts enabled a scripture passage already available in print-form in the local language (Uzbek) to become clearer and more relatable to people's experiences.

Reports indicate that whenever access is possible, people of all faiths enjoy watching films/videos such as these, drawn by the growing sensitisation amongst global Christian agencies to create materials that are both culturally appropriate and engaging for Central Asia. Increasing attention is being given to the contextualising of materials for intended audiences, using local artists for illustrations, filming in-country where possible, and considering choices of language, music and arts, materials and other cultural markers.

Conclusion

Considering the value given to the arts in this part of the world, it is fitting that artistic practices, whether old, new or interfused,[71] are contributing towards the survival and reinvigoration of a deeply persecuted body of believers. The complexity of contexts in Central Asia invites a complex strategy for sharing the Christian faith, and the difficulties for outside Christian workers to maintain a long-term presence in the region does not mean that the evangelical churches are closed to external help. What needs to be acknowledged is that, increasingly, local Christians are searching for their own ministry approaches, open to positioning the gospel message in combination with their own expressions and those of other faiths around them. It is these expressions that the Lausanne Forum "Redeeming the Arts (2004)" saw as the artistic yeast speaking to the future of this and every other church:[72]

> God's act of breaking into history in Jesus is brilliantly creative … One of the ways that the yeast of kingdom presence can be at work in the world is through the arts. Art that is born out of an understanding of the biblical narrative can speak eloquently to a world that has forgotten the story that offers the hope of a new reality. The arts engage our imaginations … They cause us to think rather than tell

---

Bride's Ten Friends], YouTube, https://youtu.be/ca9mm9AnOmk; "Дониёр мақбараси" [Daniel's Tomb], YouTube, https://youtu.be/_wR9Uml7Z1Y; and "Чашмаи Аюб" [Job's Spring], YouTube, https://youtu.be/s_7LF_vB68M – all accessed Jun 7, 2021.

[70] Interview – email and online with "NA" in Dec 2018 and Mar 2021.

[71] See earlier comments on translanguaging, transmusicking and *estrada*.

[72] Lausanne Movement, "Redeeming the Arts: The Restoration of the Arts to God's Creational Intention," Lausanne Occasional Paper, no. 46 (2004), accessed Aug 26, 2021, https://lausanne.org/content/lop/redeeming-arts-restoration-arts-gods-creational-intention-lop-46, Act III: Transformation.

us what to think. So like yeast, they are able to generate newness that will serve to nurture us in heart and mind.

This chapter has gone a small way in identifying some of the missional issues relating to Central Asia, as well as illustrating how the arts are contributing to the imagining and resilience of the evangelical church in this region. Andrew Walls speaks of Christianity as "reordering the elements that are already there so that they may face toward Christ,"[73] and although he may not only have had arts in mind, their presence at every turn of the turbulent history of Central Asia causes us to consider how faith in partnership with the arts can survive and even thrive in oppressive situations. The complacency of Christianity that Bosch sees in the west cannot be applied to the evangelical church in Central Asia.[74] Its members consistently evidence hallmarks of hope, courage and patience, and further studies relating Christian faith to the arts within Central Asia are greatly needed.

Questions for Reflection/Discussion
1. How might the creative interactions and proliferation of artistic expressions within the religions in Central Asia along the Silk Road and the examples from Russian Orthodoxy suggest opportunities for contemporary artists?
2. The paradigm shift to self-directed missional activities shows *local* approaches to the arts. What lessons can be drawn from the importance of "the local" in this discussion?
3. How might terms such as "translanguaging," "transmusicking" and "*estrada*" suggest challenges and opportunities for artists as they consider identity in Central Asian cultures?
4. The final section contrasts "traditional" arts with the possibilities of modern digital media. How does this shed light on the comment about how "artistic practices, whether old, new or interfused, are contributing towards the survival and reinvigoration" of the Christian community?

---

[73] Quote by Andrew Walls, used in Werner Ustorf, "A Missiological Postscript," in *The Decline of Christendom in Western Europe, 1750-2000*, eds. Hugh McLeod and Werner Ustorf (Cambridge: Cambridge University Press, 2003), 224.
[74] David J. Bosch, *Transforming Mission: Paradigm Shifts in Theology of Mission*, American Society of Missiology 16 (Maryknoll, NY: Orbis Books, 1991), 476.

8. A Practical Approach to Arts and Mission Courses:
Reflections on "Arts for a Better Future"
Robin Harris and Brian Schrag

Robin Harris and Brian Schrag show the importance of developing relevant arts and mission training courses. Using the "Arts for a Better Future" course as a case study, they show how well-crafted training gives participants the skills to empower local communities to use their arts for meeting community goals that extend the kingdom of God.[1]

When People Learn the Truth about Arts and God's Kingdom

In January 2020, our team of four arrived at Singapore Bible College to teach the first full "Arts for a Better Future" course to be held in Asia. We were amazed to learn that our course roster was packed to bursting with thirty-two students from nine countries: Philippines, India, Indonesia, China, Myanmar, Malaysia, Thailand, South Korea, and Singapore. Many of these students held positions of leadership in organisations and churches back home, and others had been serving in difficult countries beyond the list just mentioned. We also enjoyed having five cross-cultural workers with WEC Singapore in the class, and with our multinational team of facilitators (Taiwan, UK and USA), the class total of over forty people represented the largest group of credit-seeking students in the nine-year history of the course. One thing that we found striking, and which reminded us of the importance of arts and mission training, was the students' descriptions us how arts were used in their ministry contexts back home. Their testimonies were remarkably similar. One student lamented:

---

[1] This chapter draws from an earlier article: Brian Schrag, "Arts for a Better Future: A Practical Approach for Energizing Ministry in Oral Cultures," *Orality Journal* 5, no. 2 (2016): 51-58, accessed Oct 14, 2021, https://orality.net/library/journals/volume-5-number-2/, as well as descriptions of the workshop at "Arts for a Better Future," Global Ethnodoxology Network, accessed Oct 14, 2021, https://www.worldofworship.org/artsforabetterfuture/.

Twenty years ago I started my first music ministry in my hometown church in Indonesia; a Reformed, multi-ethnic congregation with a strong Chinese mentality that was surrounded by Javanese culture and art. One day I asked an elder, "Why don't we use gamelan in our worship services?" and I got this reply, "Because only hymns and Western music are appropriate for God. Ethnic music is for pagan gods and idolatry." As a newcomer in worship and music ministry, I had no arguments I could use to answer. Then, for the following twenty years in ministry, I almost always had these questions: "What is true worship and godly music according to my artistic context? As an Indonesian, why cannot I be an Indonesian when I worship God?"

This student's comments were echoed again and again by other students in the course. A student from Nagaland in India wrote:

This [training] made me realize the importance of studying cultures and being able to connect with them before engaging in the Word and spreading the good news. Most of the time it's all about our system and beliefs, and we forget to do the most important aspect – knowing them. I believe if this method [of arts in mission] is imparted in our society, there will be a shift in how we worship God by bringing out our best and also having a clear understanding of our culture and tradition.

These two testimonies express what *all* of the students shared: an eagerness to learn how to deal with the complexities of context and culture in relation to the arts, and the need for new approaches and attitudes towards arts in ministry in their home contexts.

Recognition of the Role of Arts and
Mission Training Courses for Cultural Learning

In *Arts Ministry*, Michael Bauer notes that artists' unusual capacity for "intuition" often remains unnoticed or disconnected from church and mission activities. This results in part from artists' lack of theological education. "This can be a problem when … they are called upon to exegete scripture or interpret a theological concept." Both artists and theologians want to be creative in their handling of the scriptures as a source, which would benefit from "the intellectual and theological resources that are needed to interpret the Christian tradition with insight and depth."[2]

Artists writing on behalf of the Lausanne Movement in "Redeeming the Arts (2004)" make similar points about the importance of learning how to understand the artistic forms of different cultures. The allusive and symbolic character of artistic products are often subtle, nuanced and sophisticated, unintelligible to those not trained to learn about arts foreign to them.

---

[2] See Bauer, *Arts Ministry*, 29.

Indigenous arts are expressive, intrinsic communication forms that are integrated within and across the structures of society where they define and sustain cultural norms and values. We must come to see that becoming acquainted with the artistic expressions of diverse cultures is as important as attending language school in preparation for mission work.[3]

In their summary of aims, these artists note specifically the importance of training for those with artistic gifts within the church. This begins by identifying people with artistic gifts, followed by creating educational courses and facilities. They further note the need to find mentors with the appropriate skills.

Echoing this call, the Lutheran World Federation, in "The Nairobi Statement on Worship and Culture (1996)," notes that the rise of the global church should encourage churches everywhere to explore "the local or contextual elements of liturgy, language, posture and gesture, hymnody and other music and musical instruments, and art and architecture for Christian worship"[4] with the aim of developing the local character of worship. This has clear implications for training in mission and evangelism globally, often requiring "scholarships for persons from the developing world to study worship, church music, and church architecture, towards the eventual goal that enhanced theological training in their churches can be led by local teachers." These documents clearly show the need to integrate the study of local arts into theological and missional training so that Christian artists can function well in evangelism and mission. Appreciation of local cultures and arts helps communicate the Christian message in ways that powerfully appeal to local people.

Theological Foundations for Incarnational Ministry in Arts and Mission

We base certain aspects of the theology and methodology of arts and mission training on Paul's counsel to the Christians in Philippi. He offers important insight into the attitudes that must deeply shape our ministry to others in their local cultural contexts. Paul's concern in Philippians is that Christians follow Jesus' example in showing humility and a concern for others in all our relationships. He writes:[5]

> In humility value others above yourselves, not looking to your own interests
>   but each of you to the interests of the others.
> In your relationships with one another, have the same mindset as Christ Jesus:
>   who, being in very nature God, did not consider equality with God
>   something to be used to his own advantage;
>   rather, he made himself nothing

---

[3] Redeeming the Arts, Act III – Scene II: The Arts, Evangelism and Contextualization in Mission – Heart Language.

[4] The Nairobi Statement on Worship and Culture, Section 6 – Challenge to the Churches.

[5] Phil. 2:3b-8 (NIV).

by taking the very nature of a servant,
being made in human likeness.
And being found in appearance as a man,
he humbled himself
by becoming obedient to death –
even death on a cross!

In developing arts and mission training courses, it is important to train missionaries and artists to reflect these attitudes towards others, including their local arts and other cultural expressions. This is not just a matter of personal spirituality, but models the respect, empathy, and understanding that must characterise Christ-like missional engagement. Beyond this description of the self-emptying of Jesus in Philippians 2, there are other aspects of the incarnation that are relevant for arts practitioners. The incarnation helps us to understand the kind of cultural identifications that Jesus made with the Jewish people in their Middle Eastern context. His parables, for example, show an intimate knowledge of the cultural settings and the way of life of his hearers living in an agrarian society.[6]

Three aspects of Jesus' incarnation point us to how we should engage in mission:

1. Be with. Jesus left his "home culture" with God the Father and joined humanity in a particular cultural context in the Middle East.

Our **first** task in mission is to live with people in the community and build relationships. Incarnational ministry, as modelled by Jesus, requires *presence* and is founded on loving relationships.

2. Learn from. Jesus learned from human beings in his Jewish community for almost thirty years before he began his public ministry.

Our **second** interaction as arts facilitators is to learn. We can do this by asking people about their community's arts and the kind of goals they would like to develop in relation to the kingdom of God. The kingdom of God has many markers but, for example, we can encourage people to think about goals related to human dignity, strengthening people's identity, well-being, or supporting the human rights of a community.[7] Or we can foster discussion about spiritual goals such as bolstering church life, scripture use, evangelism, or the personal spiritual

---

[6] For the Middle Eastern context see Kenneth E. Bailey, *Jesus through Middle Eastern Eyes: Cultural Studies in the Gospels* (Downers Grove, IL: IVP Academic, 2008). For the process of contextualisation that is already active in the New Testament itself, see Dean E. Flemming, *Contextualization in the New Testament: Patterns for Theology and Mission* (Downers Grove, IL: IVP Academic, 2005).

[7] Brian Schrag and Kathleen J. Van Buren, *Make Arts for a Better Life: A Guide for Working with Communities* (New York: Oxford University Press, 2018).

life of people in a community.[8] We show communities love by learning from them about their own culture and its related artistic expressions. Though this requires intentional asking and listening that may take a long time, it is essential to mission methods and in nurturing authenticity in our mutual relationships.

3. Work towards. Only after going to humans and learning from them for three decades did Jesus announce and fulfil his purpose publicly (Matthew 4:23). He worked side by side with his disciples towards the goals of the kingdom of God.

Jesus healed, taught, and exorcised those with demons. He rebuked, comforted, affirmed, endured torture and ridicule, died, rose from the dead, and sent his people to preach and act out the good news of the kingdom all over the world.

Our ***third*** missional activity, after going *to* people and learning *from* them, is to work towards kingdom goals *with* them. As arts facilitators, we do this by exploring with our friends and colleagues in the community how we might work together to use their local arts to meet the goals they would like to accomplish. These three elements dovetail beautifully with a bedrock of missiological best practice: contextualisation, which Wilbur Shenk[9] describes as

"… a process whereby the gospel message encounters a particular culture, calling forth faith and leading to the formulation of a faith community, which is culturally authentic and authentically Christian …. Control of the process resides within the context rather than with an external agent or agency."

The term "local arts" reminds us that we are interested in engaging with arts that already exist within the local community. "Creating" speaks of the generative process that takes artistic ideas and shapes them in intriguing, purpose-filled ways. "Together" reminds us that arts advocates need to work alongside local communities, catalysing creativity from within, not imposing their will from without.

From Theology to Methodology: Creating Local Arts Together

Thus grounded, artists transform the "be with," "learn from," and "work towards" theological framework into a seven-stage process called Creating Local Arts Together (also known as CLAT).

---

[8] See further Brian Schrag, *Creating Local Arts Together: A Manual to Help Communities Reach Their Kingdom Goals* (Pasadena, CA: William Carey Library, 2013).

[9] Wilbert R. Shenk, *Changing Frontiers of Mission*, American Society of Missiology 28 (Maryknoll, NY: Orbis Books, 1999), 56.

The Seven Steps of Creating Local Arts Together

The CLAT process is a flexible model, rich in elements of participatory community interaction. An arts advocate – someone from within, outside, or most likely a unique combination of insider/outsider identities – adopts a role primarily as a facilitator in which communities choose, evaluate, and implement activities that will result in the growth of the kingdom of God in their midst. Though presented as seven sequential steps (or just as accurately, conversations), real life contexts almost always require changing the order and repeating certain elements. Nevertheless, this format bolsters teaching the method and provides a starting place and conceptual structure to refer to during engagement with communities. The seven steps of the Creating Local Arts Together process follow.

Communities and arts advocates together perform these activities:

1. *Meet* a Community and Its Arts.

Explore artistic and social resources that exist in the community. Performing *Step 1* allows you to build relationships, involve and understand the people, and discover the hidden treasures of the community.

2. *Specify* Goals.

Discover the goals that the community wants to work towards. Performing *Step 2* ensures that you are helping the community work towards aims that they have agreed on together.

3. *Connect* Goals to an Artistic Genre.

The community chooses an artistic genre that can help it meet its goals and find activities that can result in purposeful creativity in this genre. Performing *Step 3* reveals the mechanisms that relate certain kinds of artistic activity to its effects, so that the activities the community performs have a high chance of succeeding.

4. *Analyse* an Event Containing the Chosen Genre.

Describe the event and its genre(s) in terms of artistic form and cultural context. Performing *Step 4* results in detailed knowledge of the art forms that is crucial to sparking creativity, improving what is produced, and integrating it into the community.

5. *Spark* Creativity.

Work with the community to encourage the creation of local arts towards their kingdom goals. Performing *Step 5* actually produces new artistic works, initiatives, or events.

6. *Improve* Results.

Together with the community, evaluate outcomes of the sparking activities and make them better. Performing *Step 6* makes sure that the new artistry exhibits the aesthetic qualities, produces the impacts, and communicates the intended messages at a level of quality appropriate to its purposes.

7. *Integrate and Celebrate* for Continuity.

Plan and implement ways with the community that this new kind of creativity can continue into the future. Identify more contexts where the new and old arts can be displayed and performed. Performing *Step 7* makes it more likely that a community will keep making its arts in ways that produce good effects long into the future.

The seven steps of this process (which are really seven conversations) are outlined and expanded and their relevance is shown to specific communities and projects. In the light of that overview and through an analysis of real-life existing projects, participants start outlining the seven steps in relation to possible projects of their own. This allows them to refine practice in the light of theory and find ways of making the training relevant to the arts of their own communities.

Texts for Teaching Creating Local Arts Together

Creating Local Arts Together: A Manual to Help Communities Reach Their Kingdom Goals[10] facilitates and offers a more nuanced account of the CLAT process. The "Manual" is structured as seven chapters that correspond to the seven steps. A condensed and simplified version of the Manual – *Community Arts for God's Purposes* – is being translated into multiple languages for use in workshops around the world.[11]

A second volume – *Worship and Mission for the Global Church: An Ethnodoxology Handbook*[12] – helps arts practitioners ground their activities even more in sound theology and methodology. Drawing from experiences from within and beyond a growing network of arts and missions practitioners called the Global Ethnodoxology Network (GEN – formerly the International Council of Ethnodoxologists), the "Ethnodoxology Handbook" offers an excellent

---

[10] Schrag, *Creating Local Arts Together*. See also the condensed version – Brian Schrag and Julisa Rowe, *Community Arts for God's Purposes: How to Create Local Artistry Together* (Pasadena: William Carey Publishers, 2020).

[11] See the English version of Schrag and Rowe, *Community Arts for God's Purposes* here: https://missionbooks.org/products/community-arts-for-gods-purposes. Other Asian languages planned for publication include Chinese, Korean, Mongolian, and Bahasa Indonesian, but several non-Asian languages are in process as well.

[12] James R. Krabill, Frank Fortunato, Robin P. Harris and Brian Schrag, eds., *Worship and Mission for the Global Church: An Ethnodoxology Handbook* (Pasadena, CA: William Carey Library, 2013).

review of theory with numerous case studies of projects which have been developed in a range of artistic forms in all the continents of the world. Asian projects include a range of settings from South East Asia through to Eurasia.

Both resources aim to be accessible to a wide audience and include the sorts of materials appropriate both for tertiary education and in churches and local communities. They guide missionaries, mission executives, project leaders, and arts advocates in planning, applying, and extending their understanding of the roles of arts in mission. When integrated into training courses, then, the materials contain theoretical foundations and provide references to a range of wider resources that deal more deeply with both theory and the real world. The book addresses aspects of ethnodoxology (arts in mission) such as biblical and cultural foundations; historical, missiological, and liturgical perspectives; stories from all the major regions of the world; and practical "how to" chapters on arts advocacy, teaching, multicultural worship, culturally appropriate worship, and integration of arts with preaching and scripture proclamation.

"Arts for a Better Future": A Case Study for Arts and Mission Training

Although there are other outstanding examples of courses that prepare people for effective service in arts and mission, we are using the "Arts for a Better Future" (ABF) course as a case study for two reasons. Firstly, it teaches the Creating Local Arts Together method that is based on grounded theological and missiological principles. Secondly, this course now has been tested over ten years with research through surveys that show its effectiveness and relevance for artists with missional vocations and interests. In what follows, ABF's content and pedagogical innovations are explored.[13]

The "Arts for a Better Future" Course: Pedagogy and Impact

"Arts for a Better Future" teaches participants how to have arts-orientated and kingdom-orientated conversations with communities they know and care about. In order to help the participants absorb this approach, we work through the process three times, with each cycle requiring more responsibility from participants than the preceding one. It concludes with "Phase Infinity," indicating that the process is ultimately open-ended and leads into the future and to a wider circle of participants and artists.

> **Phase One:** One of the instructors shares with the students a story of following this model with a real community somewhere in the world.[14] This phase shows students

---

[13] See Appendix 1 for assessments of ABF on six continents of the world, with people from over 60 countries, discussion of venues and the numbers of people trained increasing since its launch in 2012, with results that are consistently encouraging.

[14] For an example, see Brian Schrag's own story, Brian Schrag, "Chorale Ayo, narrated by Brian Schrag," YouTube, accessed Aug 2, 2021, https://youtu.be/AocDAQb4vQ8

that the teacher has personally seen the model work, and what the results would look like in a context different from their own. It also exposes the student for the first time to the seven steps (or conversations) that comprise the core of this model of community engagement through arts.

Phase Two: The instructors guide the participants through practising the approach with the representative of a community that is unfamiliar to them. Choosing an unfamiliar culture to study in Phase Two is key, since it motivates students to learn about the community and does not distract them by its similarity to something they think they understand. This phase requires two instructors, one who plays the role of Facilitator, guiding the conversation and making sure that each student participates, and a Community Representative who is carefully trained and prepared to respond to the students' questions in a way that helps them practise the skills of ethnographic inquiry that undergird the seven conversations of the method.

Phase Three: Participants break into groups of four to six people and apply the process with a community that one or more people in the group knows well. After working through the seven steps, each group leaves with a concrete plan they have created to help them connect their arts to their kingdom goal. This phase involves more independent work, since the facilitators, the community representatives, as well as those asking questions, are all present in the small group. The course instructors, instead of being highly involved in the process, are merely available nearby for questions or for getting the group "unstuck" if they experience problems in the process.

Phase Infinity: We are developing ways for participants to get the support they need to follow through with implementing their plans so that they can convey these principles to others. This stage connects to a wider range of groups – existing Christian communities, churches, mission organisations and artists. Students who take the course for graduate credit do the full process with a community of their choice, with the opportunity to receive support and feedback from the course professor during the process. Non-credit students have sought out support in a variety of ways: Facebook and WhatsApp groups, online member forums from the Global Ethnodoxology Network, and personal contacts with others in the workshop.

From the point of view of pedagogy, the "going deeper" multiple-phased methodology of "Arts for a Better Future" is an effective way to increase students' skills in the methodology gradually. First, it allows students to merely listen to the steps in story form (Phase One), then to practise the steps with significant guidance from the facilitators (Phase Two), then to work in teams with more independence (Phase Three), followed by a completely independent project if the student is doing the course for credit (Phase Infinity).

(Available in English, Spanish, and Swahili on Brian Schrag's YouTube channel). See also for similar projects, Global Ethnodoxology Network, YouTube, accessed Aug 2, 2021, https://www.youtube.com/user/ethnodoxology.

Another key aspect leading to the efficacy of the course is the way it uses the arts in the teaching process. For example, students interact in a role play with a community representative during Phase Two, an exercise using drama that makes the process of learning fun and engaging. In addition, we always include an arts sharing night in which students are encouraged to bring something they have created to share with others – a dance, a song, a piece of visual or craft art, a skit, photography, poetry of any genre, a story, ethnic cuisine or dress. In short, any kind of creative expression they have worked on. We have found that the atmosphere in class is always different after these evenings of sharing. We see increased mutual respect between participants, a new appreciation of the broad variety of arts for kingdom purposes, and a more positive view of how the arts can impact our relationship with God.

Finally, the Arts with God devotional times are a key aspect of effective pedagogy, ensuring that participants come away with a new appreciation of how they can engage with God and his Word in powerful ways beyond music – that accessible forms of arts and scripture engagement can revitalise personal and corporate worship in their faith communities.

Developing Goals to Impact the Kingdom of God through the Arts

To reiterate, one of the distinctives of "Arts for a Better Future" is that participants are trained to help local communities create plans to use their local arts in working towards goals that reflect the values, presence, and impact of the kingdom of God. Here are examples of some concrete plans connecting arts and kingdom goals that have been created as a result of "Arts for a Better Future":

- Scripture-infused *Yuraq* (dance) helps a Yupik community in Alaska affirm traditional values and brings the community together. This, in turn, decreases alcohol and drug dependency and helps people to engage with God.
- Trauma healing classes for refugee children can facilitate expressions of lament through storytelling, poetry, calligraphy and music, bringing healing, hope and increased shalom to their traumatised communities.
- Grandmothers tell Bible stories and sing songs in indigenous styles to their grandchildren and the women of their compound, moving believers to identify as fully indigenous followers of Christ and embedding the Word of God into the community.
- The deaf community in Singapore will hold a festival with performances and workshops, including enactment of song-signing, percussion, dance, visual arts, and crafts-making. These arts will include messages about loving, helping and connecting with each other as a family, with the goal of producing a sense of belonging that helps the deaf community in Singapore move towards social justice for the deaf, where they are being welcomed, recognised and included in family life.

- A Thai-Chinese student who serves in an arts camp made plans to include song writing, dance, painting and drama workshops with Bible study at this camp, with the goal of encouraging Thai-Chinese youth to express their voice and reflect on the scriptures through the arts, so that they will move towards applying scripture in their personal spiritual life.
- Students from the Lotha Naga community in India made plans for Christian worship that will include enactment of *Eisa* (a call and response folk genre) infused with cultural elements and Christian values to produce appreciation for Naga culture, with the hope that it would help Naga Christians move towards reclaiming their cultural identity as Christians.
- Several students from the Batak Toba tribe of Indonesia planned a song composition competition, with the goals of increasing the effectiveness of discipleship and helping Batak churches move towards deeper communication with God and spiritual growth.

What Kind of Training Does the
"Arts for a Better Future" (ABF) Course Offer?

ABF is a rich experience, integrating participatory teaching methods throughout and helping students to engage with God through multiple accessible arts exercises. Participants on the course include a broad range of people, from those with a degree of artistic skill to those who do not consider themselves artists but who see the value of arts engagement in mission. Many artistic participants are thrilled to learn – some for the first time – ways they can grow in their journey of engaging the arts towards missional goals and kingdom outcomes.[15] Most importantly, because of the intense time of training, participants come away sharing three extraordinary conclusions and commitments:

1. Hundreds of thousands of artists with God-given gifts to extend heaven on earth are invisible to the vast majority of the world. *I'm going to make it my personal goal to find some of these hidden artists.*
2. These artists' traditions are qualitatively different from anything I've known, carry unique genius, beauty, and value, and are not to be trifled with or ignored. My first guesses are always wrong. *I am not going to make the mistake of underestimating the complexity, value, and efficacy of arts I don't understand. I will not assume that I understand any meaning or form until I have studied the genre for a substantial amount of time.*
3. These artists have the capacity to heal, rebuke, educate, worship in community contexts to a depth and extent that I cannot imagine. *I will encourage these artists to create for the Kingdom in their own communities*

---

[15] Such activities may not be the *only* goal for all artists who are Christians – some may choose to engage in a range of artistic projects not all of which are directly connected with the church and with mission. See further Redeeming the Arts, Act III: Transformation – The Arts, Mission and the Marketplace.

whenever I can, and not let myself get in the way. I now know how to do this, using CLAT.

Enveloping these activities are our sacred moments of *Arts with God*. Every morning we provide a framework for participants to respond to God and scripture in diverse artistic forms. Participants are guided in accessible forms of dance, drama, visual arts, storytelling and other arts, opening up new ways for them to know God. Many participants say *Arts with God* is their favourite part of ABF, since it opens their minds, hearts and bodies to let God change them.

"Arts for a Better Future": Global Dimensions and Orality

This section considers ABF's relevance and effectiveness in relationship to global socio-artistic trends and the orality movement.[16] In our contemporary world, artistic ideas and techniques are subject to what are called "global flows."[17] Whether well-known popular forms of contemporary Christian music such as Hillsong melodies or less well-known dance forms such as Bharatanatyam,[18] they are all capable of travelling along the global cultural highways and being adopted by Christians in different parts of the world in liturgy or in mission. Michelle Petersen calls these *Arts of Wider Communication*, a phrase adapted from linguistics terminology (*Languages of Wider Communication*).[19]

How Does ABF Connect with Contemporary Globalised Cultures?

ABF encourages all kinds of local creativity, so projects often appear in forms related to Arts of Wider Communication (AWM). For example, participants often create in forms such as spoken word poetry, graphic novels, video productions, rap, gospel music, and other forms of Christian contemporary music. Events such as arts and mission training courses allow participants to share ideas on the contemporary approaches to arts and technology. At one ABF, a participant showed how an artistic event such as a flash mob was used to great effect in Central Asia and how technology can be used to share this event and

---

[16] See Appendix 2 for further information on training options.

[17] See, for example, "global flows" in relation to the church – Kevin J. Vanhoozer, "Theological Method," in *Global Dictionary of Theology: A Resource for the Worldwide Church*, eds. William A. Dyrness and Veli-Matti Kärkkäinen (Downers Grove, IL; Nottingham: IVP Academic; IVP, 2008), 891. Roberta R. King looks at the relevance of this to the arts in King, "Christ Plays in Ten Thousand Places," 13.

[18] See the work of the dancer Susanna Harrington, "Bharatanatyam on Christian themes with Shrimathi Susanna," accessed Aug 2, 2021, http://www.indian-dance.co.uk/index.html.

[19] See Petersen's outstanding article on this subject – Michelle Petersen, "Arts Development for Scripture Engagement," *Global Forum on Arts and Christian Faith* 5, no. 1 (2017): 58-86, accessed Aug 2, 2021, http://www.artsandchristianfaith.org/index.php/journal/article/view/31/43.

this idea with a wider global audience. However, context is still important and arts and mission training should prepare participants to ask the kinds of questions that encourage communities to explore the communicative power of historically-grounded arts as well as the ubiquitous Arts of Wider Communication. Ultimately, any form of local creativity can be used towards that community's kingdom goals, and the decision as to which forms to use should be made by the community.

By contrast, there are some contexts in the world where local cultures are under severe pressure in this globalised age. As Bill Harris has shown, for some Asiatic peoples such as the Sakha, in the Siberian context, reaction to the forces of globalisation is driving a resurgent revitalisation of ethnic identity. Where those engaged in mission favour international or global approaches it can be a disadvantage, bringing not only a foreign approach but unwelcome attention. By contrast, he suggests that "missionaries encourage local artists to examine their own culture and decide for themselves which elements of their indigenous arts might be appropriate to bring into worship services."[20] The use of the local round dance, the local language in prayer and local musical instruments will show that the local church:

> … is Sakha and that God accepts Sakha worshippers. Where before, Sakha people were dismissive of the Gospel as a foreign religion, now they are showing renewed interest. Why? Because their heart music, dance, instruments and costumes are appearing in churches and festivals celebrating Jesus Christ and a life of union with him.

How Does ABF Connect with Training for Orality Movements?

In relation to oral cultures, the International Orality Network has already identified arts as one of the seven disciplines of orality, providing ABF an immediate connection for those working in oral preference contexts.[21] Furthermore, in 2016, two issues (Volume 5) of the *Orality Journal* were dedicated to the topic of orality, arts, and missional training, including ABF.[22] Effective arts and mission training focuses on the arts that people use in their daily lives, and these arts are often oral in nature. As a result, ABF emphasises characteristics common to oral cultures: primacy of relationships, spontaneity, mnemonic devices, holistic viewpoints, integration of emotions and bodies, and orientation to the present. We assume orality, but the method can include literacy

---

[20] Bill Harris, "The Church Planter and Artist," 34-35.
[21] For an overview of the seven disciplines see "Archive: Seven Disciplines of Orality," International Orality Network (ION), accessed Aug 2, 2021, https://orality.net/library/seven-disciplines-of-orality/.
[22] For access to two issues of *Orality Journal* 5 dedicated to arts and mission see "Archive: Journals," accessed Aug 2, 2021, https://orality.net/library/journals/.

and written arts where they are important. In addition, we treat local artistic expression as communication:[23]

> Like all communication systems, the arts are connected to particular times, places and social contexts. They have their own symbols, grammars, and internal structures. This means that just as you have to learn how to ask directions in a language foreign to you, you must also learn how to move your arms and neck and eyebrows to tell a story in Thai dance. There is no one artistic language that communicates completely across lines of time, place and culture. So to understand any art form, you have to interact with its practitioners and study it. Getting to know local artists and their arts is our first job.

> [A]rtistic forms of communication differ from other kinds of communication in several important ways. First, artistic communication places greater emphasis on manipulating form than do everyday interactions. Poetic speech, for example, may rely on patterns of sound and thought like rhyme, assonance, and metaphor that a simple exchange of information will not. Circling a drum while repeating a sequence of foot movements relies on form more heavily than simply walking from one place to another. Adopting the facial expressions of a mythical character draws on form to communicate more than allowing a person's face to remain at rest.

> Such communication is embedded in culture, and so touches many important aspects of a society. It marks messages as important, separate from everyday activities; it touches not only cognitive, but also experiential and emotional ways of knowing; it aids memory of a message; it increases the impact of a message through multiple media that often include the whole body; it concentrates the information contained in a message; it instils solidarity in its performers and experiencers; it provides socially acceptable frameworks for expressing difficult or new ideas; it inspires and moves people to action; it can act as a strong sign of identity; and it opens spaces for people to imagine and dream. Perhaps most importantly, local artistic communication exists and is owned locally; there's no need to translate foreign materials, and local artists are empowered to contribute to the expansion of the kingdom of God.

Effective arts and mission training also helps participants think through the wide-ranging impacts of artistic creativity in the kingdom of God. In ABF projects, we see communities connecting their arts to all sorts of kingdom goals: people coming to Christ, knowing and remembering scripture, becoming healthier and safer, valuing their God-given identities, stopping abuse, loving their spouses, recovering from trauma, and many more outcomes. No matter what form the current ministry of participants takes, well-designed training in arts and mission can add to their effectiveness because it accounts for all artistic forms of communication, imagines all kinds of kingdom growth, and emphasises the context of community. Participants learn how to empower other local people to use their own forms of communication, which are easier, quicker, and more

---

[23] These observations are drawn from the *ABF Manual* (2013), xv. This is an unpublished document available to trainers.

effective for their context, and they strengthen local people by affirming their God-given identity.

Arts and Mission Training Courses

The opening section considered the way in which selected important statements on mission have included reflections on the potential role that the arts can play in mission.[24] They also show that training is an important element for those who cross cultures in mission – whether in multicultural churches in plural societies, in mission agencies, or in contexts such as the one described where local or indigenous cultures have been marginalised and overlooked. Whether within the church in liturgy and services or beyond in evangelism, outreach and transformation, there is real scope for the arts as part of the mission of God's church in our contemporary world.

However, adequate training is required that encourages artists to develop their missional capacities and those involved in mission to cultivate their skills in facilitating artistic creation. Thoughtful training courses will hold both of these elements in tension and will provide biblical, theological, missional and artistic frameworks that allow participants to develop ways of functioning effectively as artists and arts advocates in missional settings, especially those that involve cross-cultural elements. This book has been written to address a gap in reflection on the relationship between arts and Christianity and implications for mission. As we help local believers explore the artistic forms available to them in the expression of their faith, one new field of study, "Ethnodoxology," can really help us.[25]

Ethnodoxology as a Discipline Supporting Arts and Mission Training

Ethnodoxology extends the insights of fields such as ethnomusicology, performance studies, worship arts, missiology, ritual studies, and anthropology to their applications for Christian communities around the world. It especially addresses the neglect and marginalisation of local arts in liturgy and worship by encouraging local artists to make plans for arts creation that enlivens and benefits their worshipping communities.[26] A recent definition of ethnodoxology – *the interdisciplinary study of how Christians in every culture engage with God and*

---

[24] See chapters 1 and 2 for further reflection on documents including "The Cape Town Commitment (2010)," "Redeeming the Arts (2004)" and "The Nairobi Statement on Worship and Culture (1996)" in relation to the arts.

[25] Robin Harris and Brian Schrag, "Ethnodoxology: Facilitating Local Arts Expressions for Kingdom Purposes," *Mission Frontiers* (Sep-Oct 2014), accessed Sep 28, 2021, http://www.missionfrontiers.org/issue/article/ethnodoxology-article.

[26] See Robin P. Harris, "Lessons Learned in the Founding of ICE: From Isolation to Community," *Connections*: *The Journal of the WEA Mission Commission* 9, no. 2-3 (2010): 79.

the world through their own artistic expressions – does not even use the word "worship," choosing instead to emphasise the breadth of engagement that arts can and should engender in a "life of worship."[27]

At the same time, in our globalising world, there are further complexities to be addressed: Does "local arts" mean only "traditional arts"? What do "local arts" look like in urban or multicultural contexts, and how can arts engagement be encouraged in these contexts? "Arts for a Better Future" is an apt case study, since it is most often taught in urban centres, with participants from multicultural and urban contexts. Therefore, during the Phase Three (small group project) part of ABF, participants often use the skills they have learned to help plan projects that will benefit their urban or multicultural contexts. Roughly 30–50 percent of the projects are urban in nature, and we find that participants often express their surprise and satisfaction that the seven-step CLAT process works just as well for their urban contexts. In one urban-based ABF alone – Kingston, Jamaica – participants made plans to foster local creativity in such globalised forms as reggae gospel, dancehall gospel, rapping, cheerleading, marching band, DJ-ing competition, and visual arts forms.

The seven-step CLAT method also addresses the complexities of multicultural and diaspora communities. Joy Kim, a Korean-American who serves as a board member of the Global Ethnodoxology Network, wrote her master's thesis[28] applying ethnodoxology theory and methods to her multi-ethnic community in Clarkston, Georgia, a town named by *Time* magazine as the most diverse square mile in America.[29] She used the seven-step CLAT process taught in "Arts for a Better Future" to plan a "Unity in Diversity" arts-creation workshop, resulting in multilingual songs and dances reflecting the diversity of her faith community. Proskuneo Ministries, the organisation that Joy and her husband Jaewoo help to lead in Clarkston, is a unique, leading voice amongst Christian organisations, encouraging the application of ethnodoxology principles and methods to multicultural and diaspora communities.[30]

In 2020, "Arts for a Better Future" at Singapore Bible College illustrated the breadth of application for ethnodoxology principles, resulting in projects focused on fostering kingdom thriving through the arts in communities such as the Singapore Christian Deaf community, in a Singapore-based mission team, amongst Thai-Chinese youth in Thailand, in Nagaland (India), and in the Batak

[27] See "Ethnodoxology = peoples + praise," Global Ethnodoxology Network, accessed Aug 2, 2021, http://www.worldofworship.org/what-is-ethnodoxology/, Section 1 – What is ethnodoxology?

[28] Joy Hyunsook Kim, "Diaspora Musicians and Creative Collaboration in a Multicultural Community: A Case Study in Ethnodoxology," (MA thesis, Graduate Institute of Applied Linguistics, Dallas International University, Dallas, TX, 2018).

[29] "Interesting Facts," City of Clarkston, accessed Aug 2, 2021, http://clarkstonga.gov/interesting-facts/.

[30] Proskuneo Ministries, accessed Aug 2, 2021, https://proskuneo.org/.

Toba tribe of Indonesia. A master's degree student at Singapore Bible College wrote:

> The seven steps of CLAT with the examples from Dr. Brian Schrag brought about a clear picture of how to implement it not just in mission but also in our local church and communities. I had thought that it would only be applied to cultures that are different from mine but I was reminded that even in our own church, each individual's context and ideas are different and as music ministers, we need to also meet the community and know their heart language, [work with them to] specify the kingdom goals of the community, connect the artistic genres to the goals, analyze the genres so that [new creations are] relevant, … inspire the community to create, improve results so that we can continue to learn and grow, and to integrate and celebrate old and new arts.

From Here to Heaven, Creation to New Creation

The arts and mission training course described here has a focus on how God's kingdom grows and reaches out through the diversity of all the wonderful languages, local cultures and artistic forms that God has facilitated since the creation of the world. The kingdom that Jesus proclaimed here on earth will not end when we die, but will grow and expand in unimaginable ways – ways that we will experience as full citizens of heaven in the new creation.[31] Like the creation itself, the new creation will embrace the creativity of God and the artistic and cultural creativity of its citizens. Our journey towards the new creation has already started.

This is how Harriette, a Christian woman from the Siberian Yupik Inupiat tribe in Alaska, describes the way in which "Arts for a Better Future" helped her on her personal journey towards the kingdom of God:

> It changes your life. It changes your view on your culture. When you're aware of a new way in the arts and in your culture to bless others and to love God, it blows your mind. It's heart-boggling!

> Sometimes when my day is over I think about this week of ABF. It just blesses me to where I start crying tears of joy. Because as a Christian and as a native woman, I look beyond the earthly… I say, Lord … this is where I'm going, and despite everything that's going on, I see the prize, I strive for it. I jump for joy inside to know that, finally, I'm aware of a way to give God the glory as a native lady.[32]

Arts and mission training courses can help arts participants and local people to develop a fuller grasp of the potential of creativity and its applications to

---

[31] See, for example, Tom Wright, *Surprised by Hope*, Reissued ed. (London: SPCK, 2011).

[32] See Harriette Slwooko's full testimony – Brian Schrag, "Harriet Slwooko Reflects on ABF," YouTube, accessed Aug 2, 2021, https://youtu.be/r5q5hvSSj10.

mission. Through mission, God is building His kingdom – local arts and cultures can be building blocks of this process.

Questions for Reflection/Discussion
1. What next step might you take to get the kind of training you need to be more effective?
2. Who else needs to know about these resources? How can you get them involved?
3. When have you seen the "Bring it – Teach it" method of arts engagement in mission? How could the "Find it – Encourage it" model improve the outcomes of that arts engagement?
4. How might your mission or training institution incorporate an intensive in arts and mission? What are the hindrances keeping this from happening, and how might you work around them?

Appendix 1:
"Arts for a Better Future": Global Overview

The Worldwide Spread of ABF, Especially in the Global South

"Arts for a Better Future" has grown to include venues in many parts of the world since its launch in 2011 at All Nations Christian College with an international gathering of more than 20 nations, made possible by a partnership between All Nations Christian College (Easneye, UK), Dallas International University (Dallas, Texas, USA), Global Ethnodoxology Network, SIL International, and the Mission Commission of the World Evangelical Alliance. (See below for statistics showing participants since 2011 by region of the world and by specific venues.)[1]

These courses were taught by different combinations of facilitators and in various languages including Spanish, Portuguese and English, and participants were drawn from entirely different populations. Research on the efficacy of the course around key learning intentions has shown remarkably similar outcomes across cultures. Data gathered from exit surveys from 2015 through to 2020 show strong levels of improvement when students rated their "before" and "after" knowledge, skills, and attitudes in seven areas.[2]

A conclusion that might be drawn from these comparisons is that since the courses are being carefully contextualised for each society, the pedagogical methods of the course produce similar outcomes even in widely varying cultures.

---

[1] Some of which are repeated for more than one year, leading to higher numbers. Passport countries of participants are far more numerous than the fourteen (14) venues listed. We know that a minimum of 70 countries on six continents have been represented amongst the participants though, unfortunately, passport country data is missing from about one eighth of the participant records.

[2] Students rated themselves on a scale of 1–5: (1 – poor; 2 – weak; 3 – acceptable; 4 – good; 5 – excellent). This indicates their ability to: 1) describe seven Create Local Arts Together (CLAT) steps; 2) interact with community representatives to learn about their local arts; 3) interact with community representatives to learn about their kingdom goals; 4) facilitate the process of helping a community make plans to use their artistic resources to achieve their goals; 5) have a desire to use a broad spread of arts in communities for kingdom goals; 6) personally engage with a variety of arts in worship; and 7) use this training in their own ministry or life contexts.

This further suggests that ABF is well suited (with normal contextual adaptations) to the Asian context.

Regions of the World	Participants
Africa	91
Asia	99
Central America & Caribbean	64
Europe	201
North America	341
South America	106
Grand Total	**902**

Venues	Participants
Alaska	58
Argentina	28
Bangalore – India	21
Bogota – Colombia	11
Brazil	55
Dallas – USA	238
United Kingdom	201
Guatemala	30
Jamaica	34
Johannesburg – South Africa	17
Kinshasa – DRC	22
Nairobi – Kenya	52
Peru	12
Singapore	35
Thailand	43

Participants (2021)

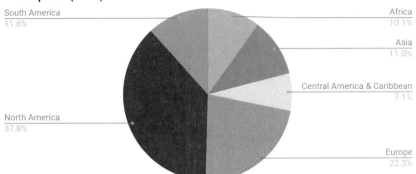

South America
11.8%

North America
37.8%

Africa
10.1%

Asia
11.0%

Central America & Caribbean
7.1%

Europe
22.3%

Appendix 2
Tertiary Colleges and Programmes
That Offer "Arts and Mission" Training

The Global Ethnodoxology Network (GEN) lists a number of training institutions offering courses on arts and cross-cultural work.[1] Whilst some institutions have just one or two courses, others offer full degrees, including bachelor's, master's, professional doctorates (e.g., DMiss, DWS, DMin, and PhD degrees).

The webpage https://www.worldofworship.org/organizations/ also lists some key mission agencies welcoming ethnodoxologists to serve at the intersection of arts and culture. In addition, the GEN site also provides information about "short courses" developed by GEN such as the "Arts for a Better Future" course described in this chapter, and the "Introduction to Ethnodoxology" course, which focuses on the applications of ethnodoxology principles to seminary students and those studying for ministry in urban and multicultural contexts.

The "Introduction to Ethnodoxology" course is a five-day intensive available for export to any training institution that wishes to adopt it. Current venues[2] for the course are outlined at https://www.worldofworship.org/introduction-to-ethnodoxology/ but the list is growing, with the first Asian venue successfully launched in March 2021 at Alliance Bible Seminary in Hong Kong.

Without appropriate training, mission agencies and churches run the risk of employing "Bring it – Teach it" methods of arts engagement in mission, rather than the "Find it – Encourage it" model that is more effective, kingdom-focused, and respectful of local culture and artists.[3] Individual artists and agencies can connect to the resources and training links at the GEN site[4]

---

[1] See the list at "GEN Organizational Members," Global Ethnodoxology Network, accessed Aug 2, 2021, https://www.worldofworship.org/organizations/. There are two tabs: one marked "Training"; the other "Agencies."

[2] "Introduction to Ethnodoxology," Global Ethnodoxology Network, accessed Aug 2, 2021, https://www.worldofworship.org/introduction-to-ethnodoxology/.

[3] See also "Seven Core Values Guide," Global Ethnodoxology Network, accessed Sep 7, 2021, https://www.worldofworship.org/core-values/.

[4] "What is GEN?" Global Ethnodoxology Network, accessed Aug 2, 2021, https://www.worldofworship.org/.

https://worldofworship.org, and the latter could profitably consider integrating either "Introduction to Ethnodoxology" or "Arts for a Better Future" into your organisation's training for arts and mission. Those who wish to serve long-term as an arts in mission facilitator should plan to begin one of the longer programmes available through the GEN organisational partners.

> "*Using a dull axe requires great strength, so sharpen the blade.*
> *That's the value of wisdom; it helps you succeed.*" (Ecclesiastes 10:10)

> Arts and mission training can serve as the "sharpened blade"
> that makes your ministry far more effective and energised.

Select Bibliography

Akçalı, P. and C. Engin-Demir, eds. *Politics, Identity and Education in Central Asia: Post-Soviet Kyrgyzstan.* Advances in Central Asian Studies 3. London and New York: Routledge, 2013.

Anderson, D. A., and M. R. Cabellon, eds. *Multicultural Ministry Handbook: Connecting Creatively to a Diverse World.* Downers Grove, IL: IVP Books, 2010.

"Arts and Orality Part 1: Foundations and Applications." *Orality Journal* 5, no. 1 (2016). Available online: https://orality.net/library/journals/.[1]

"Arts and Orality Part 2: Equipping for Ministry." *Orality Journal* 5, no. 2 (2016). Available online: https://orality.net/library/journals/.

"Arts in Mission." *Connections: The Journal of the WEA Mission Commission* 9, no. 2-3 (2010). Available online: https://weamc.global/archive/Vol09No2-3_Arts.pdf.

Asay, P. *Burning Bush 2.0: How Pop Culture Replaced the Prophet.* Nashville, TN: Abingdon Press, 2015.

ATS Forum on Theology, compiler. *Doing Theology in the Philippines.* Manila: OMF Literature and Asian Theological Seminary, 2005.

Bailey, K. E. *Jesus through Middle Eastern Eyes: Cultural Studies in the Gospels.* Downers Grove, IL: IVP Academic, 2008.

Bass, A. *The Creative Life: A Workbook for Unearthing the Christian Imagination.* Downers Grove, IL: IVP, 2001. Kindle.

Bauer, M. J. *Arts Ministry: Nurturing the Creative Life of God's People.* Calvin Institute of Christian Worship Liturgical Studies. Grand Rapids, MI: Eerdmans, 2013.

Beattie, W. R. "Creating a Community for Contextual Learning." In *Ministry Across Cultures: Sharing the Christian Faith in Asia*, edited by W. R. Beattie, 113-29. Regnum Studies in Mission. Oxford: Regnum Books, 2016.

Beattie, W. R., ed. *Ministry Across Cultures: Sharing the Christian Faith in Asia.* Regnum Studies in Mission. Oxford: Regnum Books, 2016.

Begbie, J. S. *A Peculiar Orthodoxy: Reflections on Theology and the Arts.* Grand Rapids, MI: Baker Academic, 2018.

---

[1] Select Bibliography includes works whose primary format is "print" rather than "electronic" – recognising these are constantly shifting designations; if available online at publication that information is added for the benefit of readers.

Begbie, J. S. *Resounding Truth: Christian Wisdom in the World of Music.*
    Engaging Culture. Grand Rapids, MI: Baker Academic, 2007.
Bell, J. L. *One Is the Body: Songs of Unity and Diversity.* Glasgow: Wild
    Goose Publications, 2002.
Bergmann, S. *In the Beginning Is the Icon: A Liberative Theology of Images,
    Visual Arts and Culture.* London and New York: Routledge, 2014.
Bergmann, S., and M. Vähäkangas, eds. *Contextual Theology: Skills and
    Practices of Liberating Faith.* London and New York: Routledge, 2021.
Bernard, S. C. *Documentary Storytelling: Creative Nonfiction on Screen.* 4th
    ed. Abingdon and New York: Focal Press, 2016. Kindle.
Bevans, S. B. *Models of Contextual Theology.* Faith and Cultures. Rev. and
    expanded ed. Maryknoll, NY: Orbis Books, 2002.
Black, K. *Culturally-Conscious Worship.* St. Louis, MO: Chalice Press, 2000.
Bosch, D. J. *Transforming Mission: Paradigm Shifts in Theology of Missions.*
    American Society of Missiology 16. Maryknoll, NY: Orbis Books, 1991.
Brand, H., and A. Chaplin. *Art and Soul: Signposts for Christians in the Arts.*
    Carlisle; Downers Grove, IL: Piquant; IVP Academic, 2001.
Cabrita, J., D. Maxwell and E. Wild-Wood, eds. *Relocating World
    Christianity: Interdisciplinary Studies in Universal and Local Expressions
    of the Christian Faith.* Theology and Mission in World Christianity 7.
    Leiden: Brill, 2017.
Castells, M. *The Power of Identity.* The Information Age: Economy, Society,
    and Culture 2. 2nd ed. West Sussex: Wiley-Blackwell, 2010.
Cherenkov, M., and W. Yoder. "The Changing Face of Church and Mission in
    Eurasia (with William Yoder's Response to Mykhailo Cherenkov)."
    Occasional Papers on Religion in Eastern Europe 36, iss. 3, article 6 (May
    2016): 50-59. Available online:
    https://digitalcommons.georgefox.edu/ree/vol36/iss3/6.
Cherry, C. M. *The Worship Architect: A Blueprint for Designing Culturally
    Relevant and Biblically Faithful Services.* Grand Rapids, MI: Baker
    Academic, 2010.
Chew, J. *When You Cross Cultures: Vital Issues Facing Christian Missions.*
    New ed., rev. & updated. Singapore: Nav Media, 2009. Available online:
    https://www.worldevangelicals.org/resources/rfiles/res3_331_link_1331061
    422.pdf.
Ching, L. T. S. *Anti-Japan: The Politics of Sentiment in Postcolonial East Asia.*
    Durham, NC and London: Duke University Press, 2019.
Chiu, H. "A Visual Re-Conception Using the Stories and Accounts of the Life,
    Death and Resurrection of Jesus Christ in John's Gospel to Encourage
    Christian Spiritual Formation for the Wa People in Yunnan Province." MA
    thesis, All Nations Christian College, Easneye, UK, 2016.
Chiu, V. "'You Are Precious' – A Series of Art-Based Workshops on the Subject
    of the 'Noble Character of a Woman' in Proverbs 31." BA Research Paper,
    All Nations Christian College, Easneye, UK, 2016.

Christian Conference of Asia. *Sound the Bamboo: CCA Hymnal 2000*. Tainan: Taiwan Presbyterian Church Press, 2000.

Chua, B. H., and K. Iwabuchi, eds. *East Asian Pop Culture: Analysing the Korean Wave*. Hong Kong: Hong Kong University Press, 2008.

Church, M., ed. *The Other Classical Musics: Fifteen Great Traditions*. Woodbridge: Boydell Press, 2015.

Collinge, I. "A Kaleidoscope of Doxology: Exploring Ethnodoxology and Theology." *Doon Theological Journal* 8, no. 1, part 1 (Mar 2011): 37-57.

Collinge, I. "Moving from Monocultural to Multicultural Worship." In *Worship and Mission for the Global Church: An Ethnodoxology Handbook*, edited by J. R. Krabill, F. Fortunato, R. P. Harris and B. Schrag, 438-42. Pasadena, CA: William Carey Library, 2013.

Colson, C., and N. Pearcey. *How Now Shall We Live?* London: Marshall Pickering, 1999.

Corbitt, J. N., and V. Nix-Early. *Taking It to the Streets: Using the Arts to Transform Your Community*. Grand Rapids, MI: Baker Books, 2003.

Dadabaev T. *Identity and Memory in Post-Soviet Central Asia: Uzbekistan's Soviet Past*. Central Asia Research Forum. London and New York: Routledge, 2016.

Davis, J., and N. Lerner. *Worship Together in Your Church as in Heaven*. Nashville, TN: Abingdon Press, 2015.

Dickens, M. "Syriac Christianity in Central Asia." In *The Syriac World*, edited by D. King, 583-624. Routledge Worlds. Abingdon and New York: Routledge, 2019.

Dowley, T., ed. *Christian Music: A Global History*. Oxford: Lion, 2011.

Drane, J. *Evangelism for a New Age: Creating Churches for the Next Century*. London: Marshall Pickering, 1994.

Duan, S. 佤族历史文化探秘 [*The Mystery of the Culture and History of the Wa*]. Kunming: Yunnan University Press, 2007. (In Chinese).

During, J. "Power, Authority and Music in the Cultures of Inner Asia." *Ethnomusicology Forum* 14, no. 2 (2005): 143-64.

Dyrness, W. A. *Christian Art in Asia*. Amsterdam: Rodopi, 1979.

Dyrness, W. A. *Poetic Theology: God and the Poetics of Everyday Life*. Grand Rapids, MI: Eerdmans, 2011.

Dyrness, W. A. *Senses of Devotion: Interfaith Aesthetics in Buddhist and Muslim Communities*. Art for Faith's Sake 7. Eugene, OR:[2] Cascade Books, 2013.

Dyrness, W. A. *Visual Faith: Art, Theology, and Worship in Dialogue*. Grand Rapids, MI: Baker Academic, 2001.

Flemming, D. E. *Contextualization in the New Testament: Patterns for Theology and Mission*. Downers Grove, IL: IVP Academic, 2005.

---

[2] U.S.A. – state code for Oregon.

Franklin, J. "Practising Hospitality: Arts and the Missional Task." *Connections: The Journal of the WEA Mission Commission* 9, no. 2-3 (2010): 6-7.

Fujimura, M. *Art and Faith: A Theology of Making*. New Haven, CT: Yale University Press, 2020.

Fujimura, M. *Culture Care: Reconnecting with Beauty for Our Common Life*. Downers Grove, IL: IVP Books, 2017.

Fujimura, M. *Refractions: A Journey of Faith, Art, and Culture*. Colorado Springs, CO: NavPress, 2009.

Fujimura. M. *Silence and Beauty: Hidden Faith Born of Suffering*. Downers Grove, IL: IVP Books, 2016.

Fujiwara, A. *Theology of Culture in a Japanese Context: A Believers' Church Perspective*. Princeton Theological Monograph Series 179. Eugene, OR: Pickwick Publications, 2012.

Gao, S., ed. 書法心理治療 [*Chinese Calligraphic Therapy*]. Hong Kong: Hong Kong University Press, 2000. (In Chinese).

García-Rivera, A. R. *A Wounded Innocence: Sketches for a Theology of Art*. Collegeville, MN: The Liturgical Press, 2003.

Gilkey, L. B. "Can Art Fill the Vacuum?" In *Art, Creativity, and the Sacred: An Anthology in Religion and Art*, edited by D. Apostolos-Cappadona, 187-92. New York: Crossroad, 1984.

Gittins, A. J. *Living Mission Interculturally: Faith, Culture, and the Renewal of Praxis*. Collegeville, MN: Liturgical Press, 2015.

Green, M. *Acts for Today: First Century Christianity for Twentieth Century Christians*. London: Hodder & Stoughton, 1993.

Gunn, T. J. "Shaping an Islamic Identity: Religion, Islamism, and the State in Central Asia." *Sociology of Religion* 64, no. 3 (2003): 389-410.

Hanciles, J. J. *Beyond Christendom: Globalization, African Migration, and the Transformation of the West*. Maryknoll, NY: Orbis Books, 2008.

Harbinson, C. "Art as Authentic Witness." *Connections: The Journal of the WEA Mission Commission* 9, no. 2-3 (2010): 9-11.

Harris, B. "The Church Planter and Artist: Becoming Partners in Ministry." *Connections: The Journal of the WEA Mission Commission* 9, no. 2-3 (2010): 34-35.

Hawn, C. M. *Gather into One: Praying and Singing Globally*. Calvin Institute of Christian Worship Liturgical Studies. Grand Rapids, MI and Cambridge, UK: Eerdmans, 2003.

Hawn, C. M. *Halle, Halle: We Sing the World Round (Teacher's Edition)*. Garland, TX: Choristers Guild, 1999.

He, Q. 基督教艺术纵横 [*Christian Art History and Today*]. Beijing: China Religious Culture Publisher, 2013. (In Chinese).

He, Q. *Look toward the Heavens: The Art of He Qi*. New Haven, CT: OMSC, 2006.

He, Q. *The Art of He Qi*. Roseville, MN: He Qi Arts, 2013.

Hernández-Pérez, M., ed. *Japanese Media Cultures in Japan and Abroad: Transnational Consumption of Manga, Anime, and Media-Mixes*. Basel: MDPI, 2019. Available online: https://doi.org/10.3390/books978-3-03921-009-1.

Hoberman, B. "Chaucer of the Turks." *Saudi Aramco World* 36, no. 1 (1985): 24-27. Available online: https://archive.aramcoworld.com/issue/198501/chaucer.of.the.turks.htm.

Horsfall, T. *Working from a Place of Rest: Jesus and the Key to Sustaining Ministry*. Abingdon: Bible Reading Fellowship, 2010.

Imam, J. F. "The Annunciation to Mary as Retold in the Qurʾān." MPhil thesis, University of Oxford, 2018. Available online: https://opac.ideo-cairo.org/append_pdf/iu716.pdf/219042.

Kassis, R. A. *The Book of Proverbs and Arabic Proverbial Works*. Leiden: Brill, 1999.

Kempe, A. *The GCSE Drama Coursebook*. 2nd ed. Cheltenham: Stanley Thornes, 1997.

Khalid, A. *Islam after Communism: Religion and Politics in Central Asia*. Berkeley, CA: University of California Press, 2007.

Kim, J. H. "Diaspora Musicians and Creative Collaboration in a Multicultural Community: A Case Study in Ethnodoxology." MA thesis, Graduate Institute of Applied Linguistics, Dallas International University, Dallas, TX, 2018. Available Online: https://www.diu.edu/documents/theses/Kim_Joy-thesis.pdf.

King, D., ed. *The Syriac World*. Routledge Worlds. Abingdon and New York: Routledge, 2019.

King, R. R. "Christ Plays in Ten Thousand Places: Challenges and Possibilities for Music and the Arts in Mission." *Connections: The Journal of the WEA Mission Commission* 9, no. 2-3 (2010): 11-13.

King, R. R. "Performing Witness: Loving Our Religious Neighbors through Musicking." In *The Arts as Witness in Multifaith Contexts*, edited by R. R. King and W. A. Dyrness, 39-68. Missiological Engagements. Downers Grove, IL: IVP Academic, 2019.

King, R. R., and W. A. Dyrness, eds. *The Arts as Witness in Multifaith Contexts*. Missiological Engagements. Downers Grove, IL: IVP Academic, 2019.

King, R. R., and S. L. Tan, eds. *(un)Common Sounds: Songs of Peace and Reconciliation among Muslims and Christians*. Art for Faith's Sake. Eugene, OR: Cascade Books, 2014.

Klenke, K. "Popular Music in Uzbekistan." In *The Music of Central Asia*, edited by T. Levin, S. Daukeyeva and E. Köchümkulova, 555-76. Bloomington: Indiana University Press, 2016.

Kobilov, U. U. "Interpretation of the Image of Masih in the Divan of Alisher Navoi "Badoyi ul-Bidoya" ("The Rarity of the Beginning")." *Theoretical and Applied Science* 72, no. 4 (2019): 40-47. Available online: http://dx.doi.org/10.15863/TAS.2019.04.72.7.

Koppett, K. *Training Using Drama: Successful Development Techniques from Theatre and Improvisation*. London: Kogan Page, 2002.

Koyama, K. *Water Buffalo Theology*. 25th anniv. ed., rev. and expanded. Maryknoll, NY: Orbis Books, 1999.

Krabill, J. R., F. Fortunato, R. P. Harris and B. Schrag, eds. *Worship and Mission for the Global Church: An Ethnodoxology Handbook*. Pasadena, CA: William Carey Library, 2013.

Küster, V. "Contextualisation through the Arts." In *Contextual Theology: Skills and Practices of Liberating Faith*, edited by S. Bergmann and M. Vähäkangas, 205-20. London and New York: Routledge, 2021.

Lamarre, T. *The Anime Machine: A Media Theory of Animation*. Minneapolis, MN: University of Minnesota Press, 2009.

Lapiz, E. *Pagpapahiyang: Redeeming Culture and Indigenizing Christianity*. The Philippines, 2010.

Lapiz, E. "Where Every Nation Has a Contribution." *Connections: The Journal of the WEA Mission Commission* 9, no. 2-3 (2010): 7-9.

Leonard, J. S. "The Church in between Cultures: Rethinking the Church in Light of the Globalization of Immigration." *Evangelical Missions Quarterly* 40, no. 1 (2004): 62-70. Available online: https://students.wts.edu/resources/westminsterspeaks/2004/01/01/The_Chur ch_Between_Cultures_Rethinking_the_Church_in_Light_of_Globalization_ of_Immigration.html.

Lerner, N. "Multicultural Worship." In *Multicultural Ministry Handbook: Connecting Creatively to a Diverse World*, edited by D. A. Anderson and M. R. Cabellon, 91-104. Downers Grove, IL: IVP Books, 2010.

Levin, T. *The Hundred Thousand Fools of God: Musical Travels in Central Asia*. Bloomington: Indiana University Press, 1996. (Includes CD recordings).

Levin, T. "The Reterritorialization of Culture in the New Central Asian States: A Report from Uzbekistan." *Yearbook for Traditional Music* 25 (1993): 51-59.

Levin, T., S. Daukeyeva and E. Köchümkulova, eds. *The Music of Central Asia*. Bloomington: Indiana University Press, 2016. (Includes online recordings).

Lewis, M., ed. *'History Wars' and Reconciliation in Japan and Korea: The Roles of Historians, Artists and Activists*. New York: Palgrave Macmillan, 2017.

Lim, S. H. *Giving Voice to Asian Christians: An Appraisal of the Pioneering Work of I-To Loh in the Area of Congregational Song*. Saarbrücken: Verlag Dr Müller, 2008.

Lin, S. C. *Spaces of Mediation: Christian Art and Visual Culture in Taiwan*. Contact Zone Explorations in Intercultural Theology 24. Leipzig: Evangelische Verlagsanstalt, 2019.

Loh, I. T. "Contextualization versus Globalization: A Glimpse of Sounds and Symbols in Asian Worship." *Colloquium: Music, Worship, Arts* 2 (2005):

125-39. Available online:
https://ism.yale.edu/sites/default/files/files/Contextualization%20versus%20
Globalization.pdf.

Loh, I. T. [M. N. C. Poon, ed.] *In Search for Asian Sounds and Symbols in Worship*. Singapore: Trinity Theological College, 2012.

Loverance, R. *Christian Art*. London: British Museum Press, 2007.

Maggay, M. P. "A Religion of Guilt Encounters a Religion of Power: Missiological Implications and Consequences." In *The Gospel in Culture: Contextualization Issues through Asian Eyes*, edited by M. P. Maggay, 24-56. Manila: ISACC and OMF Literature, 2013.

Maggay, M. P. "Introduction – The Task of Contextualization: Issues in Reading, Appropriating, and Transmitting the Faith." In *The Gospel in Culture: Contextualization Issues through Asian Eyes*, edited by M. P. Maggay, 5-23. Manila: ISACC and OMF Literature, 2013.

Maggay, M. P. "Towards Contextualization from Within: Some Tools and Culture Themes." In *Doing Theology in the Philippines*, compiled by ATS Forum on Theology, 37-50. Manila: OMF Literature and Asian Theological Seminary, 2005.

Maggay, M. P. *Global Kingdom, Global People: Living Faithfully in a Multicultural World*. Carlisle: Langham Global Library, 2017.

Maggay, M. P., and W. A. Dyrness. "Art and Aesthetics." In *Global Dictionary of Theology: A Resource for the Worldwide Church*, edited by W. A. Dyrness and V. M. Kärkkäinen, 64-70. Downers Grove, IL; Nottingham: IVP Academic; IVP, 2008.

Maggay, M. P., ed. *The Gospel in Culture: Contextualization Issues through Asian Eyes*. Manila: ISACC and OMF Literature, 2013.

McCullough, J. *Sense and Spirituality: The Arts and Spiritual Formation*. Eugene, OR: Cascade Books, 2015.

McLeod, H., and W. Ustorf, eds. *The Decline of Christendom in Western Europe, 1750-2000*. Cambridge: Cambridge University Press, 2003.

Mead, G. *Coming Home to Story: Storytelling beyond Happily Ever After*. London and Philadelphia: Jessica Kingsley Publishers, 2017.

Merridale, C. *Red Fortress: The Secret Heart of Russia's History*. London: Allen Lane, 2013.

Milne, B. *Dynamic Diversity: The New Humanity Church for Today and Tomorrow*. Nottingham: IVP, 2006.

Miranda-Feliciano, E. *Of Songs, Words and Gestures*: *Rethinking Filipino Liturgy*. Manila: ISACC, 2000.

Moffett, S. H. *A History of Christianity in Asia 1: Beginnings to 1500*. American Society of Missiology. 2nd rev. and corrected ed. Maryknoll, NY: Orbis Books, 1998.

Murray, R. *Symbols of Church and Kingdom: A Study in Early Syriac Tradition*. Cambridge: Cambridge University Press, 1975.

Navoi, A. "Badoyi ul-Bidoya." In *A Collection of Navoi's Completed Works 1*. Tashkent: Fan Publishing, 1987. (Editor unknown).

Nicholls, K. D. *Asian Arts and Christian Hope*. New Delhi: Select Books, 1983.

Noble, A. *Disruptive Witness: Speaking Truth in a Distracted Age*. Downers Grove, IL: IVP Books, 2018.

Nouwen, H. *Spiritual Formation: Following the Movements of the Spirit*. New York: HarperCollins, 2010.

Oswald, J. *A New Song Rising in Tibetan Hearts: Tibetan Christian Worship in the Early 21st Century*. Chiang Mai: Central Asia Publishing, 2001.

Patten, M. *Leading a Multicultural Church*. London: SPCK, 2016.

Pelkmans, M., ed. *Conversion after Socialism: Disruptions, Modernisms and Technologies of Faith in the Former Soviet Union*. Oxford: Berghahn Books, 2009.

Pelkmans, M. "Introduction: Post-Soviet Space and the Unexpected Turns of Religious Life." In *Conversion after Socialism: Disruptions, Modernisms and Technologies of Faith in the Former Soviet Union*, edited by M. Pelkmans, 1-16. Oxford: Berghahn Books, 2009. Available online: http://eprints.lse.ac.uk/id/eprint/28056.

Peterson, E. "The Pastor: How Artists Shape Pastoral Identity." In *For the Beauty of the Church*: *Casting a Vision for the Arts*, edited by W. D. O. Taylor, 89-96. Grand Rapids, MI: Baker Books, 2010.

Peyrouse, S. "Why Do Central Asian Governments Fear Religion? A Consideration of Christian Movements." *Journal of Eurasian Studies* 1 (2010): 134-43. Available online: https://journals.sagepub.com/doi/pdf/10.1016/j.euras.2010.04.006.

Poon, M. N. C. "Music among Christians in South-East Asia." In *Christian Music: A Global History*, edited by T. Dowley, 219-20. Oxford: Lion, 2011.

Pospielovsky, D. V. *Soviet Antireligious Campaigns and Persecutions*. A History of Soviet Atheism in Theory and Practice, and the Believer 2. New York: St Martin's Press, 1988.

Postman, N. *Amusing Ourselves to Death: Public Discourse in the Age of Show Business*. 20th anniv. ed. London: Penguin Books, 2006. Kindle.

Quakenbush, J. S., and G. F. Simons, eds. *Language and Identity in a Multilingual Migrating World*. Dallas, TX: SIL International Pike Center, 2019. Available online: http://leanpub.com/languageandidentity.

Radford, D. "Religious Conversion and Its Impact on Ethnic Identity in Post-Soviet Kyrgyzstan." In *Politics, Identity and Education in Central Asia: Post-Soviet Kyrgyzstan*, edited by P. Akçalı and C. Engin-Demir, 118-30. Advances in Central Asian Studies 3. London and New York: Routledge, 2013.

Reily, S. A., and J. M. Dueck, eds. *The Oxford Handbook of Music and World Christianities*. Oxford Handbooks. Oxford: Oxford University Press, 2016.

Rookmaaker, H. R. *Art Needs No Justification*. Vancouver: Regent College Publishing, 2010.

Root, J. *Worship in a Multi-Ethnic Society*. Grove Worship 236. Cambridge, UK: Grove Books, 2018.

Sanneh, L. *Translating the Message: The Missionary Impact on Culture.* American Society of Missiology 42. Rev. and expanded ed. Maryknoll, NY: Orbis Books, 2009.

Schrag, B. "Becoming Bi-musical: The Importance and Possibility of Missionary Involvement in Music." *Missiology: An International Review* 17, no. 3 (Jul 1989): 311-19.

Schrag, B. *Creating Local Arts Together: A Manual to Help Communities Reach Their Kingdom Goals.* Pasadena, CA: William Carey Library, 2013.

Schrag, B. "Why Local Arts Are Central to Mission." *Connections: The Journal of the WEA Mission Commission* 9, no. 2-3 (2010): 15.

Schrag, B., and J. Rowe. *Community Arts for God's Purposes: How to Create Local Artistry Together.* Pasadena, CA: William Carey Publishing, 2020.

Schrag, B., and K. J. Van Buren. *Make Arts for a Better Life: A Guide for Working with Communities.* New York: Oxford University Press, 2018.

Schreiter, R. J. *Constructing Local Theologies.* 30th anniv. ed. Maryknoll, NY: Orbis Books, 2015.

Scott, J. *Tuning in to a Different Song: Using a Music Bridge to Cross Cultural Differences.* Pretoria: University of Pretoria Institute for Missiological and Ecumenical Research, 2000.

Sedmak, C. *Doing Local Theology: A Guide for Artisans of a New Humanity.* Maryknoll, NY: Orbis Books, 2002.

Seerveld, C. *Bearing Fresh Olive Leaves: Alternative Steps in Understanding Art.* Carlisle: Piquant, 2000.

Seerveld, C. *Rainbows for the Fallen World: Aesthetic Life and Artistic Task.* Toronto, Ontario: Toronto Tuppence Press, 1980.

Shamgunov, I. "Listening to the Voice of the Graduate: An Analysis of Professional Practice and Training for Ministry in Central Asia." PhD thesis, University of Oxford, 2009. Available online: https://pdfs.semanticscholar.org/1b04/a51c21ad358c42b6558274eae735f2fc4498.pdf.

Shenk, W. R. *Changing Frontiers of Mission.* American Society of Missiology 28. Maryknoll, NY: Orbis Books, 1999.

Shi, L. 佤族审美文化 [*The Cultural Aesthetics of the Wa*]. Kunming: Yunnan University Press, 2008. (In Chinese).

Shiloah, A. *Music in the World of Islam: A Socio-Cultural Study.* Detroit, MI: Wayne State University Press, 1995.

Son, S. "Translanguaging, Identity, and Education in Our Multilingual World." In *Language and Identity in a Multilingual Migrating World*, edited by J. S. Quakenbush and G. F. Simons, 124-43. Dallas, TX: SIL International Pike Center, 2019. Available online: http://leanpub.com/languageandidentity.

Spinetti, F. "Tradition-Based Popular Music in Contemporary Tajikistan." In *The Music of Central Asia*, edited by T. Levin, S. Daukeyeva and E. Köchümkulova, 586-95. Bloomington: Indiana University Press, 2016.

Spradlin, B. "Worship and the Arts in Ministry and Missions." *Connections: The Journal of the WEA Mission Commission* 9, no. 2-3 (2010): 49-50.

Takenaka, M., and R. O'Grady. *The Bible through Asian Eyes*. Auckland: Pace Publishing, 1991.

Tansuğ, F. "A Bibliographic Survey of Kazakh and Kyrgyz Literature on Music." *Yearbook for Traditional Music* 41 (2009): 199-200.

Taylor, C. *A Secular Age*. Cambridge, MA and London: The Belknap Press of Harvard University Press, 2007.

Taylor, W. D. O., ed. *For the Beauty of the Church: Casting a Vision for the Arts*. Grand Rapids, MI: Baker Books, 2010.

Taylor, W. D. O. *Glimpses of the New Creation: Worship and the Formative Power of the Arts*. Grand Rapids, MI: Eerdmans, 2019.

Teague, D. *Godly Servants: Discipleship and Spiritual Formation for Missionaries*. N.p.: Mission Imprints, 2012.

Tizon, A. *Transformation after Lausanne: Radical Evangelical Mission in Global-Local Perspective*. Oxford: Regnum Books, 2008.

Turnau, T. *Popologetics: Popular Culture in Christian Perspective*. Phillipsburg, NJ: P&R Publishing, 2012.

Ustorf, W. "A Missiological Postscript." In *The Decline of Christendom in Western Europe, 1750-2000*, edited by H. McLeod and W. Ustorf, 218-25. Cambridge: Cambridge University Press, 2003.

Van Opstal, S. M. *The Next Worship: Glorifying God in a Diverse World*. Downers Grove, IL: IVP Books, 2016.

Vanhoozer, K. J., C. A. Anderson and M. J. Sleasman, eds. *Everyday Theology: How to Read Cultural Texts and Interpret Trends*. Grand Rapids, MI: Baker Academic, 2007.

Walls, A. F. *The Cross-Cultural Process in Christian History: Studies in the Transmission and Appropriation of Faith*. Maryknoll, NY: Orbis Books, 2002.

Walls, A. F. *The Missionary Movement in Christian History: Studies in the Transmission of Faith*. Maryknoll, NY: Orbis Books, 1996.

Watanabe, Y., and D. L. McConnell, eds. *Soft Power Superpowers: Cultural and National Assets of Japan and the United States*. London and New York: Routledge, 2008.

Weatherford, J. *Genghis Khan and the Making of the Modern World*. New York: Three Rivers Press, 2004.

Weaver, G., ed. *In Every Corner Sing: Songs of God's World*. Salisbury, Wiltshire: RSCM, 2008.

Wilson-Dickson, A. *The Story of Christian Music: From Gregorian Chant to Black Gospel*. Oxford: Lion, 2003.

Woodward, K. *Identity and Difference*. Culture, Media and Identities 3. London: Sage, 1997.

Wright, T. *Surprised by Hope*. Reissued ed. London: SPCK, 2011.

Yoneyama, S. *Animism in Contemporary Japan: Voices for the Anthropocene from Post-Fukushima Japan*. Abingdon and New York: Routledge, 2019. Kindle.

Yoshida, M. "The Power of Imaging – Art as Love and Struggle as Beauty." *The Asia Journal of Theology* 22, no. 2 (Oct 2008): 278-93.

Yung, H. *Mangoes or Bananas? The Quest for an Authentic Asian Christian Theology*. Regnum Studies in Mission. Oxford: Regnum Books, 1997.

Zatayevich, A. *1000 Songs of Kyrgyz/Kazakh People: Tunes and Melodies*. Orenburg: Kyrgyz State Publishing House, 1925.

Zhang, W. 滇文化与民族审美 [*The Culture and Folk Aesthetics of the Dian*]. Kunming: Yunnan University Press, 1992. (In Chinese).

Zhao, F. 中国佤族文化 [*The Culture of the Wa in China*]. Beijing: Ethnic Publishing House, 2005. (In Chinese).

Electronic Resources

About CGNTV. Accessed Sep 9, 2021. http://eng.cgntv.net/.[3]

Anime Forums. Accessed Aug 13, 2020. https://animeforums.net/.

Arts Release. "Language Selection Songs Playlist." Accessed Sep 15, 2020. https://artsrelease.org/en/resources/language-selection-songs-playlist.

Arts Release. "Music and Worship." Accessed Oct 22, 2020. https://artsrelease.org/en/music-worship.

Artway. "Chinnawong, Sawai – VM – Sawai Chinnawong." Accessed Aug 4, 2021. https://www.artway.eu/content.php?id=959&action=show&lang=en.

Barkman, A. "Anime, Manga and Christianity: A Comprehensive Analysis." *Journal for the Study of Religions and Ideologies* 9, no. 27 (Winter 2010): 25-45. Accessed Aug 11, 2020. https://www.academia.edu/30207502/_Anime_Manga_and_Christianity_A_Comprehensive_Analysis.

Beneath the Tangles. Accessed Aug 13, 2020. https://beneaththetangles.com/.

BibleProject. "The story of the Bible in your language." Accessed Aug 13, 2020. https://bibleproject.com/languages/.

Booker, B. "12 Top Storytelling Marketing Examples: How Brands Tell Stories." Attest (Sep 19, 2019). Accessed Aug 13, 2020. https://www.askattest.com/blog/marketing/12-top-storytelling-marketing-examples.

Chang, P. L., and H. Lee. "The Korean Wave: Determinants and Its Impacts on Trade and FDI." *Singapore Management University* (May 9, 2017). Accessed Aug 11, 2020. https://economics.smu.edu.sg/sites/economics.smu.edu.sg/files/economics/Events/SNJTW2017/Hyojung%20Lee.pdf.

Covel, C. "Interview: Kenneth Bright Jr. – Creator of Christian Anime, Prince Adventures." *Geeks under Grace* (Jul 26, 2015). Accessed Aug 13, 2020. https://geeksundergrace.com/anime-cosplay/interview-kenneth-bright-jr-creator-of-christian-anime-prince-adventures/.

---

[3] N.B.: Full-stops are included as punctuation for the bibliography list – they are not part of the internet links.

Crunchyroll. Accessed Aug 10, 2020. https://www.crunchyroll.com/.

Dramabeans. Accessed Aug 13, 2020. https://www.dramabeans.com/.

Eberhard, D. M., G. F. Simons and C. D. Fennig, eds. "Wa – Parauk." In *Ethnologue: Languages of the World*. 24th ed. Dallas, TX: SIL International, 2021. Accessed Aug 2, 2021. http://www.ethnologue.com/language/prk.

Ethnic China. "The Wa Nationality." Accessed Aug 2, 2021. http://www.ethnic-china.com/Wa/waindex.htm.

Fandom. "VOCALOIDs." Accessed Aug 10, 2020. https://vocaloid.fandom.com/wiki/VOCALOIDs.

Fries, S. "Cultural, Multicultural, Cross-Cultural, Intercultural: A Moderator's Proposal." TESOL-France. Accessed Sep 15, 2020. https://www.tesol-france.org/uploaded_files/files/susan-fries.pdf.

GemStone Media. "The Traveler – English." Vimeo. Accessed May 14, 2021. https://vimeo.com/327554260.

Gibbs, C. R. S. "Breaking Binaries: Transgressing Sexualities in Japanese Animation." PhD thesis, University of Waikato, Hamilton, New Zealand, 2012. Accessed Oct 6, 2021. https://hdl.handle.net/10289/6746.

Global Ethnodoxology Network. "Arts for a Better Future." Accessed Oct 14, 2021. https://www.worldofworship.org/artsforabetterfuture/.

Global Ethnodoxology Network. "Introduction to Ethnodoxology." Accessed Aug 2, 2021. https://www.worldofworship.org/introduction-to-ethnodoxology/.

Global Ethnodoxology Network. "Seven Core Values Guide." Accessed Sep 7, 2021. https://www.worldofworship.org/core-values/.

González, M. D. "Cross-Cultural vs. Intercultural." IXMATI Communications (Feb 3, 2011). Accessed Sep 15, 2020. https://ixmaticommunications.com/2011/02/03/cross-cultural-vs-intercultural.

Harbinson, C. "Restoring the Arts to the Church: The Role of Creativity in the Expression of Truth." Colin Harbinson. Accessed Aug 11, 2020. https://www.colinharbinson.com/teaching/resthearts.html.

Harrington, S. "Bharatanatyam on Christian themes with Shrimathi Susanna." Accessed Aug 2, 2021. http://www.indian-dance.co.uk/index.html.

Harris, R., and B. Schrag. "Ethnodoxology: Facilitating Local Arts Expressions for Kingdom Purposes." *Mission Frontiers* (Sep-Oct 2014). Accessed Sep 28, 2021. http://www.missionfrontiers.org/issue/article/ethnodoxology-article.

Heart of the City. Accessed Sep 15, 2020. https://www.heartofthecity.org/home.

Hillsong Team. "Why Do We Have a Multicultural Ministry?" Hillsong Collected (Jan 31, 2017). Accessed Sep 15, 2020. https://hillsong.com/collected/blog/2017/01/why-do-we-have-a-multicultural-ministry/#.XDx8o_zgpJ9.

Hong, S. M. "Uncomfortable Proximity: Perception of Christianity as a Cultural Villain in South Korea." *International Journal of Communication* 10 (2016): 4532–49. Accessed Aug 11, 2020. https://ijoc.org/index.php/ijoc/article/viewFile/4505/1783.

IndigiTube. Accessed Aug 13, 2020. http://www.indigitube.tv/.

Intercultural Church Plants EU. Accessed Aug 13, 2020. https://www.icpnetwork.eu.

International Orality Network (ION). "Archive: Seven Disciplines of Orality." Accessed Aug 2, 2021. https://orality.net/library/seven-disciplines-of-orality/.

Kaloob Dance. "This isn't dance; this is breathtaking research." Accessed Jul 26, 2021. http://www.kaloobdance.com/Vision.html.

KidsHubTV. Accessed Aug 13, 2020. https://kidshubtv.com/.

Kincaid, C. "Are You Addicted to Anime?" *Japan Powered* (May 21, 2017). Accessed Aug 13, 2020. https://www.japanpowered.com/otaku-culture/are-you-addicted-to-anime.

Lapiz, E. "The Christian and Dance: The Redemption of Dance for Use in Christian Worship." *Inspire* 2 (Jul 2001): 22-31. Accessed Jul 26, 2021. https://icdf.com/sites/default/files/documents/redemption-of-dance-jan08.pdf.

Lausanne Movement. "Making Disciples of Oral Learners." Lausanne Occasional Paper, no. 54 (2004). Accessed Aug 11, 2020. https://www.lausanne.org/content/lop/making-disciples-of-oral-learners-lop-54.

Lausanne Movement. "Redeeming the Arts: The Restoration of the Arts to God's Creational Intention." Lausanne Occasional Paper, no. 46 (2004). Accessed Sep 6, 2021. https://lausanne.org/content/lop/redeeming-arts-restoration-arts-gods-creational-intention-lop-46.

Lausanne Movement. "The Cape Town Commitment (2010)." Accessed Sep 6, 2021. https://lausanne.org/content/ctcommitment.

Lausanne Movement. "The Lausanne Covenant (1974)." Accessed Sep 6, 2021. https://lausanne.org/content/covenant/lausanne-covenant.

Lausanne Movement. "The Willowbank Report: Consultation on Gospel and Culture." Lausanne Occasional Paper, no. 2 (1978). Accessed Sep 6, 2021. https://lausanne.org/content/lop/lop-2.

Lerner, J. A., and T. Wide. "Who Were the Sogdians, and Why Do They Matter?" The Sogdians: Influencers on the Silk Roads. Accessed Jul 19, 2021. https://sogdians.si.edu/introduction/.

Lewendon, A. "Worship Music: How Should We Sing?" Eden.co.uk (Apr 11, 2012). Accessed Sep 15, 2020. https://www.eden.co.uk/blog/worship-music-how-should-we-sing-p1481.

Lutheran World Federation. "The Nairobi Statement on Worship and Culture: Contemporary Challenges and Possibilities (1996)." Calvin Institute of Christian Worship (Jun 16, 2014). Accessed Jul 27, 2021. https://worship.calvin.edu/resources/resource-library/nairobi-statement-on-worship-and-culture-full-text.

McKee, R. "The Legendary Story Seminar." McKee Seminars. Accessed Aug 13, 2020. https://mckeestory.com/seminars/story/.
Mobile Ministry Forum. Accessed Aug 13, 2020. https://mobileministryforum.org/.
Molnár, V. "Reframing Public Space through Digital Mobilization: Flash Mobs and Contemporary Urban Youth Culture." *Space and Culture* 17, no. 1 (2014): 43-58. Accessed Sep 25, 2021. https://doi.org/10.1177/1206331212452368.
Morehead, J. "Unpacking Anime's Thematic and Spiritual Depth." *Christian Research Journal* 37, no. 6 (2014). Accessed Aug 13, 2020. http://www.equip.org/PDF/JAF5376.pdf.
Moving Works. Accessed Aug 13, 2020. https://movingworks.org/.
Muyiwa. "Albums." Accessed Oct 16, 2020. https://muyiwa.co.uk/albums/.
Nakky. "Korean Web Dramas." MyDramaList (Feb 16, 2020). Accessed Aug 11, 2020. https://mydramalist.com/list/O3odrv04.
Naver TV. Accessed Sep 9, 2021. https://tv.naver.com/.
Noble, A. "How Stories Unsettle Our Secular Age." *The Gospel Coalition* (Feb 4, 2019). Accessed Aug 13, 2020. https://www.thegospelcoalition.org/article/stories-unsettle-secular-age/.
Noble, A. "The Disruptive Witness of Art." *The Gospel Coalition* (Oct 21, 2017). Accessed Aug 13, 2020. https://www.thegospelcoalition.org/article/the-disruptive-witness-of-art/.
OneHallyu. Accessed Aug 13, 2020. https://onehallyu.com/.
Operation World. Accessed May 14, 2021. https://operationworld.org/locations/.
Petersen, M. "Arts Development for Scripture Engagement." *Global Forum on Arts and Christian Faith* 5, no. 1 (2017): 58-86. Accessed Aug 2, 2021. http://www.artsandchristianfaith.org/index.php/journal/article/view/31/43.
Pew Research Center. "Russians Return to Religion, But Not to Church." (Feb 10, 2014). Accessed May 17, 2021. https://www.pewforum.org/2014/02/10/russians-return-to-religion-but-not-to-church/.
Pew-Templeton Global Religious Futures Project. Accessed May 14, 2021. http://www.globalreligiousfutures.org/countries.
Peyrouse, S. "Christians in Central Asia." *East-West Church Ministry Report* 17, no. 4 (Fall 2009): 9-11. Accessed Jun 8, 2021. https://www.eastwestreport.org/pdfs/ew17-4.pdf.
Poushter, J., and N. Kent. "The Global Divide on Homosexuality Persists." Pew Research Center (Jun 25, 2020). Accessed Aug 12, 2020. https://www.pewresearch.org/global/2020/06/25/global-divide-on-homosexuality-persists/.
Prensky, M. "Digital Natives, Digital Immigrants Part 1." *On the Horizon* 9, no. 5 (2001): 1-6. Accessed Aug 11, 2020. https://doi.org/10.1108/10748120110424816.
Proskuneo Ministries. Accessed Aug 2, 2021. https://proskuneo.org/.

Rogers, E. "hEvan Songs." SoundCloud. Accessed Sep 15, 2020.
  https://soundcloud.com/hevans-songs.

Schriefer, P. "What's the Difference between Multicultural, Intercultural, and
  Cross-Cultural Communication?" Spring Institute (Apr 18, 2016). Accessed
  Oct 22, 2021. https://springinstitute.org/whats-difference-multicultural-
  intercultural-cross-cultural-communication/.

SIL International Media Services. "Story Producer App." Accessed Aug 26,
  2021. https://www.internationalmediaservices.org/story-producer.

SIL International. "What is the "Heart Language" in Multilingual
  Communities?" (Aug 2017). Accessed May 3, 2021.
  https://www.sil.org/about/multilingual-communities.

Soh, A. "k drama." *Faith, Worship, Arts*. Accessed Aug 13, 2020.
  https://faithworshiparts.blogspot.com/search/label/k%20drama.

Songs2Serve. Accessed Nov 14, 2021. https://songs2serve.eu.

Taizé. "Songs." Accessed Sep 15, 2020.
  https://www.taize.fr/en_rubrique2603.html.

Takamizawa, E. "A Missiological Analysis of the "Love Sonata" Project in
  Japan." *Torch Trinity Journal* 11, no. 1 (2008): 147-58. Accessed Sep 9,
  2021. http://www.ttgst.ac.kr/upload/ttgst_resources13/20124-238.pdf.

TrueLove.Is. Accessed Aug 13, 2020. https://truelove.is/.

Vatican. "Sancrosanctum Concilium (1963)." Accessed Jul 27, 2021.
  https://www.vatican.va/archive/hist_councils/ii_vatican_council/documents/
  vat-ii_const_19631204_sacrosanctum-concilium_en.html.

Viu. Accessed Aug 10, 2020. https://www.viu.com/.

Wa Dictionary Project. "The Young Family's Work with the Wa People."
  Humanities Computing Laboratory. Accessed Aug 2, 2021.
  http://www.humancomp.org/wadict/young_family.html.

Williams, K. ""Mobilizing" the Story of His Glory (Part 1)." *Orality Journal* 2,
  no. 2 (2013): 95-104. Accessed Jul 2, 2020. https://orality.net/wp-
  content/uploads/2015/11/V2N2-Orality-Journal.pdf.

Wise, D. "Multi-Ethnic Worship." *Ministry Today* 63 (Apr 2015). Accessed
  Aug 15, 2020. https://www.ministrytoday.org.uk/magazine/issues/63/482/.

Filmography

A-1 Pictures. *Erased*. Animated series. Directed by Tomohiko Itō. 2016.

A-1 Pictures. *Silver Spoon*. Animated series. Directed by Tomohiko Itō and
  Kotomi Deai. 2013-2014.

A-1 Pictures. *Sword Art Online*. Animated series. Directed by Tomohiko Itō.
  2012.

A-1 Pictures. *Wotakoi: Love Is Hard for Otaku*. Animated series. Directed by
  Yoshimasa Hiraike. 2018.

A-1 Pictures. *Your Lie in April*. Animated series. Directed by Kyōhei Ishiguro.
  2014-2015.

AIC. *Now and Then, Here and There*. Animated series. Directed by Akitaro
   Daichi. 1999-2000.
Aura Media. *Doctor Stranger*. TV series. Directed by Jin Hyuk and Hong
   Jong-Chan. Performed by Lee Jong-Suk and Jin Se-Yeon. 2014.
Barunson E&A. *Parasite*. Film. Directed by Bong Joon-Ho. Performed by
   Song Kang-Ho and Choi Woo-Shik. 2019.
Bon Factory Worldwide. *Her Private Life*. TV series. Directed by Hong Jong-
   Chan. Performed by Park Min-Young and Kim Jae-Wook. 2019.
C Story. *The Greatest Marriage*. TV series. Directed by Oh Jong-Rok.
   Performed by Park Si-Yeon and No Min-Woo. 2014.
CGNTV. 교회오빠의 연애 *QT*[4] [*Church Oppa's QT Romance*]. Web series.
   Directed by Hong Hyeon-Jeong. Performed by Im Ji-Kyu and Im Seong-
   Eon. 2016.
CGNTV. 고고송 [*Go Go Song*]. Web series. Directed by Hong Hyeon-Jeong.
   Performed by Yoon Eun-Hye and Ji Il-Joo. 2019.
CGNTV. 두근두근 마카롱 [*Heart-Pounding Macarons*]. Web series. Directed
   by Na Eun-Joo. Performed by Lim Jae-Min and Gabin. 2016-2018.
CGNTV. 계도왕 [*King of Enlightenment*]. Web series. Featuring Shim Gyu-
   Bo. 2020-2021.
CGNTV. 미니 휴먼다큐 [*Mini Human Documentary*]. Web series. Directed
   by Hwang Ji-Soo *et al*. Featuring Joseph Butso and Shim Gyu-Bo. 2016-
   2020.
CGNTV. 여행의 이유 [*Reason to Travel*]. Web series. Featuring Kim In-
   Kwon and Park Ji-Heon. 2019.
Cheer Up SPC and Content K. *Cheer Up!* TV series. Directed by Lee Eun-Jin.
   Performed by Jung Eun-Ji and Lee Won-Keun. 2015.
CJ ENM. *The World of My 17*. Web series. Directed by Choi Sun-Mi.
   Performed by Arin and Hwang Bo-Reum-Byeol. 2020.
CloverWorks. *Rascal Does Not Dream of Bunny Girl Senpai*. Animated series.
   Directed by Sōichi Masui. 2018.
CoMix Wave Films and Story Inc. *Weathering with You*. Animated film.
   Directed by Makoto Shinkai. 2019.
CoMix Wave Films. *Your Name*. Animated film. Directed by Makoto Shinkai.
   2016.
CY Film. *Underground Rendezvous*. Film. Directed by Kim Jong-Jin.
   Performed by Im Chang-Jung and Park Jin-Hee. 2007.
Daehong Communications, Creative Leaders Group Eight and Thank You Very
   Much Contents Company. *7 First Kisses*. Web series. Directed by Jung
   Jung-Hwa. Performed by Lee Cho-Hee and Choi Ji-Woo. 2016-2017.
Drama House. *Dazzling*. TV series. Directed by Kim Suk-Yoon. Performed by
   Han Ji-Min and Kim Hye-Ja. 2019.

---

[4] Korean title ends with "QT" (in English); CGNTV series listed alphabetically under
the English title.

Drama House. *Somehow 18*. TV series. Directed by Kim Do-Hyung. Performed by Choi Min-Ho and Lee Yu-Bi. 2017.

Filmmaker R & K. *The Battleship Island*. Film. Directed by Ryoo Seung-Wan. Performed by So Ji-Sub and Song Joong-Ki. 2017.

Gaina. *Forest of Piano*. Animated series. Directed by Gaku Nakatani, Ryūtarō Suzuki and Hiroyuki Yamaga. 2018-2019.

Gainax and Production I.G. *The End of Evangelion*. Animated film. Directed by Hideaki Anno. 1997.

Gainax and Tatsunoko Production. *Neon Genesis Evangelion*. Animated series. Directed by Hideaki Anno. 1995-1996.

Gainax, Tatsunoko Production and Production I.G. *Neon Genesis Evangelion: Death and Rebirth*. Animated film. Directed by Hideaki Anno. 1997.

Group 8 and DramaFever. *Naeil's Cantabile*. TV series. Directed by Han Sang-Woo and Lee Jung-Mi. Performed by Joo Won and Shim Eun-Kyung. 2014.

HB Entertainment, Drama House and JTBC. *Sky Castle*. TV series. Directed by Jo Hyun-Tak. Performed by Yum Jung-Ah and Lee Tae-Ran. 2018-2019.

Hofilm. *The Last Princess*. Film. Directed by Hur Jin-Ho. Performed by Son Ye-Jin and Park Hae-Il. 2016.

Huayi Brothers. *Lucky Romance*. TV series. Directed by Kim Kyung-Hee. Performed by Hwang Jung-Eum and Ryu Jun-Yeol. 2016.

Hwa & Dam Pictures. *Guardian: The Lonely and Great God*. TV series. Directed by Lee Eung-Bok. Performed by Gong Yoo and Kim Go-Eun. 2016-2017.

J.C. Staff. *Food Wars!* Animated series. Directed by Yoshitomo Yonetani. 2015-2020.

KAFA Films. *Socialphobia*. Film. Directed by Hong Seok-Jae. Performed Byun Yo-Han and Lee Joo-Seung. 2015.

KBS and IHQ. *Page Turner*. TV series. Directed by Lee Jae-Hoon. Performed by Kim So-Hyun and Ji Soo. 2016.

KBS and Netflix. *One More Time*. Web series. Directed by Song Hyu-Wook. Performed by Kim Myung-Soo and Yoon So-Hee. 2016.

KBS. *Come to Me Like a Star*. TV drama. Directed by Hwang In-Hyuk. Performed by Kim Ji-Suk and Jung So-Min. 2013.

KBS. *Jungle Fish 2*. TV series. Directed by Kim Jung-Hwan and Min Doo-Sik. Performed by Hong Jong-Hyun and Park Ji-Yeon. 2010.

KBS. *Soul Plate*. Web series. Directed by Kim Sung-Moon. Performed by Cha Eun-Woo and Ahn Sol-Bin. 2019.

Kim Jong-Hak Production. *Thumping Spike*. Web series. Directed by Kim Jin-Yeong. Performed by Song Jae-Rim and Hwang Seung-Eon. 2016.

Kyoto Animation. *A Silent Voice*. Animated film. Directed by Naoko Yamada. 2016.

Kyoto Animation. *The Melancholy of Haruhi Suzumiya*. Animated series. Directed by Tatsuya Ishihara. 2006-2009.

Kyoto Animation and Animation Do. *Free! – Iwatobi Swim Club*. Animated series. Directed by Hiroko Utsumi. 2013.

Lerche. *Classroom of the Elite*. Animated series. Directed by Seiji Kishi and Hiroyuki Hashimoto. 2017.

Madhouse. *No Game No Life*. Animated series. Directed by Atsuko Ishizuka. 2014.

Madhouse. *Rail of the Star*. Animated film. Directed by Toshio Hirata. 1993.

Madhouse. *The Girl Who Leapt through Time*. Animated film. Directed by Mamoru Hosoda. 2006.

MBC and Naver. *Queen of the Ring*. TV and web series. Directed by Kwon Sung-Chan. Performed by Kim Seul-Gi and Ahn Hyo-Seop. 2017.

MBC. *Coffee Prince*. TV series. Directed by Lee Yoon-Jung. Performed by Yoon Eun-Hye and Gong Yoo. 2007.

MBC. *Dae Jang Geum* [*Jewel in the Palace*]. TV series. Directed by Lee Byung-Hoon. Performed by Lee Young-Ae and Ji Jin-Hee. 2003-2004.

MBC. *My Secret Terrius.* TV series. Directed by Park Sang-Hun. Performed by So Ji-Sub and Jung In-Sun. 2018.

MediaCorp Raintree Pictures. *I Not Stupid Too*. Directed by Jack Neo. Performed by Shawn Lee, Joshua Ang and Ashley Leong. 2006.

Moho Film and Yong Film. *The Handmaiden*. Film. Directed by Park Chan-Wook. Performed by Kim Min-Hee and Kim Tae-Ri. 2016.

Movie Rock. *Midnight Runners*. Film. Directed by Jason Kim. Performed by Park Seo-Joon and Kang Ha-Neul. 2017.

Myung Films. *Joint Security Area*. Film. Directed by Park Chan-Wook. Performed by Lee Young-Ae and Lee Byung-Hun. 2000.

Nippon Sunrise. *Mobile Suit Gundam*. Animated series. Directed by Yoshiyuki Tomino. 1979-1980.

Novus Mediacorp and Invent Stone. *Innocent Thing*. Film. Directed by Kim Tae-Kyun. Performed by Jang Hyuk and Jo Bo-Ah. 2014.

OLM, Inc. *Pokémon*. Animated series. Directed by Kunihiko Yuyama and Daiki Tomiyasu. 1997-2021.

Pierrot and TV Tokyo. *Naruto*. Animated series. Directed by Hayato Date. 2002-2007.

PlayList. *A-Teen*. Web series. Directed by Han Soo-Ji. Performed by Shin Ye-Eun and Lee Na-Eun. 2018.

PlayList. *A-Teen 2*. Web series. Directed by Han Soo-Ji. Performed by Shin Ye-Eun and Lee Na-Eun. 2019.

PlayList. *Ending Again*. Web series. Directed by Park Dan-Hee. Performed by Jo Soo-Min and Kim Geon-Won. 2020.

PlayList. *Flower Ever After*. Web series. Directed by Shin Wan-Suk. Performed by Choi Hee-Jin and Jung Gun-Joo. 2018.

PlayList. *Love Playlist*. Web series. Directed by Shin Jae-Rim, Jung Eun-Ha, Kim Seo-Yoon and Yoo Hee-On. Performed by Kim Hyung-Suk and Jung Shin-Hye. 2017-2019.

Production I.G. *Kuroko's Basketball*. Animated series. Directed by Shunsuke Tada. 2016.

Project No.9. *And You Thought There Is Never a Girl Online?* Animated series. Directed by Shinsuke Yanagi. 2016.

Samhwa Networks. *The Fiery Priest*. TV series. Directed by Lee Myung-Woo. Performed by Kim Nam-Gil and Kim Sung-Kyun. 2019.

Samhwa Networks and SidusHQ. *Uncontrollably Fond*. TV series. Directed by Park Hyun-Suk and Cha Young-Hoon. Performed by Kim Woo-Bin and Bae Suzy. 2016.

School 2017 SPC and Production H. *School 2017*. TV series. Directed by Park Jin-Suk and Song Min-Yeob. Performed by Kim Jung-Hyun and Kim Se-Jeong. 2017.

Shaft. *Arakawa under the Bridge*. Animated series. Directed by Yukihiro Miyamoto and Akiyuki Shinbo. 2010.

Shaft. *Sayonara, Zetsubou-Sensei*. Animated series. Directed by Akiyuki Shinbo. 2007.

Shinyoung E&C Group and Hunus Entertainment. *Come Back Mister*. TV series. Directed by Shin Yoon-Sub. Performed by Rain and Oh Yeon-Seo. 2016.

Silkwood and Will Entertainment. *The Time*. TV series. Directed by Jang Joon-Ho. Performed by Kim Jung-Hyun and Seohyun. 2018.

Soo Jack Films. *No Breathing*. Film. Directed by Jo Yong-Sun. Performed by Lee Jong-Suk and Seo In-Guk. 2013.

Studio Dragon. *Memories of the Alhambra*. Directed by Ahn Gil-Ho. Performed by Hyun Bin and Park Shin-Hye. 2018.

Studio Dragon. *The Guest*. TV series. Directed by Kim Hong-Seon. Performed by Kim Dong-Wook and Kim Jae-Wook. 2018.

Studio Dragon and Culture Depot. *Crash Landing on You*. TV series. Directed by Lee Jung-Hyo. Performed by Hyun Bin and Son Ye-Jin. 2019-2020.

Studio Dragon and Hwa&Dam Pictures. *Mr Sunshine*. TV series. Directed by Lee Eung-Bok. Performed by Lee Byung-Hun and Kim Tae-Ri. 2018.

Studio Ghibli. *Grave of the Fireflies*. Animated film. Directed by Isao Takahata. 1988.

Studio Ghibli. *Kiki's Delivery Service*. Animated film. Directed by Hayao Miyazaki. 1989.

Studio Ghibli. *My Neighbor Totoro*. Animated film. Directed by Hayao Miyazaki. 1988.

Studio Ghibli. *Princess Mononoke*. Animated film. Directed by Hayao Miyazaki. 1997.

Studio Ghibli. *Spirited Away*. Animated film. Directed by Hayao Miyazaki. 2001.

Studio&NEW. *Ms Hammurabi*. TV series. Directed by Kwak Jung-Hwan. Performed by Go Ara and Kim Myung-Soo. 2018.

Sunrise and Ascension. *Colorful*. Animated film. Directed by Keiichi Hara. 2010.

Taehung Pictures. *Seopyeonje*. Directed by Im Kwon-Taek. Performed by Oh Jung-Hae, Kim Myung-Gon and Kim Kyu-Chul. 1993.

Taewon Entertainment. *Backstreet Rookie*. TV series. Directed by Lee Myung-Woo. Performed by Ji Chang-Wook and Kim Yoo-Jung. 2020.

Telecom Animation Film. *Orange*. Animated series. Directed by Hiroshi Hamasaki and Naomi Nakayama. 2016.

Tezuka Productions. *Astro Boy*. Animated series. Directed by Osamu Tezuka, Noboru Ishiguro and Kazuya Konaka. 1963-1966, 1980-1981, 2003-2004.

The Story Works. *Hymn of Death*. TV series. Directed by Park Soo-Jin. Performed by Lee Jong-Suk and Shin Hye-Sun. 2018.

The Unicorn and Studio Dragon. *Chicago Typewriter*. TV series. Directed by Kim Cheol-Kyu. Performed by Yoo Ah-In and Im Soo-Jung. 2017.

Toei Animation. *One Piece*. Animated series. Directed by Kōnosuke Uda, Munehisa Sakai, Hiroaki Miyamoto, Toshinori Fukazawa and Tatsuya Nagamine. 1999-2021.

Toei Animation. *Sailor Moon*. Animated series. Directed by Junichi Sato. 1992-1993.

Tokyo Theaters Co. and The Television Inc. *Roujin Z*. Animated film. Directed by Hiroyuki Kitakubo. 1991.

Tower Pictures. *As One*. Film. Directed by Moon Hyun-Sung. Performed by Ha Ji-Won and Bae Doona. 2012.

Victory Contents and Monster Union. *Angel's Last Mission: Love*. TV series. Directed by Lee Jung-Sub. Performed by Shin Hye-Sun and Kim Myung-Soo. 2019.

Woollim Entertainment. *Student A*. Film. Directed by Lee Kyung-Sub. Performed by Kim Hwan-Hee and Suho. 2018.

List of Contributors

Warren R. Beattie (*editor*) serves as an ordained minister and theological educator in the Highlands of Scotland. He has a PhD in World Christianity from the Centre for the Study of World Christianity, New College, University of Edinburgh (currently an Associate), and is a part-time lecturer at the Highland Theological College, University of the Highlands and Islands. Formerly, he was the Master's Programme Leader at All Nations Christian College (UK) (now an Associate) during which time he supervised the creation of an MA in Arts with Mission. In Asia, he was Director for Mission Research at OMF International's headquarters, a faculty member at the Discipleship Training Centre, Singapore, and worked in South Korea in mission mobilisation and leadership training. His arts interests have included presentations at the international Christian Congregational Music Network on aspects of Scottish church music and being director of The Prinsep Players (an instrumental ensemble) at his Presbyterian church in Singapore and of the All Nations Singers (a vocal chamber ensemble). He has presented on Mission Studies topics in the Asia-Pacific region and in Europe, contributed to three volumes of the WEA Globalization of Mission Series, and was editor of the journal *Mission Round Table: The OMF Journal for Reflective Practitioners* (2006-12) and the companion volume to this book *Ministry Across Cultures: Sharing the Christian Faith in Asia* (Regnum Books, 2016).

Hennie Chiu has been a member of Wycliffe Bible Translators (Hong Kong) since 2000. Her first role was as Literacy Specialist for Mother Tongue Education, living and working in the Philippines; latterly, she has been an Arts Consultant for the Mainland Southeast Asia Group (MSEAG) with SIL International, based in Thailand and working with ethnic minority people groups in Asia. She completed the MA in Arts with Mission at All Nations Christian College (UK), where she wrote her thesis: "A Visual Re-Conception Using the Stories and Accounts of the Life, Death and Resurrection of Jesus Christ in John's Gospel to Encourage Christian Spiritual Formation for the Wa People in Yunnan Province." She is currently a candidate on the doctoral programme at the Robert E. Webber Institute for Worship Studies (USA). Her ministry has a focus on two spheres of activity: EthnoArts and Scripture Engagement, and Arts and Trauma Healing in Asia.

Vivian Chiu worked as a counsellor and youth worker in Hong Kong where she conducted leadership training for young adults and worked with the Christian youth organisation Breakthrough for fifteen years. She has experience of volunteering to provide support in areas affected by earthquakes in China, Japan and Nepal. She graduated from All Nations Christian College (UK) in 2016 and served with refugees in the Middle East exploring the integration of a range of arts and crafts activities with trauma healing processes. Since 2021, she has been serving amongst diaspora communities in the UK with WEC International.

Ian Collinge is an ethnodoxologist with the global mission agency WEC International, the founder of WEC's arts ministry Arts Release (https://artsrelease.org) and a member of the Executive Committee of the Global Consultation on Arts and Music in Missions. He is based in Leeds, England, and has a master's degree in Ethnomusicology from the School of Oriental and African Studies, a graduate degree in Music from the Royal Academy of Music and a bachelor's degree in Theology from Spurgeon's College, all in London. After teaching violin and pastoring a church-plant in London, he spent several years in Asia, researching indigenous music and developing music and arts resources for local churches. He is a visiting tutor in Ethnodoxology and Multicultural Worship, especially at All Nations Christian College (UK), the London School of Theology and the Eastwest College of Intercultural Studies (New Zealand). What especially thrills Ian is to train people to run arts and songwriting workshops and to come alongside local church and worship leaders seeking to develop intercultural worship. He has contributed to various books, including several chapters in *Worship and Mission for the Global Church: An Ethnodoxology Handbook* (William Carey Library, 2013).

Jill Ford is the Arts Programme Leader and Lecturer at All Nations Christian College (UK), with special responsibility for the design and delivery of creative arts modules at both the undergraduate and postgraduate levels. She has a doctorate in Worship Studies from the Robert E. Webber Institute for Worship Studies (USA). Her research focused on the areas of contextual worship, ethnodoxology and the importance of learning how to embrace culturally-diverse forms of artistic expression in Christian liturgy. She is Chair for the WEA Arts in Mission Task Force; Executive Board Member of the Arts+Europe Network; and Chair for the Multicultural Worship Forum (a partnership of All Nations, London School of Theology, Arts Release, and Integrity Music). She has contributed to *Worship and Mission for the Global Church: An Ethnodoxology Handbook* (William Carey Library, 2013).

Robin Harris currently serves as Associate Professor and Director of Center for Excellence in World Arts at Dallas International University, Texas (USA). She has master's degrees in Intercultural Studies and Ethnomusicology and a PhD in Music/Ethnomusicology from the University of Georgia, Athens (USA). She is currently the President of the Evangelical Missiology Society (EMS), President of the Global Ethnodoxology Network (GEN) and a member of the Global Leadership Council of the WEA Mission Commission. She served in cross-cultural contexts for many years, including a decade spent in the Russian Federation, and now lectures at colleges and conferences about topics such as ethnodoxology and ethnomusicology, with a special focus on the "Arts for a Better Future" training course. Her publications include co-editing *Worship and Mission for the Global Church: An Ethnodoxology Handbook* (William Carey Library, 2013) and an academic monograph, *Storytelling in Siberia: The Olonkho Epic in a Changing World* (University of Illinois Press, 2017).

Brian Schrag is a Senior Ethnomusicology and Arts Consultant with SIL International, and Founder of the Center for Excellence in World Arts at Dallas International University, Texas (USA). He has an MA in Intercultural Communications and Ethnomusicology from Wheaton College and a PhD in Ethnomusicology from the University of California, Los Angeles. Brian served as linguist/Bible translator and ethnomusicologist in Central Africa in the 1990s and 2000s, was SIL's Ethnomusicology and Arts Coordinator from 2006 to 2019, and served for 12 years on the board of the Global Ethnodoxology Network (GEN). He developed the "Arts for a Better Future" course based on the book he wrote which serves as the course text: *Creating Local Arts Together: A Manual to Help Communities Reach Their Kingdom Goals* (William Carey Library, 2013). His other publications include *Artistic Dynamos: An Ethnography on Music in Central African Kingdoms* (Routledge, 2021) and *Make Arts for a Better Life: A Guide for Working with Communities* (Oxford University Press, 2018), with Kathleen Van Buren. He has contributed articles to many conferences, journals, and edited volumes, including *De-colonization, Heritage, and Advocacy*, An Oxford Handbook of Applied Ethnomusicology 2 (Oxford University Press, 2019). Brian's core life project is promoting arts-energised community engagement for futures more like heaven.

Anne M. Y. Soh (*co-editor*) is a music educator from Singapore who taught in a secondary school as well as worked as a curriculum specialist for music in the Ministry of Education, Singapore where she oversaw the publication of music syllabuses, textbooks and teaching resources. Anne's choral compositions have been performed and recorded by various vocal ensembles and choirs in Singapore, including the *a cappella* group In Transit which she co-founded. She has extensive experience in children and youth ministries in both local and overseas contexts. As the Regional Director of the Generations of Virtue ministry, she often speaks on parenting topics and current issues faced by families and the younger generation. Having completed the MA in Arts with Mission at All Nations Christian College (UK) in 2016, she joined WEC International (Singapore) in 2019 where she serves in the Arts Release team. Her role centres on mobilising and training artists for mission, and organising local and overseas arts outreach activities. Anne keeps a blog where she occasionally writes on K-drama theology, and other faith/arts-related subjects. She is a regular contributor to the *Biblical Wisdom for Parents* online magazine published by Our Daily Bread Singapore.

Julie Taylor is a certified Senior Ethnomusicology and Arts Consultant with SIL International and SIL Eurasia, and Adjunct Faculty at Dallas International University, Texas (USA) where she teaches Research Methods in World Arts. She has also taught at universities within Thailand, Kenya and Moldova, and shorter arts courses in England, the Netherlands, Ethiopia and Russia. From 1993 to 2017 she was Coordinator of Anthropology and EthnoArts for SIL Africa Area, and held nearly 60 workshops with local artists in remote minority language locations across Africa. Prior to this, she was a professional violinist for many years with the Scottish Chamber Orchestra and Guadagnini String Quartet. Her PhD in Ethnomusicology is from the University of Edinburgh, and current academic interests include artistic expressions of oral-preference cultures in Asia, and the roles of the arts in immigrant movements. She has contributed to many publications on ethnomusicology, the most recent being a chapter in *The Oxford Handbook of Music and World Christianities* (Oxford University Press, 2016).

Missional Church in Asian Contexts Series

The series *Missional Church in Asian Contexts* aims to help Christians to think afresh about the challenges that face the church in Asia:

> We are concerned with the **church** because we view local communities of Christians as the foundation and core of God's work in the world. All the themes addressed will be of relevance to the church and its communal life.

> We want to stress the **missional** character of the church because the church's task is to look inwards and outwards – inwards to build communities of the kingdom, but outwards to represent the kingdom to the whole of society and to present the "good news" to others.

> We have an interest in **Asian contexts** because the local communities of Asia are found in many people groups and nations and form a rich diversity of cultures which embrace more than two billion people across the face of the globe.

Against that backdrop, *Missional Church in Asian Contexts* seeks to show that the interplay between church and mission involves a dynamic, ongoing dialogue. We want to contribute to a robust understanding of "missional": a missional church is not just concerned with local contexts, but is a church that looks out to "the ends of the earth"; a missional church does not just empower local people, but is a church that partners with the global church.

This volume in the series *Missional Church in Asian Contexts* aims to show the importance for missional artists of forging links between the arts in Asian contexts and local cultures and developing sensitivity to the needs and aspirations of local Christians against the contemporary global backdrop with all its creative energies and pressures. We include contributions that demonstrate a healthy balance between theory and practice: the need for the artist to make tangible art forms is informed by theological and cultural reflection, and the ideas of artistic educators are shaped by realities "on the ground." We hope that by drawing on writers from east and west, we can point the way to missional communities that partner in the work of the missional church in Asian contexts in the 21st century.

BV - #0074 - 050922 - C6 - 229/152/11 - PB - 9781914454431 - Gloss Lamination